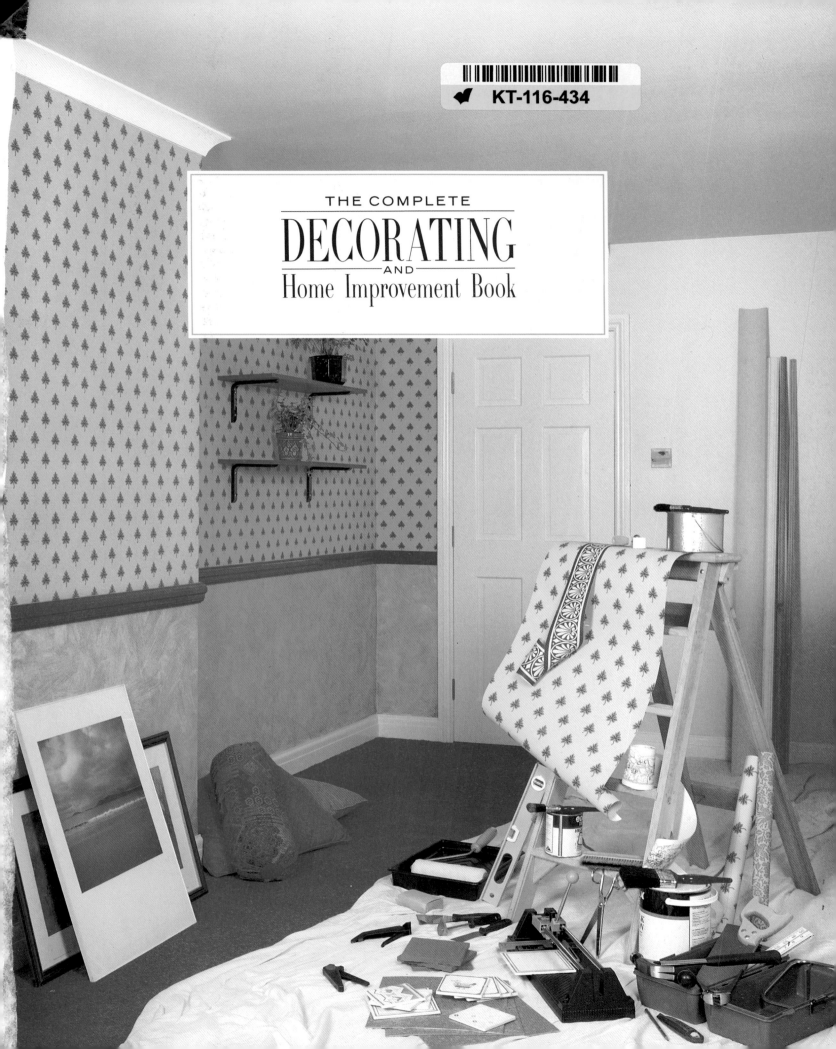

THE COMPLETE

DECORATING

AND

Home Improvement Book

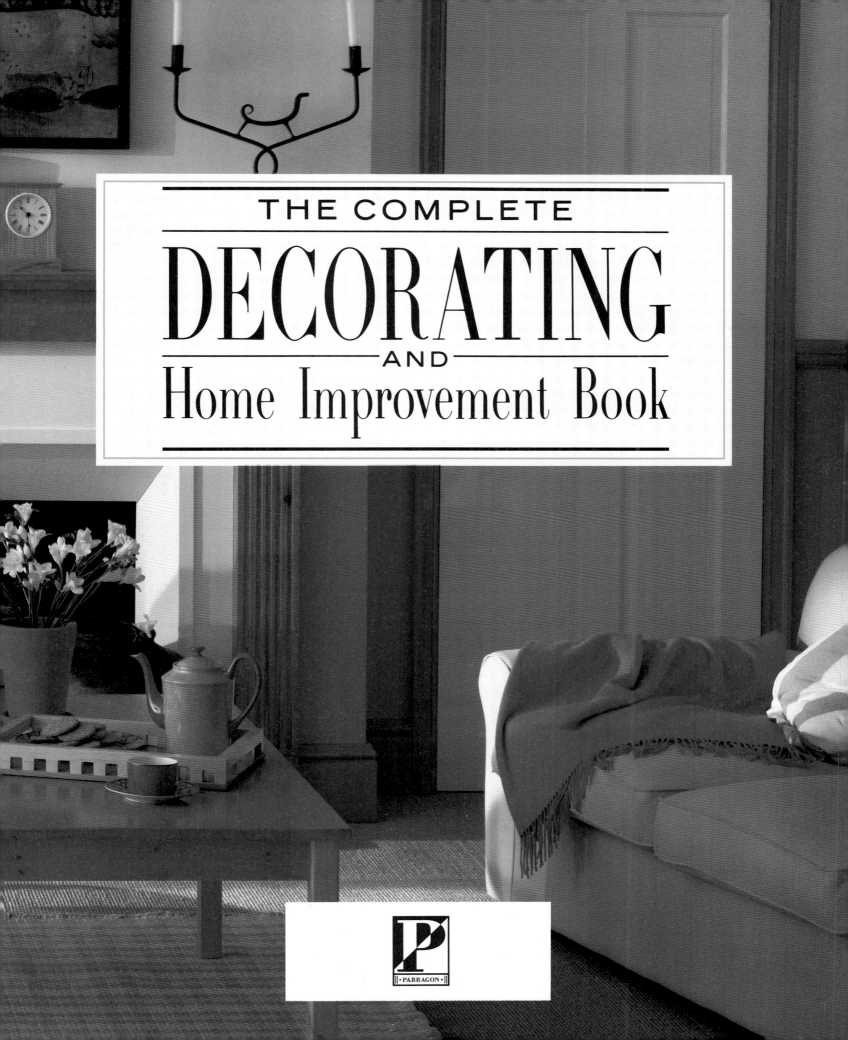

THE COMPLETE
DECORATING
AND
Home Improvement Book

P
PARRAGON

This edition published in 1998 by
Parragon
Avonbridge Trading Estate
Atlantic Road
Avonmouth
Bristol BS11 9QD

Produced by Anness Publishing Limited
Hermes House, 88-89 Blackfriars Road
London SE1 8HA

ISBN 0 75252 469 0 (hardback)
ISBN 0 75252 470 4 (paperback)

Publisher: Joanna Lorenz
Project Editor: Judith Simons
Designer: Michael Morey
Photographer: John Freeman
Illustrator: Andrew Green

Printed and bound in Italy

3 5 7 9 10 8 6 4 2

PUBLISHER'S NOTE
The author and publishers have made every effort to ensure that all instructions
contained within this book are accurate and safe, and cannot accept liability for
any resulting injury, damage or loss to persons or property however it may arise.
If in any doubt as to the correct procedure to follow for any home
improvements task, seek professional advice.

CONTENTS

INTRODUCTION

The interior of someone's home is like a giant mirror,
reflecting their character, taste, aspirations and
interests, and their little foibles. The purpose of this
book is to help in making decisions that will create a
home which reflects the personality of the owners, and
one which they are happy to live in.
It starts by explaining how to examine the present
state of things, and to work out what should be retained
and what would be better changed. This first chapter
assesses the benefits of some basic internal alterations
such as reorganizing the use of space or how the
furniture is arranged, and goes on to plan new
decorating and furnishing schemes in conjunction with
another very important but often overlooked factor:

lighting. The next stage is to plan how to carry out the
work in a well-organized and methodical way – always
the secret of success.

The rest of the book contains chapters that deal with
the use of paint, wall coverings, tiles, floor coverings,
features and fittings, soft furnishings and storage, and
closes with a look at the everyday maintenance and
repair jobs that every householder has to face from time
to time. Each chapter gives full information on the
tools and materials that will be used, and covers a wide
range of techniques and projects. Full-colour step-by-
step photographs appear throughout the book, plus
explanatory illustrations, useful charts and a wealth of
practical advice on creating the ideal interior.

DECORATING DECISIONS

The hardest part of any do-it-yourself project is deciding precisely what is wanted and planning how to achieve it. The decision may simply involve a choice of colour or pattern, or may be more complex, perhaps involving major changes to the style, layout, features and fittings of a room or rooms.

For example, it may seem likely that better use can be made of the interior space that is available. An easy way of doing this is to rearrange or change some of the furniture, whether it is freestanding or built-in – but a more radical approach may bring even more dramatic gains. Partitioning some rooms, linking others, even changing the use to which individual rooms have previously been put, can revolutionize the way a home works. This approach is particularly relevant as the occupants' needs alter over the years, since a house that worked well with young children will not suit a family with teenagers, and once the children have flown the nest their parents will want to use the house in a different way again.

On a smaller scale, even the way in which individual rooms are decorated and furnished can have a major effect on the way they look and feel. Many people find that achieving the style they want is often a process of evolution rather than revolution; few people can get everything right first time. The secret of success lies in understanding the basic rules of colour scheming and in learning how to make the best use of the wide range of materials and techniques available to the interior designer today.

Lastly, it also means taking a close look at what lighting contributes to the scheme. Few homes make use of the possibilities explored so imaginatively in many public buildings, yet some minor changes to lighting could bring a home alive. Some interior designers even dream of the day when they can create and change interior colour schemes with the flick of a switch. However, until that day the big decorating decisions are still the same as they always were; this chapter should render them somewhat easier to make.

OPPOSITE
The art of successful decoration lies in marrying materials that protect and enhance the various surfaces around the home with a touch of decorative flair and originality that will give every room a style all its own and reflect the owner's personal taste and lifestyle.

MAKING AN ASSESSMENT

The best way to get an objective view of a home's interior condition is to imagine that it is up for sale and to view it in the role of a prospective purchaser. The aim of the exercise is not to give rise to a severe bout of depression, but to make it clear what exists in the home and what could be done to change or improve it.

Start at the front door, and step into the hallway. Is it bright and well lit, or gloomy and unwelcoming? A lighter colour scheme could make a narrow room appear more spacious, and better lighting would make it seem more inviting. Decorating the wall opposite the front door would make a long hall appear shorter, while changing the way the staircase is decorated could make it a less – or more – dominant feature. Is the staircase well lit, for safety's sake as well as for looks? Opening up the space beneath the stairs could get rid of what

ABOVE Choose an integrated decorating scheme for hallways, stairs and landing areas. Bring down the apparent ceiling height using a dado (chair) rail or decorative border.

BELOW The living room has to be light and airy during the day, yet cosy and comfortable in the evening. The fireplace and a central table provide the main focal points here.

is typically an untidy gloryhole (storage room), taking up space without saving any. Lastly, are the wall and floor coverings practical? The hall floor is bound to be well trodden, and needs to be durable and easy to clean as well as looking attractive.

Now move into the main living room. This is always the most difficult room in the house to decorate and furnish successfully because of its dual purpose. It is used both for daily life and to entertain visitors. It must be fresh and lively by day, yet cosy and peaceful in the evening. One of the chief keys to success is flexible lighting that can be altered to suit the room's different uses, but the decorations and furnishings all have their part to play too.

Look at the colour scheme. How well does it blend in with the furnishings, the curtains and drapes, the floor covering? Are there any interesting features such as a fireplace, an alcove, an archway into another room, even an ornate cornice around the ceiling? Some might benefit from being highlighted, other less attractive ones would be better disguised.

Next, examine how the room works. Are traffic routes congested? Are the seating arrangements flexible? Are there surfaces where things can easily be put down? Does any storage or display provision look good and work well? Can everyone who is seated see the television? Does everyone want to? Assessing the room in this way reveals its successes and failures, and shows how to eliminate the latter.

Continue the guided tour with the dining room – or dining area, if it is part of a through room. This is often the least used room in the house, so its design tends to be neglected. Since it is usually used for just one purpose –

LEFT Bedrooms are the most private of rooms, and their colour schemes and furnishings should reflect the personal whims of their occupants.

BELOW The kitchen is the engine room of the house. It must be well-planned with plenty of work and storage space, and be pleasant to work in and easy to clean.

eating – it needs to be decorated in a way that avoids visual indigestion. Warm, welcoming colour schemes and flexible lighting work best in this location; strident patterns and harsh colours are to be avoided.

Now turn to the kitchen. Whatever type of room it is, the most important thing is that it should be hygienic, for obvious reasons. Are the various surfaces in the room easy to keep clean, and to redecorate when necessary? Are there dust and grease traps? Is the lighting over the hob (burners) and counter tops adequate? Is the floor covering a practical choice? Since the kitchen is often the hub of family life, it needs to be functional but adaptable, and also pleasant to be in so that the cook does not mind the time spent slaving over a hot stove.

Bathrooms have their own special requirements, mainly revolving around combining comfort with a degree of waterproofing, especially if there are young children in the family. Are the decorations and floor covering suitable? How do they complement the bathroom suite? What about the space available within the room? Could congestion be relieved by moving

things around? – or by moving them out altogether: having a shower instead of a bath could create lots of extra space. Could a second bathroom be created elsewhere in the house? Otherwise, putting washbasins in some of the bedrooms could take the pressure off the family bathroom during the morning rush hour.

Lastly, bedrooms. In most, the bed is the focal point of the room, so the way it is dressed will be the main influence on the room's appearance. The colour scheme also has its part to play in making the room look comfortable and relaxing; remember that the room's occupant will see it from two viewpoints – on entering, and from the bed – so take this into account when assessing it. What about the ceiling? In the one room where people actually spend some time staring at it, does it deserve something a little more adventurous than white paint? Is the floor covering warm to the touch of bare feet? In children's rooms, is it also capable of withstanding the occasional rough and tumble or a disaster with the finger paints? Lastly, is the lighting satisfactory? Most bedrooms need a combination of subdued general

lighting and brighter local task lighting for things such as reading in bed, putting on make-up or tackling school homework. Some changes may make the room work a great deal more satisfactorily.

Once the tour of the house is complete there should be a clear picture of its condition and how well it works; and some ideas as to how it might be improved. Above all, it will have been viewed as a whole, not just as a series of individual rooms. That is the first step towards creating an attractive, stylish and above all practical home.

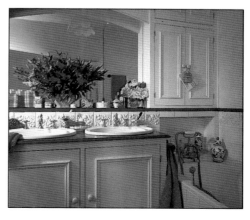

ABOVE Bathrooms need tailoring to family needs. Here a double vanity unit provides valuable extra washing facilities for busy couples or growing families.

REORGANIZING SPACE

If a home does not function well, there are three choices. Two of these are thoroughly defeatist and may also be impractical: learn to live with it, or move to a more suitable house. The third is much more positive; alter it so that it gives the extra living space and the additional features needed.

The average home is basically a box, within which internal partitions create individual rooms, doors allow movement and windows let in light and air. Various services are included within the structure – heating, plumbing, wiring and so on. All these features can be altered, within reason, to make them work better.

When planning alterations, there are two considerations which should constantly be borne in mind. Are the changes feasible? And are they legal? It is essential to check with the local planning (zoning) and building control bodies to find out whether the work requires official approval.

Where to improve

Alterations to the use of space in the home are of two kinds. The first is to create new living space. The second is to alter the present layout of the interior and to change or improve the services. Here are some of the possibilities.

In the attic, unused space beneath a pitched roof could well become valuable extra living space. Remember, though, that providing access to the new rooms will mean losing some space on the floor below.

In the existing upstairs rooms, rearranging internal walls could create an extra bedroom or bathroom, while providing plumbing facilities in bedrooms could ease the pressure on the existing bathroom.

ABOVE Subdividing large rooms can help to create more effective use of space, by redefining traffic zones and providing more wall space for furniture.

LEFT Bathing facilities are often over-stretched, especially in family homes. Finding space for an extra shower cubicle can greatly relieve the traffic jams.

Downstairs, removing dividing walls to create large through rooms or partitioning large rooms to create two smaller ones, moving doorways to improve traffic flow, or altering the kitchen layout could all be considered. It might even be possible to turn an integral garage into extra living space.

Look at the possibility of changing the use to which individual rooms are put, especially if the family is increasing or decreasing in size. Reorganization can bring dramatic improvements to the way the house works.

CONVERTING AN ATTIC

A full-scale conversion into one or more habitable rooms – that is, bedrooms and the like rather than just play or hobby space – is one of the biggest and most complex indoor home improvement projects. It involves altering the roof structure to make space for the rooms, strengthening the existing attic floor, providing access from the floor below, installing roof or dormer windows and extending existing services into the new rooms. Professional advice is needed here, and it is advisable to hand over the main structural alterations to a builder or specialist conversion firm. That still leaves plenty of scope for do-it-yourself finishing and fitting of the new rooms.

In many older homes, the space beneath a pitched (sloping) roof can be used to provide valuable extra living space, often with spectacular results.

Creating a through room

Creating a through room means removing an existing dividing wall, and may also require the repositioning of existing doorways and the formation of new windows. If the existing wall is loadbearing, a steel beam will have to be installed to carry the load, and lintels will also be needed over new windows and over new doors in other loadbearing walls. It may be necessary to reroute existing plumbing and electrical services that cross the wall that will be removed. Once the new opening has been formed, there will be extensive replastering to be done, and the floors in the two rooms will have to be linked smoothly. The original colour schemes of the two rooms will also probably be different, which may entail complete redecoration.

Partitioning an existing room

Subdividing an existing room into two smaller ones means building a new wall, possibly adding a door or window to one of the new rooms, and perhaps altering or extending existing plumbing, heating and electrical services to serve the two separate rooms.

The new dividing wall will generally be built as a timber-framed partition wall faced with plasterboard (gypsum board), but a solid blockwork wall could be built on suitable foundations, which may well need to be inserted.

Creating a new door opening

If the new opening is to be made in a loadbearing wall, a lintel must be used to bridge the opening. However, if the wall is a non-loadbearing partition, simple alterations to the wall framing are all that will be needed. The job will also involve some replastering work, making alterations to skirtings (baseboards) and floor surfaces, the fitting of architraves (trims) around the opening, and possibly alterations to existing plumbing, heating and electrical services if pipes or cables cross the area where the door will be installed.

Altering the kitchen layout

The amount of work depends on how extensive the rearrangement will be. At the very least there will be new base and wall units (cabinets) and counter tops, and these will probably involve some work on wall and floor surfaces. If repositioning sinks, cookers (stoves), dishwashers and the like, there will have to be alterations to plumbing and electrical services.

USING COLOUR, PATTERN AND TEXTURE

After redesigning the house layout and reorganizing each room, the next task is to start planning the colour schemes. To do this successfully, it helps to understand the basics of colour theory, and how to use pattern and texture to good effect.

When putting a colour scheme together, a device called the *colour wheel* can be used to help plan the various decorative effects. All colours are made by mixing together varying proportions of the three *primary* colours – red, yellow and blue. Mixing them in pairs creates three new *secondary* colours, with red and yellow making orange, yellow and blue making green, and blue and red making violet. Imagine these six colours making up segments of a circle in the order red, orange, yellow, green, blue and violet. Mix adjacent pairs together again, and you create six *tertiary* colours – red/orange, orange/yellow, yellow/green, green/blue, blue/violet and violet/red. Adding these to the circle gives the basic colour wheel of twelve segments.

There is one more ingredient to add to these colours: colour intensity or tone. By adding different amounts of white or black, you can produce lighter or darker shades of the original colours in almost infinite variety. And you can also, of course, use white, black and varying shades of grey as colours in their own right.

On the wheel, the twelve colours split into two groups. The colours from violet/red round to yellow are known as *advancing* colours because they appear to make wall and ceiling surfaces look nearer to the viewer than they really are. They make a room seem warm and welcoming, but also smaller. The remaining colours are known as *receding* colours because they have the opposite

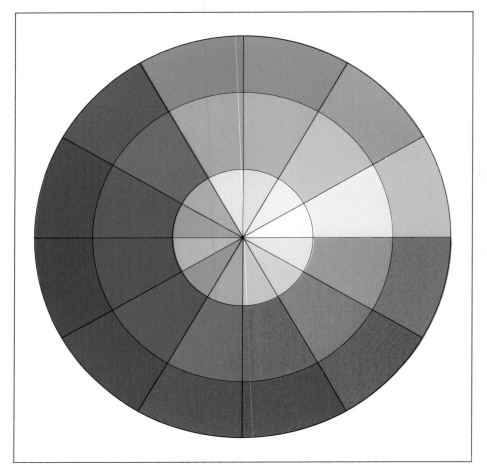

An understanding of colour and colour mixing will be invaluable when choosing a new colour scheme. The colour wheel is divided into 12 segments, and the central ring shows the primary, secondary and tertiary colours described in the text. The outer ring shows darker tones of these colours and the inner one lighter ones.

LEFT Blues, greys and plenty of white space create a cool, airy colour scheme that is the perfect complement for wooden fixtures and furnishings in a light shade of pine.

Blues and greens are naturally cool, receding colours, ideal for well-lit south-facing rooms, but can be warmed by splashes of contrast in orange and yellow.

visual effect, making a room look cool, and also larger than in reality. Which group is chosen as the basis for a colour scheme depends on the overall effect that is wanted in that particular room.

The colour wheel also helps to create colour *harmony* or *contrast*. Colours next to or near each other are said to be in colour harmony, giving a restful effect. However, too much colour harmony can become visually rather dull; it needs livening up with some elements of colour contrast, which come from using colours at opposite sides of the wheel. Colours exactly opposite each other, such as red and green, are called *complementary*. The ideal colour scheme is usually considered to be a basically harmonious one, with contrast added by the judicious use of contrasting or complementary colours for some elements of the design. Soft furnishings, such as scatter cushions or blinds and shades, chosen in a fabric to contrast with the overall colour scheme can add just the right amount of contrast to brighten up a room.

BELOW Nothing succeeds in creating a feeling of cosiness as well as the red/pink section of the colour wheel. Surface texture plays its part too, as does warm, natural wood fittings.

ABOVE Neutral tones – beiges, creams and browns – create a colour scheme that is restful on the eye and can be teemed with almost any accessory shades.

DECORATING DECISIONS

BELOW Bold splashes of colour can add interest and definition to a colour scheme that is basically neutral.

BELOW Wall coverings with a vertical pattern element can help to make rooms appear taller, but work well only when the walls are perfectly square.

ABOVE Small, random patterns are a better choice than larger motifs for small rooms, and are ideal for decorating areas where perfect pattern matching can be difficult.

Colour can also play tricks on the eye, which can be used to good effect in colour scheming. For example, painting a high ceiling in a dark colour makes it appear lower. The same effect applies on walls, where using dark colour on opposite walls makes a wide room seem narrower; conversely, using it on the end wall of a long, thin room and lighter colours on the side walls helps to make the room seem wider to the eye.

Using pattern

Pattern on walls, ceilings and floors adds visual interest to a colour scheme, either in harmony with the overall effect or to provide contrast – for example, by having a patterned wall covering on one wall, and the rest painted. Pattern as well as colour can cheat the eye and alter the apparent dimensions of a room. Wall coverings with a distinct horizontal pattern make walls seem wider and ceilings lower; strong vertical designs such as stripes have the opposite effect. The same applies to pattern in floor coverings, which can make a room look wider or narrower depending on which way the pattern element runs.

Pattern size has its own contribution to make. Wall and floor coverings with large pattern motifs make the surface they are on seem to advance and so make the room appear smaller, while tiny motifs have the opposite effect of making the surface appear to recede from the eye. Choosing patterned fabrics for cushions, curtains and drapes or bed linen is an ideal way of enlivening a decor with plain walls and woodwork.

Luxurious fabrics used for curtains, cushions and upholstery are often the ideal medium for adding patterned elements to a decor.

Using texture

Surface texture – in other words, a surface that is not completely smooth – helps to add variety and visual interest to your colour schemes. Wall coverings with a textured or embossed surface generally have a comparatively low relief which helps to soften the decorative effect of the material, while texture paints can be used to create effects that have quite a high relief and consequently look particularly striking when lit from the side. Textured finishes also have another benefit, of helping to disguise slightly irregular wall and ceiling surfaces.

RIGHT Sometimes richly textured upholstery and floor coverings benefit from the simplest of settings. Here textured walls and painted floorboards in pure white are the perfect backdrop.

BELOW Where lamps are visible, it is best to use types such as candles and globes that look attractive whether lit or unlit.

Good lighting can play an important role in bringing a home to life, as well as making it easier for the occupants to work and engage in leisure activities. Few homes take advantage of the design possibilities that good lighting can offer, preferring to rely on the traditional central pendant light in each room and the occasional table or standard (standing) lamp.

The following pages show some of the many versatile and attractive lighting effects that can be achieved in different rooms. Before embarking on a radical redesign of a lighting scheme it is important to understand some of the basics of lighting design.

Light is provided by lamps and tubes of various types and wattages. *Wattage* is a measurement of the amount of electricity the lamp consumes. The amount of light each emits is measured in units called *lumens*. Conventional

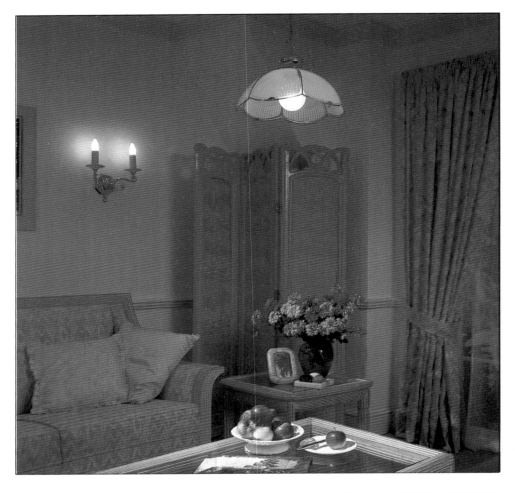

HOW LAMPS EMIT LIGHT

Fluorescent tubes (1) and GLS (general lighting service) lamps (2) emit light in all directions. Silvered reflectors emit it either forwards (3, 4 and 5) or backwards (6).

tungsten-filament lamps – that is, ordinary lightbulbs – are much less efficient at producing light than are fluorescent tubes. For example, a 40-watt lamp emits about 400 lumens, or 10 lumens per watt of power used, while a 40-watt tube emits almost 2000 lumens, or 50 lumens per watt.

The amount of light that is needed depends on the surface area being lit. As a general guide something in the region of 200 lumens per sq m (20 lumens per sq ft) is needed in work areas such as kitchens, half that figure in other living rooms, bathrooms and in access areas such as halls, landings and stairs, and a quarter of the amount – 50 lumens per sq m (5 lumens per sq ft) in bedrooms.

ABOVE Individual spotlights on ceiling- or wall-mounted track provide the maximum flexibility when highlighting particular room features.

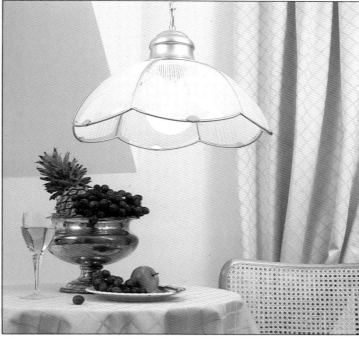

There are other factors to take into consideration when working out how much light is needed, such as the colour and reflectivity of the surfaces being lit and whether lighting is direct or indirect, but they are somewhat complex for the lay person to work with. As a rough guide for general background lighting, using filament lighting emitting around 10 lumens per watt, aim to provide about 20 watts per sq m (2 watts per sq ft) of floor area. As an example, a living room measuring 6 × 4 m (20 × 13 ft) would need 6 × 4 × 20 = 480 watts of lighting. For fluorescent tubes giving 50 lumens per watt, you need 4 watts per sq m (0.4 watts per sq ft) – that is, just under 100 watts of lighting for the same room. Regard any additional local task lighting in the room, for reading or studying perhaps, as supplementary to this basic figure.

LEFT Globe lamps have an opaque spherical envelope that is perfect for use with pendant fittings, and look good whether the light is on or off.

ABOVE Downlighters (**left**) and PAR reflectors (**right**) can cast a narrow spotlight beam or create a border floodlit effect, according to the type of lamp fitted.

HOW LIGHT FITTINGS EMIT LIGHT

The type of light fitting or lampshade used affects the way light is distributed. Shown here are a pendant lampshade (1), a ceiling-mounted diffuser (2), wall lights with diffusers (3), spotlights on ceiling-mounted track (4), a downlighter (5), a recessed eyeball (6), a wallwasher (7) and an uplighter (8).

ABOVE Wall-mounted uplighters are used to wash ceilings with light. When fitted with a crown-silvered lamp, the light source is invisible even with the lamp at eye level.

LIGHTING FOR LIVING AND DINING ROOMS

The key to success with any lighting scheme is to ensure that it meets two criteria: it must give light where it is needed; and the effect it creates should enhance the room's appearance by creating a balanced mixture of light and shadow. The type of light fittings chosen has a major part to play, and so does the positioning of the fittings. The illustration shows how the type and positioning of ceiling lights can create different lighting effects on room walls.

The first basic guideline to observe is to ensure that naked lamps or tubes cannot be seen, by the judicious choice of shades and diffusers. The second is always to provide an acceptable level of background lighting throughout the room, even when additional local lighting is employed, to avoid creating pools of hard, dark shadow. The third is to use lighting to highlight individual features of the room – an attractive alcove, for example, lit by a spotlight, or a run of curtains (drapes) illuminated by perimeter lighting.

In addition, many rooms in the house will probably need local task lighting, for reading, writing, sewing or other work. The kitchen in particular has its own special lighting requirements. Some task lighting requirements can be satisfied by the use of portable plug-in lamps, while others may need more permanent arrangements.

Living rooms are among the most difficult areas to light successfully, because of the many different uses to which the room is put. The aim should be to provide background lighting that can be bright or dim according to the

ABOVE A rise-and-fall fitting provides glare-free light over the dining table, while a freestanding uplighter casts a gentle glow across the ceiling.

RIGHT Recessed eyeball spotlights allow light to be focussed closely on individual features or objects in a room, and can be adjusted as required.

ABOVE For lighting with minimal glare, team an opaque central fitting with strip lights behind pelmets (valances) to light up a cornice (crown molding) and the ceiling surface above.

OPPOSITE Pastel-shaded lamps in opaque lampshades help to create soft background lighting effects that complement the room's colour scheme.

mood of the moment, and then to add separately controllable feature lighting to highlight the room's focal points, and local task lighting where required. The accent is on flexibility. Choosing fittings in keeping with the style of the room will help to ensure that its lighting looks good by day or by night.

Dining rooms have slightly different needs. The main requirement is a table that is well lit without glare, which you can satisfy with a rise-and-fall fitting or carefully targeted downlighters. The background lighting should be subdued, preferably under dimmer control – note that fluorescent lights cannot be easily dimmed. Additional lighting from wall lights or wallwashers can be used to illuminate the serving and carving area, and uplighters for dramatic effect.

WASHING WALLS WITH LIGHT

A row of wallwashers of the same wattage create a perfect wash (1); decreasing wattages along the row give a graded wash (2). A row of downlighters can create a scalloped effect (3); a single downlighter casts a parabola (4).

LIGHTING FOR KITCHENS AND BATHROOMS

BELOW Kitchens are difficult to light because most tasks take place round the perimeter of the room. Lights above counter tops are the perfect solution.

Kitchens pose special lighting problems mainly owing to the wide use of the fitted kitchen. In the old days most food preparation was done on a central table, so a central light was generally adequate. Now almost every task is carried out close to the perimeter of the room, and a central light – still the standard fitting in many homes – is now useless, condemning the cook to working in his or her own shadow.

What a modern kitchen needs is lighting tailored to provide good illumination at each of the main work stations – the cooker (stove), the sink and the food preparation area. There should also be a reasonable level of general background lighting, plus lighting to illuminate the insides of cupboards (closets). These requirements can only be achieved by separate, flexible and independently controllable light sources.

If the cooker has an extractor hood over it, one containing a downlighter will illuminate the hob (burners) satisfactorily. Otherwise the aim should be to provide ceiling-mounted lights positioned so that they shine directly on the hob without casting a shadow. The same is needed over the sink. Ideally each of these lights or sets of lights should have its own switch so that it can be switched on and off as required. For counter tops below wall storage units, lighting is best provided by striplights fixed beneath the wall units and shielded by baffles to prevent glare. Walk-in cupboards and open display units can be lit by recessed downlighters, and base units can be lit by small interior lights with automatic switches worked by opening the doors. If the kitchen is also used for eating, provide a rise-and-fall fitting or recessed downlighters over the kitchen table so

that the rest of the kitchen lighting can be turned off – not least to hide the cooking debris during the meal.

Bathrooms are much less demanding. The basic requirement is for a modest level of background lighting, provided by a close-mounted central light or some recessed fittings. If the washbasin area is used for shaving or applying

make-up, add a wall strip (fluorescent) light over the basin to provide good, glare-free illumination there. Do not install a fluorescent light if it is to be used for applying make-up. Even the best types give a slightly inaccurate rendering of some colours. There may also be a need for a splashproof recessed light fitting in a shower cubicle.

ABOVE Track lighting is a versatile solution for kitchens and utility rooms, since individual spots can be adjusted to cast light where it is most wanted.

ABOVE In bathrooms, enclosed fittings are a must for safety reasons. A central fitting with an opaque diffuser will cast a soft overall light.

LEFT Recessed downlighters can be used in bathrooms to provide some additional illumination above areas such as vanity units.

LIGHTING IN BEDROOMS

Bedroom lighting requires a combination of restful background lighting and easily controllable local lighting to cover separate activities such as dressing and undressing, applying make-up, reading in bed, or perhaps watching television. Remember that every fitting must look as good from the viewpoint of the bed as from elsewhere in the room.

Background lighting can be provided by wall lights, by table lamps on bedside tables, by recessed downlighters or, very appropriately for bedrooms, with the wall- or ceiling-mounted fittings known as uplighters, which throw light onto the ceiling and completely conceal the lamp when viewed from below. The general light level can be lower than for living rooms, as long as the task lighting does its job. Bright,

glare-free lighting is needed at a dressing table, and good light from above to check clothes. Fluorescent lighting should not be used here, because it falsifies certain colours, so choose ordinary lightbulbs.

Bedside reading lights should be directional so that they illuminate the page adequately but do not disturb a sleeping partner. Lastly, make full use of two-way switching so that lights can be turned on and off without having to get out of bed. Again, choose light fittings to complement the room's decor and colour scheme.

Children's rooms, especially nurseries, have slightly different requirements. Good task lighting is essential for jobs such as changing or dressing a baby, and young children will want a higher overall lighting level

than in an adult's room when playing. They may also need a low-wattage night light for comfort and safety. Finally, older children will want portable task lighting for activities such as hobbies and homework.

The landing and stairwell should not be forgotten. This is one area of the home where good bright lighting is essential; safety is more important than mood here, ensuring that all parts of the staircase are clearly lit without glare. For the best effect, fittings should be positioned so that treads are lit but risers are in shadow. Make sure that any suspended fittings do not impede passage up and down the staircase, and check that recessed fittings are readily accessible – it is irritating to have to get a ladder out to reach a high-level fitting whenever a lamp fails.

ABOVE Recessed downlighters are the ideal light source for children's rooms, providing good illumination of play and storage areas yet remaining safely out of harm's way.

LEFT An opaque shade on a bedside light prevents glare while providing gentle background uplighting and enough downlighting for bedtime reading.

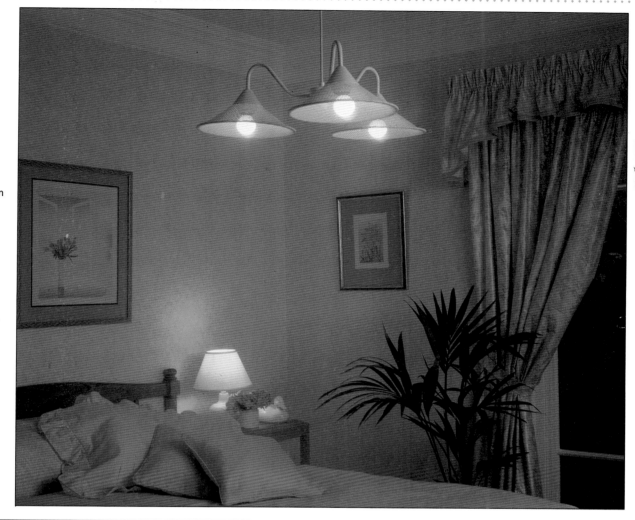

RIGHT In bedrooms, light fittings need careful selection because they must look as attractive from the bed as from elsewhere in the room. Globe lamps look good and are free from glare.

BELOW In nurseries, low-energy fluorescent lamps offer the ideal combination of long life and safety, since the lamp envelope is cool to the touch.

ABOVE Halls and stairwells need good illumination for safety reasons. Here recessed downlighters illuminate every tread of the staircase and highlight the hall's features too.

ABOVE A wall-mounted downlighter can also be used to light a staircase, casting the risers into shadow and so making the treads more clearly visible.

Most of the lighting schemes mentioned so far have concentrated on illuminating individual rooms and providing good task lighting for the various activities carried out in them. However, lighting can also be used as a means of decorating rooms and highlighting their best features.

Spotlights offer great flexibility here. They are available as single, double and triple spot units for wall or ceiling mounting, as individual spotlights designed to fit on lighting track, or as recessed 'eyeball' ceiling fittings. The beam direction can be adjusted to 'wash' walls, curtains (drapes) or ceilings with light, which may be coloured instead of white; or to illuminate an individual area of the room such as a fireplace, an arch, an alcove, a display unit (cabinet) or some other feature.

Small spotlights, especially the recessed eyeball types, can be used to illuminate individual pictures or picture groups on your walls. Alternatively, a traditional picture light – a small strip light in a wall-mounted holder – may be set above or below the picture.

Shelves or closed cabinets displaying china, glass or other *objets d'art* can be lit in several ways. Spotlighting is one, but this can look harsh. What often works better is either backlighting via small tungsten filament strip lights fitted beneath the shelves or, where glass shelves are used, a lamp behind a frosted glass panel at the top or bottom of the unit.

That last area of lighting that is well worth considering is indoor security lighting. It is well known that intruders are deterred by good lighting outside the house; this also applies indoors, for several reasons. The first is that if a would-be intruder sees an indoor light,

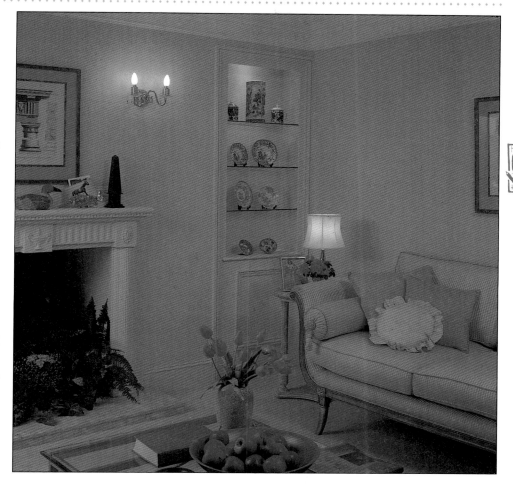

he can never be sure whether the house is occupied or not, especially if the curtains are drawn. Even if the owners are out, he will be less keen to break in and risk being seen from outside.

There are several types of programmable controls which can be used to switch both fixed lighting and plug-in lights on, either at preset times or at sunset. Some can then mimic human behaviour by turning lights on and off at random during the night, and will switch off at dawn. Others turn lights on – and can also trigger a burglar alarm – if they detect the body heat of an intruder, much like the sensors used out of doors. All give extra protection, especially if combined with electrically controlled curtain closers.

ABOVE Pictures can be brought to life if highlighted by an individual spotlight or a linear picture light.

OPPOSITE Low-voltage tungsten halogen lighting sheds a crisp white light that is perfect for highlighting a collection of ornamental glass.

ABOVE Coloured lamps can help to accentuate a room's colour scheme, while concealed lighting in alcoves makes the most of china and other treasures.

LEFT Use a combination of small clip-on spotlights and freestanding fittings to cast individual pools of light on objects within an alcove.

PLANNING THE WORK

Once it is clear exactly what work is to be carried out in the home, it is essential to plan the job properly so as to do things in a sensible order. This will not only ensure that the work proceeds smoothly, with the minimum of disruption to family life; it will also help in estimating accurately the quantities of materials needed for each phase of the job, and to check that all the necessary tools and materials are to hand, including hired equipment.

Where to start depends on how extensive the work is. Begin with any major internal alterations such as building partition walls; creating through rooms; relocating rooms; adding or blocking off windows and doorways; removing, blocking or opening up chimney breasts; and lowering ceilings. Then carry out any alterations that are needed to the services – for example electric wiring, plumbing or heating pipework – whether this is to improve them generally or to cope with the alterations. If merely repainting or covering a wall, remove existing furniture, fixtures and fittings in order to strip out any materials that are to be replaced, or to prepare existing surfaces. At this stage, there is an opportunity to tackle any general repairs that may be required to make good the wall, floor, ceiling and woodwork surfaces, before starting work on the new scheme.

Finally, complete the work in each room by replacing the fixtures and fittings, followed by bringing in existing or replacement furniture and adding the soft furnishings.

STEP-BY-STEP CHECKLIST

Use this checklist to help in organizing
each numbered stage of the work and to
draw up a record of the tools, equipment
and materials required.

Task	Materials	Tools/equipment
1 Remove furniture from affected room(s)		
2 Remove fixtures and fittings: go to 7 if not carrying out major work		
3 Carry out structural alterations		
4 Relocate room contents		
5 Alter/extend/improve services		
6 Replace features (doors, mouldings/trims etc.) being altered		
7 Remove old wall and floor covering materials being replaced		
8 Make good any damaged surfaces		
9 Wash or rub down painted wall/ceiling surfaces		
10 Wash or rub down painted woodwork		
11 Clean floors, level surface if uneven		
12 Paint or paper ceilings		
13 Paint or cover walls		
14 Paint woodwork		
15 Fix wall tiles/cladding (panelling)		
16 Add decorative mouldings, borders etc.		
17 Replace fixtures and fittings (light switches shelf brackets, curtain (drapery) track, built-in furniture etc.)		
18 Lay new floor coverings		
19 Reposition furniture		
20 Add soft furnishings (curtains/drapes, blinds/shades, cushions etc.)		

PAINTING

Painting walls, woodwork and other surfaces is, so all the surveys reveal, by far the most popular do-it-yourself job. Modern paints and improvements in the design and manufacture of decorating tools have certainly made the task less arduous than it was in the days of traditional oil-bound paints and distemper, and have also made it easier for the amateur decorator to get professional-looking results.

One major shift in paint technology is the trend away from using solvent-based varnishes and paints for wood, towards water-based products which do not give off harmful vapours as they dry. Water-based finishes are not as durable as solvent-based ones, but are no longer as far behind them in performance terms as they once were, and they have other advantages such as faster drying times, virtually no smell and easier cleaning of brushes, rollers and pads. It is therefore likely that their use in the home will become much more widespread.

No amount of clever technology can eliminate the need for proper preparation of the surfaces to be decorated, even though this part of the job is far less enjoyable and often more time-consuming than the actual painting. In many cases it involves little more than washing the surface down, but sometimes more thorough preparation will be called for.

This chapter describes the various types of paint, varnish and stain on the market; which to use where; how to prepare surfaces for redecoration; how to apply the new finish – especially to the more awkward surfaces such as windows and panelled doors – and how to create a range of special paint effects that can be a dramatic and inexpensive alternative to wall coverings.

OPPOSITE
Paint offers a huge palette of colours, and complementary and contrasting shades can create the subtlest and most restful of colour schemes. It is the easiest finish to change too when a room needs a new look.

TYPES OF PAINT, VARNISH AND STAIN

Paint works by forming a film on the surface to which it is applied. This film has to do three things: it must hide the surface underneath; it must protect it; and it must stay put. All paint has three main ingredients: pigment, binder and carrier. The *pigment* gives the film its colour and hiding power. The *binder* binds the pigment particles together into a continuous film as the paint dries, and also bonds the film to the surface beneath. In traditional paint this was a natural material such as linseed oil in oil paints, or glue size in distemper; but modern paints use synthetic resins such as alkyd, acrylic, vinyl and polyurethane. The third ingredient, the *carrier*, makes the paint flow smoothly as it is applied, and evaporates as the paint dries.

The ratio of pigment to binder in a paint affects the finish it has when it dries; the higher the pigment content, the duller the finish. By adjusting this ratio, paint manufacturers can produce paints that dry to a flat *matt* finish; to a silky sheen, *eggshell*; or to a high *gloss*. The choice depends on personal preference, tempered by the condition of the surface: high-gloss finishes highlight any imperfections, while matt finishes tend to disguise them.

Paint types

The paint types used in the home have different carriers. Water-based paint has the pigment and binder suspended in water as tiny droplets. It is an emulsion, like milk, and is usually called *emulsion* paint. (In the USA it is

ABOVE The yellow water-based paint chosen for the walls of this kitchen creates a basically warm colour scheme that is off-set by the gloss paint in cool colours selected for the woodwork. Solvent-based (oil) paint is ideal for surfaces which need washing down regularly.

LEFT There is nothing like a hint of strong contrast to bring a neutral colour scheme to life, as the bright red bedposts and picture rail do so dramatically here. Paints specially formulated for steamy locations should be used in en-suite bathrooms.

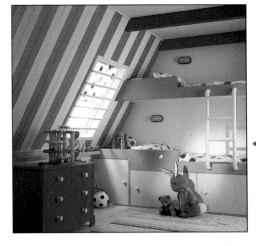

RIGHT Blues and greys are cool, fresh colours that particularly suit a well-lit children's room. The brightly painted ladder provides the perfect contrast. Painted surfaces need to be able to withstand some rough treatment in these locations.

Paint systems

A single coat of paint is too thin to form a durable paint film. To provide adequate cover and performance there must be a paint system consisting of several coats. What these are depends on the type of paint used, and on the surface being painted.

The first coat is a *sealer*, which is used where necessary to seal in things such as the natural resin in wood, or to prevent the paint from soaking into a porous surface.

The second is a *primer*, which provides a good key for the paint film to stick to. On metal surfaces, this also stops the metal corroding or oxidizing. A primer can also act as a sealer.

The third is the *undercoat*, which builds up the film to form a flexible,

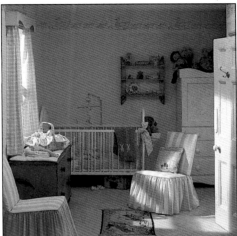

ABOVE A palette of yellow shades adds up to an irresistibly welcoming colour scheme for a baby's nursery.

often called *latex* paint.) As the water evaporates the droplets coalesce to form the paint film. Solvent-based *alkyd* paints have pigment and binder dissolved in a petroleum-based solvent, and take longer to dry than water-based paints. (In the USA these are known as *oil* or *oil-base* paints, though the term 'alkyd' is used for some primers of this kind.) These paints give off a characteristic 'painty' smell as they dry, which many people find unpleasant and to which some are actually allergic. Because of growing awareness of the health risks of inhaling some solvents, the use of these paints is declining in popularity and is already legally restricted in some countries.

Paint also contains a range of other additives to improve its performance. The most notable is one that makes the paint *thixotropic* or non-drip, allowing more paint to be loaded onto the brush and a thicker paint film to be applied; one coat is often sufficient.

LEFT Paint is not only for walls, ceilings and woodwork; it can also help to enhance the crisp lines of ornamental plasterwork.

BELOW Plain painted walls can be given a personal touch with hand-painted embellishments. Decorators with unsteady hands can use stencils instead.

ABOVE Sponging a second colour over a complementary base coat creates a soft broken-colour effect.

ABOVE Rag-rolling is another broken-colour effect that can look especially attractive when applied in stripes over the base colour.

non-absorbent base of uniform colour close to that of the fourth and final layer, the *top coat*, which gives the actual finish and colour.

On walls, for which water-based paint is generally used, the system consists simply of two or three coats of the same paint unless there is a need for a sealer or primer to cure a fault in the surface such as dustiness, high alkalinity or excessive porosity. The first coat is a *mist* coat of thinned paint. A primer is also used if walls are being painted with solvent-based paints.

On woodwork, the first step is to apply a liquid called *knotting* (shellac) to any knots to prevent resin from bleeding through the paint film. Then comes a wood primer, which may be water-based or solvent-based, followed by an undercoat and then the top coat. To speed up the painting process, paint manufacturers have now perfected

combined primer/undercoats, and have also introduced so-called *self-undercoating* gloss paint which just needs a primer.

On metal, a primer is generally needed. A zinc phosphate primer is used for iron or steel, and there are special primers for aluminium. This is then followed by an undercoat and top coat, as for wood. Copper, brass and lead can be painted directly without the need for a primer so long as they are brought to a bright finish first and are thoroughly degreased with white spirit (paint thinner).

Varnishes and wood stains

Varnish is basically paint without the pigment. Most contain polyurethane resins and are solvent-based (like oil paint), although water-based acrylic varnishes are becoming more popular for health and environmental reasons,

CLEANING PAINTING EQUIPMENT

Paint is thinned or diluted if necessary with water or white spirit (paint thinner) according to the paint type. Wash tools and equipment in soapy water if using a water-based paint, and with white spirit or a proprietary brush cleaner for solvent-based (oil) paint. Soak hardened paint in paint remover overnight, then wash out the softened paint with hot soapy water.

ABOVE Coloured varnishes help to enhance the colour of the wood grain without obliterating it completely, as paint does.

ABOVE Varnish is a hardwearing alternative to paint on wood with an attractive grain pattern, and the surface shows marks less readily than paint too.

just as solvent-based paints are losing ground to water-based types. Varnishes are available with a satin/silk or a high-gloss finish, either clear or with the addition of small amounts of colour. These coloured varnishes are intended to enhance the appearance of the wood, or to give it some extra colour without obliterating the wood grain, as paint would do.

Varnish is its own primer and undercoat, although it is best to thin the first coat with about 10 per cent white spirit (paint thinner) for solvent-based types, or water for acrylic types, and to apply it with a lint-free cloth rather than a brush so that it can be rubbed well into the wood grain. When this first coat has dried, it is *keyed* or roughened by rubbing very lightly with fine abrasive paper (sandpaper), dusted off, and a second, full-strength coat brushed on. For surfaces likely to get a lot of wear, it is advisable to key the second coat as before and apply an additional coat.

Wood stains, unlike paint and varnish, are designed to soak into the wood. They may subsequently be sealed

with clear varnish to improve the finish and make the surface more durable. They are available in water-based or solvent-based types in a wide range of colours and wood shades; different colours of the same type can be blended to obtain intermediate shades, and the stain can be thinned with water or white spirit as appropriate to give a paler effect.

Stains are often applied with a brush or a paint pad, but it is often quicker and easier to get even coverage by putting them on with a clean lint-free cloth. Quick work is needed to blend wet edges together, and to avoid overlaps which will leave darker patches as the stain dries. A water-based stain will raise fibres on the surface of the wood, which will spoil the evenness of the colour. The solution is to sand the surface perfectly smooth first and then dampen it with a wet cloth. This will raise the surface fibres. When the wood is dry these fibres are sanded off with extra-fine abrasive paper, ready to receive the application of stain.

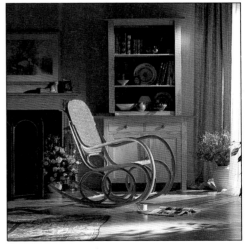

ABOVE Varnish can be used to enhance the natural beauty of wood throughout the home, from floors and fire surrounds to storage units and other items of furniture.

PAINTING TOOLS AND EQUIPMENT

Two groups of tools are needed, one for preparing the surface and one for actually putting the paint on. For a masonry wall, the minimum preparation is to wash down any previously painted surface. This calls for a bucket, sponges and cloths, strong household detergent or sugar soap (all-purpose cleaner), and rubber gloves to protect the hands.

If the washed-down surface has a high-gloss finish, or feels rough to the touch, use fine abrasive paper (sandpaper) and a sanding block to smooth it down. Wet-and-dry (silicon carbide) paper, used wet, is best for sanding down existing paintwork; rinse off the resulting fine slurry of paint with water afterwards. Use ordinary abrasive paper for bare wood.

Defects in the surface need filling. Use a traditional cellulose filler (spackle) for small cracks, chips and other surface blemishes, and an expanding filler foam which can be shaped and sanded when hard for larger defects. To apply filler paste use a filling knife (putty knife).

To strip existing paintwork, use either a heat gun – easier to control and much safer to use than a blowtorch – or a chemical paint remover, plus scrapers of various shapes to remove the softened paint. For removing wall coverings in order to apply a painted wall or ceiling finish, a steam wallpaper stripper will be invaluable. The small all-in-one strippers which resemble a large steam iron are the easiest type to use.

Painting tools

The paintbrush is still the favourite tool for applying paint to walls, ceilings, woodwork and metalwork around the house. Most are made with natural bristle, held in a metal ferrule which is attached to a wooden or plastic handle, but there are also brushes with synthetic fibre bristles which are sometimes recommended for applying water-based (latex) paints.

Brushes come in widths from 12 mm (½ in) up to 150 mm (6 in). The smallest sizes are used for fiddly jobs such as painting glazing bars (muntins), while the widest are ideal for flat uninterrupted wall and ceiling surfaces. However, a wide brush can be tiring to use, especially with solvent-based (oil) paints. There are also long-handled

PREPARATION EQUIPMENT

The following tools and equipment are the general items needed to prepare for repainting: steam wallpaper stripper (1), liquid paint remover (2), paste paint remover (3), cellulose filler (spackle) (4), expanding filler foam (5), rubber gloves (6), bucket (7), sugar soap (all-purpose cleaner) (8), sponge (9), cloth (10), spray gun (11), abrasive paper (sandpaper) (12), sanding block (13), shavehooks (triangular scrapers) (14), scrapers (15), heat gun and attachments (a directional nozzle and two integral scrapers) (16).

brushes with angled heads for painting behind radiators, and narrow brushes called *cutting-in* (sash) brushes, which have the bristle tips cut off at an angle for painting into internal angles. For the best results, buy good-quality brushes and look after them, rather than buy cheap ones and throw them away after finishing the job.

Paint rollers are used mainly for painting walls and ceilings with water-based paints, although they can be used with solvent-based types too. They consist of a metal roller cage mounted on a handle, plus a hollow sleeve that fits onto the cage and actually applies the paint. Some can be fitted with an extension pole, which is useful if there are high ceilings or stairwells to paint. Most rollers are 180 mm (7 in) wide;

larger sizes are available, but can be harder to 'drive'. There are also slim mini-rollers for painting awkward-to-reach areas such as walls behind radiators. For any type, a roller tray is used to load paint onto the sleeve. Solid water-based paint is sold in its own tray.

The sleeves are waterproof tubes with a layer of foam plastic or cloth stuck to the outside. The second type may be made from natural or synthetic fibre, and have a short, medium or long pile. Choose the pile length to match the surface being painted: short for flat surfaces, medium for those with a slight texture and long for heavily embossed or sculpted surfaces.

Paint pads are squares or rectangles of short-pile cloth stuck to a foam backing

and mounted on a plastic or metal handle. The pad is dipped in a shallow container, or loaded from a special paint container with a roller feed, and then drawn across the surface. Pads come in a range of sizes.

Paint and varnish are also sold in *aerosol* form. This is ideal for small areas or fiddly materials such as wickerwork, but too expensive to use on large areas.

Lastly, do not forget the decorating sundries. A *paint kettle* is needed for decanting the paint and straining out any foreign bodies. Hand-held *paint masks* or *masking tape* are invaluable aids to getting straight edges and keeping paint off adjacent surfaces. Above all, remember to provide *dust sheets* (drop cloths), which perform better than plastic sheets.

PAINTING EQUIPMENT

This selection of equipment includes: brushes in various sizes (**1**), aerosol paint (**2**), long-handled brush for use behind radiators (**3**), hand-held skirting (baseboard) masks (**4**), slimline mini-roller (**5**), roller extension pole (**6**), a full-sized roller with short-pile sleeve and roller tray (**7**), dust sheet (drop cloth) (**8**), white spirit (paint thinner) (**9**), long pile and textured roller sleeves (**10**), paint shield (**11**), masking tape (**12**), paint kettle (**13**), paint pads in various sizes and shapes (**14**), paint-loading containers for paint pads (**15**).

PREPARING SURFACES FOR PAINTING

Modern paints have excellent adhesion and covering power, but to get the best performance from them they must be given a good start by preparing the surface thoroughly.

Wash surfaces, which have previously been painted, using a solution of strong household detergent or sugar soap (all-purpose cleaner). Rinse them very thoroughly with clean water, and allow them to dry completely before starting repainting.

Remove areas of flaking paint with a scraper or filling knife (putty knife), and then either touch in the bare area with more paint or fill it flush with the surrounding paint film by using fine filler (spackle). Sand this smooth when it has hardened.

If the surface shows signs of mildew growth due to persistent condensation, wipe it over with household bleach, or refrigerator cleaner containing a fungicide, to kill off the spores. Wash down the surface with detergent and rinse thoroughly.

If knots are showing through on painted woodwork, sand the paint film back to bare wood and apply knotting (shellac) to the knot, then prime and undercoat to bring the new paint film level with the surrounding paintwork. Sand between coats. Resinous knots may produce stains which can only be prevented by drying the knot out with a blowtorch.

PREPARING PAINTED WOODWORK

1 Use fine-grade abrasive paper (sandpaper) wrapped around a sanding block to remove 'nibs' from the paint surface and to key the paint film ready for repainting.

2 Wash the surface down with detergent or sugar soap (all-purpose cleaner) to remove dirt, grease, finger marks and the dust from sanding it. Rinse with clean water, ensuring that no detergent residue is left as this will inhibit the new paint film.

3 Use a proprietary tack rag or a clean cloth moistened with white spirit (paint thinner) to remove dust from recessed mouldings and other awkward corners.

FILLING DEFECTS IN WOOD

1 Fill splits and dents in wood using filler (spackle) on painted surfaces, and tinted wood stopper (patcher) on new or stripped wood that will be varnished.

2 Use the corner of a filling knife (putty knife), or even a finger, to work the filler into recesses and other awkward-to-reach places. Smooth off excess filler before it dries.

3 When the filler or wood stopper has hardened completely, use abrasive paper (sandpaper) wrapped around a sanding block to sand the repair down flush.

FILLING CRACKS IN PLASTER

1 Use the corner of a filling knife (putty knife) to rake out loose material along the line of the crack, and to undercut the edges slightly so that the filler has a better grip.

2 Brush out dust and debris from the crack, using an old paintbrush. Alternatively, use the crevice nozzle attachment of a vacuum cleaner.

3 Dampen the surrounding plaster with water from a garden spray gun to prevent it from drying out the filler too quickly and causing it to crack.

4 Mix up some filler on a plasterer's hawk (mortarboard) or a board offcut to a firm consistency. Alternatively, use ready-mixed filler or wallboard compound.

5 Use a filling knife to press the filler well into the crack, drawing the blade across it and then along it. Aim to leave the repair slightly proud.

DEALING WITH STAINS

If ceilings have been stained by plumbing leaks, seal the affected area with a proprietary aerosol stain sealer to prevent the stain from showing through the new paint film. Alternatively, paint the affected area with white gloss (oil) paint – it will seal just as well and is usually already on hand. It can be overpainted with water-based (latex) paint.

6 When the filler has hardened, use fine-grade abrasive paper (sandpaper) wrapped around a sanding block to smooth the repair flush with the surrounding wall.

STRIPPING PAINT

Every time a surface is repainted, this adds a little more thickness to the paint layer. It does not matter much on wall or ceiling surfaces, but on woodwork (and, to a lesser extent, on metalwork) this build-up of successive layers of paint can eventually lead to the clogging of detail on mouldings. More importantly, moving parts such as doors and windows start to bind and catch against their frames. If this happens, it is time to strip off the paint back to bare wood and build up a new paint system from scratch.

It may also be necessary to strip an old paint finish if it is in such poor condition – from physical damage, for example – that repainting will no longer cover up the faults adequately.

There are two methods of removing paint from wood and metal surfaces. The first is using *heat*, traditionally from a blowtorch but nowadays more often an electric heat gun. The second is to use a *chemical paint remover*, which contains either dimethylene chloride or caustic soda. Heat works well on wood, but may scorch the surface and can crack the glass in windows; it is less successful on metal because the material conducts heat away as it is applied. Chemicals work well on all surfaces, but need handling with care; always follow the manufacturer's instructions to the letter.

HOMEMADE PASTE REMOVER

Add caustic soda to water until no more will dissolve. Thicken to a paste with oatmeal and use as for proprietary paste remover. Be particularly careful when using this corrosive solution. If it splashes on the skin, rinse at once with plenty of cold water.

USING A HEAT GUN

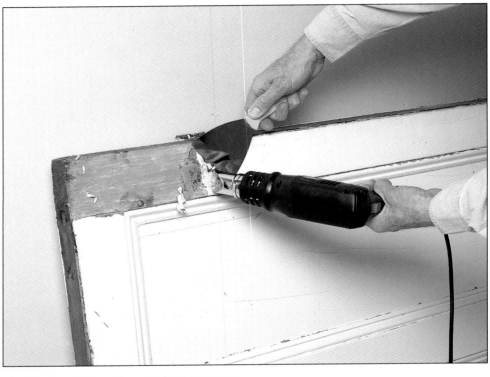

1 Play the air stream from the heat gun over the surface to soften the paint film. Scrape it off as it bubbles up, and deposit the hot scrapings in an old metal container.

2 Use a shavehook (triangular scraper) instead of a flat scraper to remove the paint from mouldings. Take care not to scorch the wood if it is to be varnished afterwards.

3 Remove any remnants of paint from the wood surface with wire wool soaked in white spirit (paint thinner), working along the direction of the grain.

4 Use a hand vacuum cleaner to remove any remaining loose particles of paint from the crevices in mouldings and from any other inaccessible areas.

5 Sand the surface of the wood lightly to remove any raised fibres or rough patches, then wipe it over with a clean cloth moistened with white spirit.

6 Seal the resin in any exposed knots by brushing on a coat of liquid knotting (shellac). Leave this to dry thoroughly before priming the wood.

7 Apply a coat of either wood primer or a combined primer/undercoat to the stripped wood surface to provide optimum adhesion for the subsequent top coats.

USING LIQUID REMOVER

1 Wear rubber gloves and old clothing. Decant the liquid into a polythene (polyethylene) container or an old can, then brush it onto the surface you want to strip. Leave it until the paint film bubbles up.

2 Use a flat scraper or shavehook (triangular scraper) as appropriate to remove the softened paint. Deposit the scrapings safely in an old container.

3 Neutralize the stripper by washing the surface down with water or white spirit (paint thinner), as recommended by the manufacturer. Leave it to dry.

USING PASTE REMOVER

1 Paste removers are especially good for removing paint from intricate mouldings because they dry very slowly. Apply the paste liberally to the surface.

2 Give the paste plenty of time to work, especially on thick paint layers. Then scrape it off and wash down the surface with plenty of water to neutralize the chemical.

USING A PAINTBRUSH

The paintbrush is the most versatile and therefore the most widely used tool for applying paint. Choose the brush size to match the surface being painted. For example, for painting glazing bars (muntins) on windows or narrow mouldings on a door, use a slim brush – or perhaps a cutting-in (sash) brush if painting up to an adjacent unpainted surface such as glass where a neat edge to the paint film is needed. For expansive, flat areas select a larger brush for quick coverage. Remember that the largest wall brushes can be tiring to use, especially with solvent-based (oil) paints.

Get rid of any loose bristles in a new brush by flicking it vigorously across the palm of the hand before using it for the first time. Wash previously used brushes that have been stored unwrapped to remove any dust or other debris from the bristles, and leave them to dry out again before using them to apply a solvent-based paint.

Always check that the metal ferrule is securely attached to the brush handle, and hammer in any projecting nails or staples. Check too that the ferrule is free from rust which could discolour the paint. To remove rust use either wire wool or abrasive paper (sandpaper).

PREPARING THE PAINT

1 Wipe the lid first to remove any dust. Then prise it off with a wide lever such as the thicker edge of a table knife to avoid damage to the lip.

2 Decant some paint into a clean metal or plastic paint kettle, or small bucket. This is easier to handle than a full container, especially one without a handle.

3 Remove any paint skin from partly used containers. Then strain the paint into the paint kettle through a piece of old stocking or tights (pantyhose), or cheesecloth.

HOLDING THE BRUSH

1 Before using a new brush, work it vigorously backwards and forwards across the palm of the hand to remove any loose bristles. Wash stored brushes.

2 The best control of a small or medium-sized brush is achieved by holding it with the fingers and thumb on the ferrule, rather than on the handle.

3 Wide wall brushes can be tiring to use, and it is usually more comfortable to grip the brush by the handle rather than by the ferrule.

1 To load the brush with paint, dip it into the paint to about a third of the bristle depth. An overloaded brush will cause drips, and paint will run down the brush handle.

2 Tie a length of string or wire across the mouth of the paint kettle between the handle supports, and use it to scrape excess paint from the bristles.

3 Apply the paint to the wood in long, sweeping strokes, brushing the paint out along the grain direction until the brush begins to run dry.

4 Load up the brush with more paint and apply it to the next area. Blend the two together with short, light strokes, again along the grain direction.

5 Repeat this process while working across the area, blending the edges of adjacent areas together with light brushstrokes to avoid leaving a visible join.

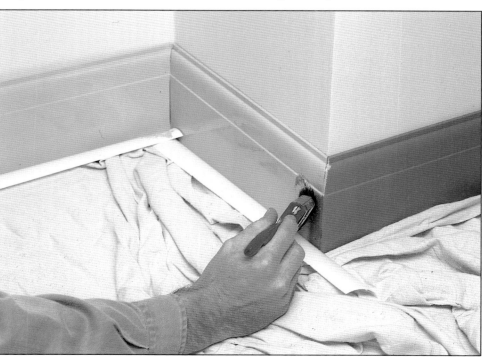

6 At edges and external corners, let the brush run off the edge to avoid a build-up of paint on the corner. Repeat the process for the opposite edge.

USING PAINT ROLLERS AND PADS

Paint rollers are generally used to apply water-based (latex) paints to large, flat areas such as walls and ceilings. Choose a sleeve with a short pile for painting plaster, a medium pile for painting embossed or textured wall coverings, and a long pile for deeply sculpted surfaces such as those created with textured finishes (texture paints). Rollers can also apply solvent-based (oil) paint to flat surfaces such as flush doors, but tend to leave a distinctive 'orange peel' texture rather than the smooth finish left by a paintbrush.

There are some drawbacks with paint rollers: they cannot paint right up to internal corners or wall/ceiling angles, so these need to be painted first with a brush or pad. They can also splash if 'driven' too fast, and the sleeves take a lot of time and effort to clean thoroughly, especially if they have been used for a long period and there is dried paint in the pile. Repeated cleaning eventually causes the sleeve to peel from its core.

People either love or loathe paint pads. They tend to apply less paint per coat than either a brush or a roller, so an additional coat may be needed in some circumstances, but they make it easy to apply paint smoothly and evenly with no risk of brush marks.

USING A ROLLER

1 Select a sleeve with the required fibre type and pile length, and slide it onto the sprung metal cage until it meets the stop next to the handle.

2 Decant some paint (previously strained if from an old can) into the roller tray until the paint level just laps up the sloping section.

3 Brush a band of paint about 50 mm (2 in) wide into internal corners and wall/ceiling angles, around doors and windows, and above skirtings (baseboards).

4 Load the roller sleeve with paint by running it down the sloping section into the paint. Then roll it up and down the slope to remove the excess.

5 Start applying the paint in a series of overlapping diagonal strokes to ensure complete coverage of the surface. Continue until the sleeve runs dry.

6 Reload the sleeve and tackle the next section in the same way. Finish off by blending the areas together, working parallel to corners and edges.

PAINTING

44

USING A PAINT PAD

1 Pour some paint into the special applicator tray. Then load the pad by running it backwards and forwards over the ridged loading roller.

2 On walls, apply the paint in a series of overlapping parallel bands. Use a small pad or a special edging pad (see step 4) to paint right up to corners or angles.

3 Use smaller pads for painting narrow areas such as mouldings on doors or glazing bars (muntins) on windows, brushing out the paint along the direction of the grain.

4 Special edging pads are designed for painting right up to internal angles, and have small wheels which guide the pad along the adjacent surface as you work.

USING AEROSOL PAINT

Aerosol paints and varnishes are ideal for hard-to-decorate surfaces such as wickerwork. Always follow the maker's instructions when using them.

5 Some larger pads can be fitted to an extension pole to make it easier to paint ceilings and high walls. Make sure the pad is attached securely.

PAINTING WALLS AND CEILINGS

Paint is a popular decorative finish for walls and ceilings because it is quick and easy to apply, offers a huge range of colours and is relatively inexpensive compared with rival products such as wall coverings. It can be used over plain plaster, or can be applied over embossed relief wall coverings and textured finishes.

Before starting painting, clear the room and prepare the surfaces. Start by taking down curtains and blinds (drapes and shades). Remove furniture to another room if possible, or else group it in the middle of the room and cover it with clear plastic sheeting. Take down lampshades and pendant light fittings (after turning off the power supply). Unscrew wall-mounted fittings and remove the hardware from doors and windows if they are being repainted at the same time.

Protect surfaces not being repainted, such as wall switches and socket outlets (receptacles), with masking tape. Finally, cover the floor with dust sheets (drop cloths), which will absorb paint splashes; vacuum-clean surfaces such as window sills, picture rails and skirtings (baseboards) where dust can settle, and turn off forced-air heating so that dust is not recirculated into the room.

Access equipment

Normally most of the surfaces to be painted can be reached from a standing or a kneeling position, but for ceilings, the tops of room walls and the upper reaches of stairwells some access equipment is needed. A simple stepladder, ideally with a top platform big enough to support a paint kettle or roller tray, will be adequate for painting walls and ceilings.

PAINTING WALLS AND CEILINGS

Paint walls and ceilings in a series of overlapping bands. Start painting the ceiling next to the window wall so that reflected light on the wet paint shows whether coverage is even. On walls, right-handed people should work from right to left, and left-handed people the other way.

For stairwells, use steps or ladder sections plus secured scaffold boards or the components of a slot-together access tower to set up a work platform that allows you to get to all the surfaces without over-reaching.

Texture paints

Texture paints are water-based (latex) paints thickened with added fillers. Once the paint has been applied to the decorating surface, a range of three-dimensional effects can be created using various patterning or texturing techniques. These paints are ideal for covering up surfaces in poor condition. Most are white, but they can be overpainted with ordinary water-based paint for a coloured effect. Avoid using them in kitchens – the textured surface will trap dirt and grease which is difficult to clean.

PAINT COVERAGE

Paint coverage depends on several factors, including the roughness and porosity of the surface to which it is being applied and the thickness of the coating. For example, the first coat of paint will soak into new plaster, so the coverage will be less than is achieved with subsequent coats. Similarly, a textured surface will hold more paint than a smooth one, again reducing the paint coverage.

The figures given here are intended as a rough guide only. Always check the manufacturer's coverage figure on the container, and use that plus the area to be painted to work out how much paint is required.

ESTIMATING QUANTITIES

Paint type	Sq m per litre	Sq ft per gallon
Liquid gloss (oil) paint	16	650
Non-drip gloss paint	13	530
Eggshell	12	490
Matt (flat) water-based (latex) paint	15	610
Silk (satin) water-based paint	14	570
Non-drip water-based paint	12	490
Undercoat	11	450
Wood primer	12	490
Metal primer	10	410
Varnish	15–20	610–820

1 Start applying the paint to the wall or ceiling surface in a series of overlapping random strokes, recharging the roller or brush at intervals.

2 When an area of about 1 sq m (11 sq ft) is covered, go over the whole area with a series of parallel roller/brush strokes for an even surface texture.

3 Give the textured finish the look of tree bark by drawing a flat-bladed scraper or similar edged tool over the surface to flatten off the high spots.

4 Use a texturing comb to create overlapping swirls, working across the area. Practise the effect on paint applied to a piece of heavy cardboard first.

5 Twist a sponge before pulling it away from the wall surface to create a series of small, overlapping swirls in the paint finish. Rinse the sponge regularly.

6 You can buy patterning roller sleeves in a range of different designs for use with texture paints. This one creates a regular diamond pattern.

7 This patterning sleeve gives a random streaked effect when rolled down the wall. Apply the texture paint with a brush first if using a patterning sleeve.

PAINTING

PAINTING DOORS

The main problem with painting doors – or indeed any woodwork with a large surface area – involves keeping what professional decorators call a *wet edge*. Obviously the door has to be painted bit by bit, and if the edge of one area begins to dry before this is joined up to the next area, the join will show when the paint dries completely.

The secret of success is to work in a sequence, as shown in the accompanying drawings of flush and panelled doors, and to complete the job in one continuous operation, working as fast as reasonably possible.

Before starting to paint a door, wedge it open so there is room to walk through the doorway without touching wet paint, and also so that the hinged edge of the door can be reached easily. Remove handles, locks and other fittings; wedge a length of dowel in the latch hole to make a temporary handle for use until the paint has dried. Slide a dust sheet (drop cloth) underneath the door to catch any drips. Finally, warn everyone else in the house that the door is covered with wet paint, and keep children and pets out of the way in another room or out of doors.

PAINTING FLUSH DOORS

1 Remove the door furniture and wedge the door open. Then divide it up into eight or ten imaginary squares, and start painting at the top of the door by filling in the first square. Brush the paint out towards the door edges so it does not build up on the external angles.

2 Move on to the next block at the top of the door, brushing paint out towards the top and side edges as before. Carefully blend the two areas together with horizontal brushstrokes, then with light vertical laying-off strokes.

3 Continue to work down the door surface block by block, blending the wet edges of adjacent blocks together as they are painted. Always aim to complete a flush door in one session to prevent the joints between blocks showing up as hard lines. Replace the door furniture when the paint is touch-dry.

PAINTING PANELLED DOORS

1 Tackle panelled doors by painting the mouldings (**1**) around the recessed panels first. Take care not to let paint build up in the corners or to stray onto the faces of the cross-rails at this stage. Then paint the recessed panels (**2**).

2 Next, paint the horizontal cross-rails (**3**), brushing lightly inwards towards the painted panel mouldings to leave a sharp paint edge. Feather the paint out thinly where it runs onto the vertical stiles at each end of the rails.

3 Finish the door by painting the vertical centre rail (**4**) and the outer stiles (**5**), again brushing towards the panel mouldings. Where the rail abuts the cross-rails, finish with light brushstrokes parallel to the cross-rails.

PAINTING DOOR EDGES

Where the two faces of a door are being painted in two different colours, the convention is to match the colour of the hinged edge to that of the closing face of the door – the one facing the next room – and to paint the leading edge to match the other door face.

1 HINGED EDGE

VARNISHING WOOD

1 On bare wood, use a clean lint-free cloth to wipe the first coat onto the wood, working along the grain direction. This coat acts as a primer/sealer.

2 Sand the first coat lightly when dry to remove any 'nibs' caused by dust particles settling on the wet varnish, then wipe off the sanding dust.

3 Apply the second and subsequent coats of varnish with a brush, applying it along the grain and linking up adjacent areas with light brush strokes.

PAINTING WINDOWS

Windows are more difficult to paint than doors because they contain so many different surfaces, especially small-paned types criss-crossed with slim glazing bars (muntins). There is also the additional problem of paint straying onto the glass. The ideal is a neat paint line that covers the bedding putty and extends onto the glass surface by about 3 mm (⅛ in) to seal the joint and prevent condensation from running down between putty and glass.

With hinged windows, the edges of the casement or top opening light (transom) should be painted to match the colour used on the inside of the window. With double-hung sliding sash windows, the top and bottom edges of each sash and the top, bottom and sides of the frame are all painted to match the inner face of the sashes.

Remove the window hardware before you start painting. On casement windows tap a nail into the bottom edge of the casement and into the lower frame rebate and link them with stiff wire to stop the casement from swinging open or shut.

For best results, sash windows should be removed from their frames before painting. Modern spring-mounted windows are easy to release from their frames. With older cord-operated types, remove the staff beads (window stops) first to free the sashes. Although quite a major task, take the opportunity to renew the sash cords (pulley ropes). This makes it possible to cut the cords to free the window. Some making good and finishing off will have to be done after the window is reassembled.

PAINTING A CASEMENT WINDOW

1 Remove the window furniture from the opening casement and wedge the window open while you work. Tackle the glazing bars (muntins) and edge mouldings first (**1**), then the face of the surrounding casement frame (**2**) and finally the hinged edge of the casement. Paint the other edges from outside.

2 Move on to paint the glazing bars and edge mouldings (**3**) of the fixed casement. Use masking tape or a paint shield to ensure neat, straight edges here and on the opening casement; the paint should overlap the glass by about 3 mm (⅛ in). Paint the face of the surrounding casement frame (**4**).

PAINTING A SASH WINDOW

1 To paint sash windows without removing the sashes from their frames, start by raising the bottom (inner) sash and lowering the top (outer) one. Paint the lower half of the top sash (**1**), including its bottom edge, and the exposed parting beads at the top and bottom (**2**) and the exposed sides of the frame itself.

2 When the paint is touch-dry, reverse the sash positions and paint the upper half of the top sash (**3**), including its top edge, and the exposed and unpainted parting beads and frame sides (**4**).

PAINTING AROUND GLASS

3 Paint the outer frame (**5**), then the centre frame member between the opening and fixed casements (**6**). Complete the job by painting the window sill (**7**) and the rebate into which the opening casement closes.

1 Stick masking tape to the glass with its edge 3 mm (⅛ in) from the wood. Paint the surrounding wood, removing the tape when the paint is touch-dry.

2 Alternatively, hold a paint shield against the edge of the glazing bar (muntin) or surrounding moulding while painting. Wipe the shield regularly to prevent smears.

USING STAIN

3 Finish off by painting the face and edges of the inner sash (**5**), the staff beads and any other trim mouldings around the window (**6**). Finally, paint the window sill (**7**). Leave the sashes ajar until the paint has dried to avoid components sticking.

Test the stain on an offcut of the same wood, or in an inconspicuous area. If necessary, dilute it. Use a clean lint-free cloth to apply stain to bare wood. If the result is too pale, apply further coats when the first is dry. Avoid overlapping parallel bands of stain; the overlap will show up as a darker area when the stain dries.

TIP

To clean up an untidy paint edge on the glass, use a ruler and a very sharp knife to cut a clean edge, and carefully scrape off the excess paint up to the cut line.

SPECIAL PAINT EFFECTS

There is no need to stick to plain colour on painted walls as there is a wide range of special paint effects that will enliven their looks. Some of these effects are purely decorative in their own right; others imitate the appearance of other materials. All can be created with the use of inexpensive tools and materials, and practice and patience will bring highly attractive results.

The special paint effects dealt with here fall into two broad groups: *broken colour* and *imitation*. In the first group a range of different techniques is used to apply a second colour over a different base colour so that the latter still shows through, providing a pleasing two-colour effect. In the second group paint is used to copy the looks of materials such as wood veneers and marble.

For either finish it is essential to prepare the surface of the wall or woodwork thoroughly first (see chart).

Glazes

Most special effects are applied as a tinted glaze which is semi-transparent and allows the underlying base colour to show through. Water-based glazes are made from water-based (latex) paint diluted with water or a proprietary emulsion glaze until the required level of translucency has been achieved. Use coloured paints or tint white paint to the required shade with artists' acrylics. Water-based glazes produce a thinner, more open, coat of colour and they dry extremely quickly, which means they are not suitable for the more complex special paint effects.

Scumble is the main component of solvent-based (oil) glazes and is generally diluted with a mixture of 1 part linseed oil to 2 parts white spirit (paint thinner). However, the proportions can be varied: a higher proportion of scumble will increase the definition of the effect and will retard the drying time; more linseed oil produces a smoother texture; white spirit thins the glaze and speeds up the drying time. Once the glaze has been mixed, pour off a small quantity and add the colour to this, using either eggshell paint or artists' oils. When the correct colour has been mixed, gradually add this to the main quantity of glaze until the required level of transparency is achieved. Solvent-based glazes have a rich, hardwearing

TOOLS AND MATERIALS

Among the tools and materials needed are a stencilling brush (**1**), a dusting brush (**2**), a small paintbrush (**3**), a softening brush (**4**), a stippling brush (**5**), artists' paintbrushes (**6**), cotton or linen rags (**7**), a natural marine sponge (**8**), a rubber rocker for graining (**9**), a large paintbrush (**10**) and a flat-bristle varnishing brush (**11**).

PREPARING SURFACES

The method of preparation varies depending on whether water-based (latex) paints or solvent-based (oil) paints are used for the final effect. Care taken at this early stage will help to ensure a satisfying end result.

Once the preparation is complete, apply the chosen base colour. Use eggshell for a good opaque and non-porous surface if using either a water- or a solvent-based finish and, when dry, rub it down with fine abrasive paper (sandpaper).

finish and the slower drying times are particularly suited to special effects.

If working over large areas – more than 2 sq m (22 sq ft) – two people will be needed to achieve the best finish: one to apply the glaze and the other to work it. This is the only way to maintain a wet edge and therefore to avoid noticeable joins between one area of colour and the next.

Stencilling

This is slightly different from the other techniques, since the stencil produces a clearly defined shape. It is very simple to do, and can be used to create effects in more than one colour by using different stencils. Ready-cut stencils can be bought, but it is easy to create designs of your own.

Surface	Water-based effect	Solvent-based effect
Bare plaster	Prime with diluted water-based paint	Prime with proprietary primer or PVA adhesive (white glue)
	Apply 1–2 water-based undercoats	Apply 1–2 solvent-based undercoats
Painted plaster	Wash down, repair defects and sand solvent-based finishes	Wash down, repair defects and sand solvent-based finishes
	Apply 1–2 water-based undercoats	Apply 1–2 solvent-based undercoats
Hardboard	Prime with diluted water-based paint	Prime with proprietary primer
	Apply 1–2 water-based undercoats	Apply 1–2 solvent-based undercoats
Bare wood	Apply knotting (shellac) to knots	Apply knotting (shellac) to knots
	Prime with diluted water-based paint	Apply proprietary primer
	Apply 1–2 water-based undercoats	Apply 1–2 solvent-based undercoats
Painted wood	As for Painted plaster	As for Painted plaster
Varnished wood	Strip and prepare as for Bare wood	Strip and prepare as for Bare wood

CUTTING STENCILS

To cut stencils, tracing paper, some special waxed paper for stencils (available from art stores), a pencil, a pin and a scalpel or sharp utility knife are needed. Trace or draw the pattern and enlarge or reduce it on a photocopier, if necessary. Tape the finished trace to the stencil paper and prick through it to mark the design outline on the stencil paper. Join up the prick marks in pencil. Alternatively, transfer the trace onto the stencil using carbon paper. Cut out the design carefully, leaving sufficient ties to bridge the separate areas of the design. Allow a large margin above and below the design so that the stencil is sufficiently strong. Reinforce any tears or accidental cuts with adhesive tape.

1 Affix the stencil to the surface with masking tape, aligning it with a true horizontal pencil guideline. Dip the stencilling brush in the paint and remove the excess on some waste paper. Use a pouncing action to apply the paint to minimize the risk of colour seeping under the stencil and marring the masked-off areas.

2 When the paint is touch-dry, release the stencil, wipe off the wet paint and reposition it farther along the wall to create the next section of the pattern.

Sponging

This technique involves dabbing irregular patches of paint onto the base coat. Two or more different sponged colours can be applied. Note that a natural marine sponge must be used to create this effect; man-made sponges do not work. Soak it in water first until it swells to its full size, then wring it out ready to start applying the paint.

2 Allow the first application to dry, then go over the surface again and add more colour if necessary to deepen the contrast with the base colour.

3 If applying a different second colour, allow the first colour to dry and then use the same technique to apply the new colour over it.

1 After testing the effect on an offcut of board, dip the sponge in the paint and apply light pressure to leave overlapping splodges of colour.

Rag-rolling

Another simple two-colour effect, rag-rolling involves brushing a diluted second colour over the base coat and then using a rolled-up 'sausage' of cloth to remove some of the second colour before it starts to dry.

The technique works best with a base coat of eggshell paint and a top coat of eggshell paint diluted with white spirit (paint thinner). Use lint-free cotton or linen rags and change them frequently before they become soaked with paint.

1 Allow the base coat to dry thoroughly. Then lightly brush on the second diluted colour in bands across the surface, aiming to leave a random pattern of brushstrokes that allows the base colour to show through.

2 Roll the rag sausage across the surface in a continuous motion. Vary the direction for a random effect and touch in small areas by just dabbing with the cloth. Replace the rag regularly.

Stippling

For an attractive mottled appearance, try stippling; apart from being used as a decorative finish in its own right it can also be used to obliterate brush marks in the base coat beneath other broken-colour effects.

The one item of specialist equipment that is needed to create this effect is a stippling brush.

1 Brush the glaze on over the base coat, applying a generous coat. Do not worry about leaving brush marks; the stippling will obliterate them.

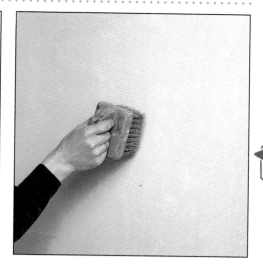

2 Hold the stippling brush with the bristle tips parallel with the surface, and simply hit the paint film. Clean paint from the brush regularly, wiping it with a dry cloth.

Colour washing

This is one of the simplest broken-colour effects. Brush on the glaze and then use a dry softening brush or an ordinary wide paintbrush to create a random pattern of brushstrokes that allow the base coat to show through. A further colour can be added.

1 Brush a liberal coat of the glaze over the base coat. The effect of colour washing is enhanced when there is a good contrast between the two paint colours.

2 Draw the softening brush over the glaze in a series of long random strokes in varying directions. Add a further toning colour if desired when this coat has dried.

SPECIAL PAINT EFFECTS (*continued*)

Graining

Graining is a technique that aims to imitate the look of natural wood, especially the more exotic and expensive species. Use a solvent-based (oil) eggshell paint for the base coat, and a solvent-based glaze.

2 Then, after a couple of minutes, draw a dry graining brush or an ordinary paintbrush lightly over the glaze to create the actual grain pattern.

3 Use a rubber rocker (as here), a graining comb or a bristle grainer to produce the individual grain characteristics of the wood you are copying.

1 Brush the glaze onto the wood surface, leaving the brush marks visible along the direction of the intended wood grain effect.

Dragging

Another very simple effect, dragging is created by drawing a dry brush over the glaze in a series of parallel strokes that allow the base colour to show through. Use a normal paintbrush in a width to suit the surface being decorated.

1 Brush a generous coat of glaze over the base coat. Always work parallel to the direction of the grain if applying the effect to wood.

2 Use a dry paintbrush to drag a series of parallel lines in the second colour. Wipe the build-up of paint off the brush at regular intervals with a dry cloth.

Marbling

As its name implies, marbling copies the appearance of marble. It is a relatively difficult technique to master, but the results can be quite spectacular. For a first attempt choose a piece of real marble to copy. For best results work with a solvent-based (oil) glaze, applied over an eggshell base coat. Add the veining details with artists' oils.

VARNISHING SPECIAL PAINT EFFECTS

Some special paint effects, especially graining and marbling, should be sealed with a coat of clear varnish once the effect has dried completely. Use satin varnish rather than gloss unless a particularly polished effect is required. When this has dried, burnish the surface with a soft cloth and add a little wax polish to create a realistic surface sheen, if wished.

1 Either brush out the glaze or apply it with a pad of lint-free cloth. Only a relatively thin coat is needed.

2 Use a dusting brush as here or a stippling brush to stipple the surface of the wet glaze. Add more colour to the glaze mixture, apply selectively to some areas for contrast and stipple the glaze again.

3 Working on the wet glaze, draw in the main areas of veining with an artists' paintbrush and a mixture of glaze and artists' oils. Use different weights of line to create a natural-looking effect.

4 Use the softening brush again to soften the outlines of the veining and to blend it into the background. Wipe the brush regularly to avoid smudges.

5 Highlight some areas of the veining by adding more colour or a second colour. Soften the effect again, as in step 4.

PAPERHANGING

The term 'wall coverings' is used to describe the whole range of decorative materials sold in roll form and designed to be stuck to wall and ceiling surfaces with a strippable adhesive. The range includes an enormous variety of designs, patterns and colourways . . . almost too many, as any home decorator will testify when confronted by an array of pattern books and trying to decide which covering to select.

The vast majority of wall coverings are either made entirely from paper, or have a plastic or cloth layer bonded to a paper backing so that they can be hung in the same way as all-paper types. The basic technology of paperhanging has changed little over the centuries, even if the products have been subtly altered and improved; people still paper the living room in a way that would be familiar to their grandparents.

The two main developments that have occurred in recent years are the introduction of ready-pasted types which are immersed in a trough of water instead of having paste brushed onto them, and of all-plastic wall coverings which are hung by pasting the wall.

This chapter gives information on the various types of wall covering available and on the tools, materials and other equipment needed to hang or strip them. There is advice on how to go about removing existing wall decorations – other wall coverings, materials such as texture paints, wall panelling and tiles of various types – and on preparing the surface. This is followed by detailed step-by-step instructions on how to hang a new wall covering on walls and ceilings, and on how to cope with awkward areas such as door and window openings, arches and stairwells.

OPPOSITE
There is virtually no limit to the versatility of modern wall coverings. This complementary match of broken colour and simple stripes is linked by a striking multicoloured border at dado (chair) rail level.

BELOW Contrasting wall coverings can help to change the proportions of a room. Here a border at picture-rail level provides a natural break, and the darker wall covering above it helps lower the ceiling, emphasizing the country-style decor.

Wall coverings fall into two basic groups: those with a printed design or a surface material which is decorative in its own right, and those with a surface texture or embossing which are designed to be painted over once they have been hung.

Printed wallpaper is exactly that – paper with a coloured design printed on it. It may also be embossed along the lines of the design, or may have a distinctive surface texture added during manufacture. Cheaper types may be awkward to hang, tearing easily or stretching so as to make accurate pattern matching difficult. More expensive types, especially hand-printed ones, are better in this respect, but care must still be taken when hanging them to keep paste off the face of the paper. The strongest printed wallpapers are called *duplex papers*, and are made by bonding two layers of paper together during the manufacturing process. Most printed papers can be wiped with a damp cloth if they become stained, but it is wise to check whether this is the case when selecting this type of wall covering. All are easy to strip, making them a good choice if you like to redecorate regularly.

Washable wallpaper is a printed wallpaper which has a thin clear plastic coating applied over the design during manufacture to render it water and stain resistant. As with printed types, the surface may be embossed or textured. Washable wallpapers are also widely available in ready-pasted form. The plastic surface will withstand gentle washing and sponging with a mild detergent, but not prolonged scrubbing or the use of abrasive cleaners. Choose them for rooms where they will be subject to moderate wear, or for steamy conditions such as are

LEFT Stencil borders with the design printed on a clear self-adhesive backing allow the wall covering beneath to show through – the perfect solution for unwilling stencillers.

LEFT In bathrooms, vinyl wall coverings resist steam and splashes well and are easy to wipe clean. Foamed types offer excellent imitations of materials such as ceramic tiles.

Tougher still are the *foamed vinyl wall coverings*, which have a surface layer aerated with tiny bubbles to produce a slightly cushioned feel. The surface may be heavily textured or embossed to imitate materials such as ceramic tiles and wood grains, and is warm to the touch thanks to the insulating effect of the air bubbles – a fact that makes such a covering a good choice for rooms which are prone to mild condensation. Because of their bulk, they are

BELOW Many collections of wall coverings feature colour-coordinated borders and fabrics to enable rooms to be given the most stylish of colour treatments.

found in kitchens and bathrooms. Their main drawback is that they are difficult to remove because the plastic coating stops water penetrating and softening the paste unless it is thoroughly scored first; a steam wallpaper stripper is advisable.

Vinyl wall coverings consist of a plastic film onto which the design is printed, laminated to a paper backing. Again, the surface may also be textured or embossed, or may have a metallic appearance – the so-called *vinyl foils*. The result is a wall covering that is much tougher than a washable type; if properly hung it can be scrubbed to remove stains and marks, although care must be taken not to lift the seams by oversoaking the surface. Vinyl wall coverings are widely available in ready-pasted form, and are extremely easy to strip since the plastic layer can be peeled off dry, leaving the paper backing on the wall. They are the ideal choice for walls that will be scuffed or brushed against – in halls and landings or on staircases, for example – and also for children's rooms, kitchens and bathrooms. They are, however, more expensive than most printed or washable wall coverings, so it is just as well that they can be expected to provide excellent wear.

sometimes sold in shorter rolls than other wall coverings.

Flock wall coverings are either printed papers or vinyls with parts of the design having a raised pile – of fine wool or silk fibres on paper types and of synthetic fibres on vinyls – that closely resembles velvet. Paper types are quite delicate and must be hung with care, but vinyl flocks are extremely tough and hardwearing.

Yet another printed wall covering is made from *foamed polythene* (polyethylene) with no paper backing, and is intended to be hung by pasting the wall and then brushing the covering into position direct from the roll – the material is very light compared to paper-backed types. The surface can be washed, but is relatively fragile and will not withstand repeated scuffing or knocks. The material can be simply dry-stripped from walls and ceilings, like the plastic surface layer of a vinyl wall covering.

An alternative to a printed surface design is a texture. This can be achieved with a paper-backed *fabric* wall covering. The commonest is hessian (burlap), but there are also

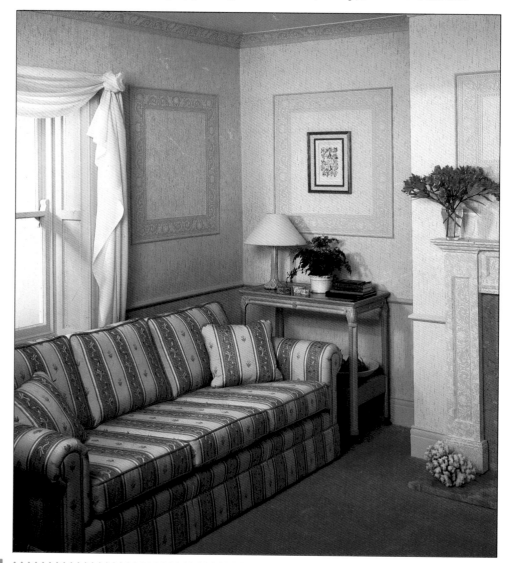

materials such as silk, tweed, wool strands, grasscloth and linen, offering a range of softly tinted or boldly coloured wall finishes. Apart from hessian, they are comparatively expensive. They can also be difficult to hang and remove, and so are best used for decorating or highlighting small and relatively well-protected areas such as alcoves. They can be vacuum-cleaned to remove surface dust, and small marks can be washed gently or lifted with special fabric cleaners.

The other kind of textured wall covering is intended for overpainting. These materials are generally known as *relief wall coverings* or 'whites'. The cheapest is *woodchip paper*, also known as oatmeal or ingrain, which has small chips of wood sandwiched at random between a heavy backing paper and a thinner surface layer. The wood chips may be fine or coarse, and the effect after painting is often likened to thinly-spread porridge.

Vinyls are also made as relief wall coverings, with a plain white aerated plastic surface layer that is moulded during manufacture into a range of random or repeating patterns.

Other relief wall coverings are embossed to produce a random or regular surface pattern. Those with a relatively low relief design are generally two-layer duplex papers which are embossed while the adhesive bonding the two layers is still wet; this helps to retain the relief during hanging. Those with more pronounced embossing are made from stronger paper containing cotton fibres rather than wood, and are also embossed wet.

All the relief wall coverings can be painted with water-based (latex) or solvent-based (oil) paints. A steam wallpaper stripper will be needed to remove them.

There is one further type of wall covering: lining (liner) paper. As its name suggests, this is a plain paper used for lining wall surfaces in poor condition or having uneven or zero porosity before a decorative wall covering is hung. It comes in various weights, from 55 g/sq m (360 lb) up to 90 g/sq m (600 lb), and in two grades, white and extra-white. The latter can also be used as an economy wall covering, and is hung in the usual way and then overpainted.

OPPOSITE Self-adhesive borders can be used to add decorative detail to any room. Here they highlight the cornice (crown molding) and form wall panels.

BELOW Borders can be used round door openings, beneath decorative features such as plate rails, and even as an unusual embellishment for panelled doors.

ABOVE Low-relief wallcoverings are the ideal cover-up for less-than-perfect wall surfaces, and are available in a wide range of random and regular designs.

ABOVE A three-dimensional frieze is an unusual way of filling in above a picture rail. The embossed panels are butt-jointed to form a continuous strip.

PAPERHANGING TOOLS AND EQUIPMENT

As for painting, there are two distinct groups of tools, equipment and materials to deal with wall coverings.

Stripping tools

The basic technique for removing an old wall covering is to soften the paste used to stick it to the wall so that it can be scraped off and discarded. To strip porous materials such as ordinary printed paper and the backing paper left behind after dry-stripping vinyl wall covering, use a bucket of water and a sponge or a garden spray gun to apply the water, dust sheets (drop cloths) to protect floor coverings, and a broad-bladed scraping knife to remove the softened paper.

To remove wall coverings with a water-resistant plastic or painted surface, it is necessary to pierce the surface film and so allow the water to penetrate. This can be done with a serrated wallpaper scraper or preferably a toothed roller or wheels, which is rolled backwards and forwards over the surface to create hundreds of little perforations. The water will take longer to penetrate this type of wall covering.

Stripping can be speeded up dramatically on coated wall coverings (and also on paper-backed fabrics and texture paints) by using a steam stripper. This consists of a perforated steaming plate and a water reservoir heated by electricity or bottled gas. Steam penetrates the surface far more quickly than water does, enabling the covering to be stripped quickly and effectively.

Paperhanging tools

There are four separate operations involved in hanging a new wall covering: cutting to length, pasting, hanging and trimming.

For cutting, the tools are a retractable steel tape measure, a pencil and a pair of scissors (or a sharp utility knife and a steel straightedge).

For pasting the wall covering, there should be a bucket in which to mix the paste (unless using ready-mixed tub paste), plus a stirrer and a brush with which to apply the paste. A 100 mm (4 in) wide paintbrush is satisfactory, but a special pasting brush can be bought.

As far as choosing the correct paste is concerned, follow the instructions for the wall covering concerned. In particular, remember that a paste containing a fungicide should be used for washable and vinyl coverings, to prevent mould from growing in the paste as it slowly dries under the impervious covering. A special overlap adhesive will be needed for lap joints in internal and external corners when using washables or vinyls.

When hanging a ready-pasted wall covering, the table, bucket and brush can be dispensed with. All that is needed is a plastic soaking trough in which to immerse the rolled-up lengths of wall covering.

Before starting hanging, a plumb bob and line are needed to mark a true vertical line on the wall against which to hang the first length.

Most wall coverings are applied with a special soft-bristled paperhanging brush. These are generally between 190 and 250 mm (7½ to 10 in) wide, and have a slim handle. The soft bristles help to make the wall covering follow the contours of the wall surface behind, and also eliminate undue hand contact with the face of the covering, which might mark it.

A sponge can be used instead of a brush for hanging washables or vinyls, especially if they are ready-pasted, since here the sponge helps mop water from the surface of the wall covering as well as smoothing it into place.

The final stage is trimming, and the best tool for this is a special pair of paperhangers' scissors. These have blades up to 300 mm (12 in) long for making long, straight cuts.

For papering walls a stepladder is needed which should be tall enough to enable the ceiling to be easily touched. For papering ceilings, set up a proper platform across the width of the room at a comfortable height, using scaffold boards or staging on trestles or other low supports to ensure complete stability. Do not step from chair to chair or set up similar makeshift arrangements.

PASTING TABLES

A flat surface is needed to lay the paper on while it is being pasted. It is best to use a proper pasting table. This is a lightweight folding table covered in hardboard or plywood on a softwood frame, and is usually about 1.8 m (6 ft) long and just wider than a standard roll of wall covering. If you cannot buy, borrow or hire a pasting table, one can be improvised by cutting a standard sheet of plywood or chipboard (particle board) down to the same width and supporting it on trestles or sawhorses.

SEAM ROLLERS

For smooth wall coverings, a tool called a seam roller can be used to make sure that the seams are well bonded to the wall. Do not use a seam roller on textured or embossed wall coverings, though, as it will flatten the embossing.

Displayed on a fold-up pasting table are a soaking trough (1), rubber gloves (2), sponge (3), pencil (4), sharp utility knife (5), paperhangers' scissors (6), plumb bob and line (7), retractable steel tape measure (8), steel straightedge (9), paste bucket (10), pasting brush (11), packet of ready-mixed paste (12), seam roller (13) and paperhanging brush (14). A spirit level (15) can do double duty in checking verticals and as a straightedge.

10

11

12

13

14

15

PREPARING FOR PAPERHANGING

Unrestricted access is a must for paperhanging. If working on just the walls, move all the furniture to the centre of the room and cover it with dust sheets (drop cloths). When tackling the ceiling too, it is best to remove all the furniture completely if there is space to store it elsewhere in the house; otherwise group it at one end of the room so that most of the ceiling can be done, and then move it to the other end to complete the job.

Next, take down curtains and blinds (drapes and shades) and remove wall-mounted or ceiling-mounted tracks. Turn off the electricity supply at the mains, then disconnect and remove wall or ceiling light fittings as necessary, covering the bare wire ends thoroughly with insulating tape before restoring the power supply to the rest of the house. In the USA, ceiling roses, wall switch plates and socket outlets can be unscrewed and removed without

disconnecting the wall receptacles or switches. Isolate, drain, disconnect and remove radiators, and unscrew their wall brackets. Call in a professional electrician or plumber for these jobs if unsure of how to do them safely.

Lift down pictures, and remove other wall-mounted fittings such as shelves and display units. To make it easy to relocate the screw holes afterwards, push a matchstick (wooden match) into each one (see Tip).

CHOOSING THE STARTING POINT

ABOVE Start paperhanging at the centre of a chimney breast (fireplace projection) if the wall covering has a large, dominant pattern. Otherwise start next to the door so the inevitable pattern break can be disguised above it.

RIGHT Work outwards from the centre of a dormer window so the design is centred on the window recess.

ESTIMATING WALL COVERINGS (WALLS)

Height	Distance around room																		
	9m 30ft	10m 33ft	12m 40ft	13m 42ft	14m 46ft	15m 50ft	16m 52ft	17m 56ft	19m 62ft	20m 66ft	21m 69ft	22m 72ft	23m 75ft	25m 82ft	26m 85ft	27m 88ft	28m 92ft	30m 98ft
2.15–2.30 m / 7–7½ ft	4	5	5	6	6	7	7	8	8	9	9	10	10	11	12	12	13	13
2.30–2.45 m / 7½–8 ft	5	5	6	6	7	7	8	8	9	9	10	10	11	11	12	13	13	14
2.45–2.60 m / 8–8½ ft	5	5	6	7	7	8	9	9	10	10	11	12	12	13	14	14	15	15
2.60–2.75 m / 8½–9 ft	5	5	6	7	7	8	9	9	10	10	11	12	12	13	14	14	15	15
2.75–2.90 m / 9–9½ ft	6	6	7	7	8	9	9	10	10	11	12	12	13	14	14	15	15	16
2.90–3.05 m / 9½–10 ft	6	6	7	8	8	9	10	10	11	12	12	13	14	14	15	16	16	17
3.05–3.20 m / 10–10½ ft	6	7	8	8	9	10	10	11	12	13	13	14	15	16	16	17	18	19

Numbers are based on a standard roll size of 10.05 m (33 ft) long and 520 mm (20½ in) wide. The measurement around the room includes all windows and doorway.

If the walls and ceiling are at present painted, they need washing down to remove dirt, grease, smoke stains and the like. If they are decorated with another wall covering, this will have to be removed and any defects in the surface put right. Finally, they need sizing – treating with a diluted coat of wallpaper adhesive to even out the porosity of the surface and to help to improve the 'slip' of the pasted wall covering during hanging.

Measuring up

The next job is to estimate how many rolls of wall covering will be needed to decorate the room. If using a material that comes in standard-sized rolls, simply measure the room dimensions and refer to the charts given here for the number of rolls needed to cover the walls and ceiling. They allow for a typical door and window area; fewer rolls are needed for a room with large picture windows or wide door openings. If using a paper-backed cloth covering which comes in a nonstandard width, measure up each wall, and ask the supplier to estimate what length of material you will need; such materials

are too expensive to waste. Wall coverings in the USA vary in width and length but are usually available in rolls sized to cover a specified area, allowing for trimming.

Buying wall coverings

Wall coverings are made in batches, with a number printed on the label, and it is important to check that there are

sufficient rolls with the same batch number; colours may not match exactly between batches.

When hanging a wall covering with a particularly large pattern repeat, wastage is often unusually high and it may be wise to purchase one or two extra rolls, over and above the numbers given in the charts. Most suppliers will take back unopened rolls.

ESTIMATING WALL COVERINGS (CEILINGS)

Distance around room		No of
m	ft	rolls
10	33	2
11	36	2
12	40	2
13	42	3
14	46	3
15	50	4
16	52	4
17	56	4
18	59	5
19	62	5
20	66	5
21	69	6
22	72	7
23	75	7

TIP

Insert a matchstick (wooden match) in each hole left when unscrewing wall-mounted fixtures and fittings that will be replaced later. It will burst through the wall covering as this is applied and make it easy to find the screw holes.

STRIPPING OLD WALL COVERINGS

In the days when ordinary printed wall coverings were all that were usually on sale, it was common practice to paper over existing wallpaper, often to the point where four or five successive layers would accumulate. This is no longer considered acceptable (and will not work at all over today's washable and vinyl wall coverings), and it is always best to strip all old coverings before hanging new ones. Even if the old material looks sound, hanging a newly-pasted wall covering over it may cause it to lift from the wall, creating ugly bubbles that are impossible to disguise. This also applies to the backing paper that is left on the wall after dry-stripping a vinyl wall covering; there is no guarantee that it is perfectly bonded to the wall, and so hanging another wall covering over it could give very poor results.

Once the room is cleared and dust sheets (drop cloths) are spread over the floor and any remaining furniture, the next step is to identify what type of wall covering is to be removed. An ordinary printed paper will absorb water splashed on it immediately; other types will not. To tell washables from vinyls, pick and lift a corner and try to strip the wall covering dry. The printed plastic layer of a vinyl wall covering will peel off dry, but the surface of a washable paper will not come off in the same way unless it is a duplex paper made in two layers. With paper-backed fabric wall coverings, it is often possible to peel the fabric away from its paper backing; try it before turning to other more complicated methods of removal.

1 To strip printed wallpapers, wet the surface with a sponge or a garden spray gun. Wait for the water to penetrate, and repeat if necessary.

2 Using a stiff wallpaper scraper – not a filling knife (putty knife) – start scraping the old paper from the wall at a seam. Wet it again while working if necessary.

3 Turn off the power before stripping around switches and other fittings, then loosen the faceplate screws to strip the wallpaper behind them.

4 After removing the bulk of the old wallpaper, go back over the wall surface and remove any remaining 'nibs' of paper with sponge/spray gun and scraper.

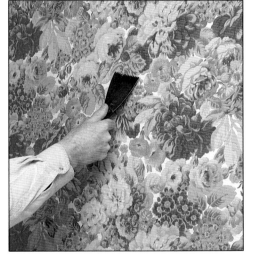

5 To strip a washable wallpaper, start by scoring the plastic coating with a serrated scraper or toothed roller, then soak and scrape as before.

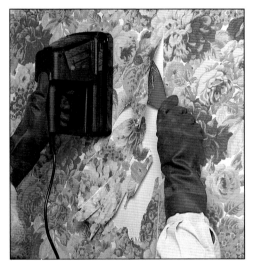

6 For quicker results, use a steam stripper to remove washable papers. Press the steaming plate to the next area while stripping the area just steamed.

STRIPPING VINYLS

1 Strip vinyl wall coverings by lifting a corner to separate the vinyl layer from the paper backing. Strip it off by pulling it away from the wall surface.

2 Always soak and remove the plain backing paper left on the wall after stripping a vinyl. It may well not be a sound lining for a new wall covering.

REMOVING OTHER OLD FINISHES

If the wall or ceiling to be given a new covering is painted or wallpapered, preparing the surface for its new finish is quite straightforward. However, if it was previously covered with materials such as texture paint, ceramic or polystyrene tiles or wall panelling, more work will be needed to remove the old finishes and return the surface to its original condition.

Textured finishes are tackled in different ways, depending on their type. Texture paints are basically thick water-based (latex) paints, normally used to create relatively low-relief effects, and can be removed with specially formulated paint removers. Some textured effects formed with a powder or ready-mixed compound are best removed with a steam wallpaper stripper, which softens the compound so that it can be scraped from the wall.

Never attempt to sand off a textured finish. There are two reasons. The first is that it will create huge quantities of very fine dust; the second is that older versions of this product contained asbestos fibres as a filler, and any action that might release these into the atmosphere as inhalable dust must be avoided at all costs.

For tiles and wall panelling, complete removal or a cover-up with plasterboard (gypsum board) are the two options available. The former will leave a surface in need of considerable renovation, while the latter will cause a slight loss of space within the room, as well as some complications at door and window openings.

REMOVING TEXTURED FINISHES

1 Strip texture paint by brushing on a generous coat of a proprietary texture paint remover. Stipple it well into the paint and leave it to penetrate.

2 When the paint has softened, scrape it off with a broad-bladed scraper. Wear gloves, and also safety goggles if working on a ceiling.

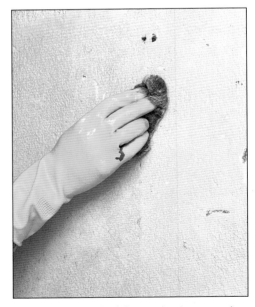

3 Once the bulk of the coating is removed, use wire wool dipped in the paint remover to strip off any remaining flecks of paint.

4 Remove powder-based or ready-mixed types using a steam stripper, which will soften the finish. Never try to sand off this type of finish.

REMOVING CERAMIC TILES

1 On a completely tiled wall, use a hammer to crack a tile and create a starting point for the stripping. On partly tiled walls, start at the tile edge.

2 Use a broad bolster (stonecutter's) chisel and a club (spalling) hammer to chip the old tiles off the wall. Have the wall replastered afterwards rather than trying to patch the surface up.

REMOVING POLYSTYRENE TILES

1 Lever the tiles away from the ceiling with a scraper. If they were fixed with a continuous coat of adhesive, consider covering the tiles with heavy lining paper as a temporary measure. For the best finish, fit a new plasterboard (gypsum board) ceiling, nailing through the tile layer into the ceiling joists.

2 If the tiles were fixed in place with blobs of adhesive, use a heat gun to soften the old adhesive so it can be removed with a broad-bladed scraper.

REMOVING WALL PANELLING

1 The last board to be fixed will have been nailed to the fixing grounds through its face. Use a nail punch to drive the nails in and free the board.

2 The other boards will have been secret-nailed through their tongues. Use a crowbar (wrecking bar) to prise them away from their grounds.

3 Finally, prise the grounds off the wall, and use a claw hammer or crowbar with some protective packing to lever the fixing nails out of the wall.

PREPARING SURFACES FOR COVERING

Once the previous wall and ceiling decorations have been removed the next task is to restore any defects in the surfaces to be covered, and then to prepare them so that they present the perfect substrate for successful paperhanging.

The first step is to put down some heavy-duty plastic sheeting on the floor to catch splashes, and then to wash down the bare wall and ceiling surfaces thoroughly with strong household detergent or sugar soap (all-purpose cleaner), working from the bottom up on walls, and then to rinse them off with clean water, working this time from top to bottom on walls. Turn off the electricity supply first in case water gets into light switches and socket outlets (receptacles). Leave the surfaces to dry out thoroughly.

Next, repair defects such as cracks, holes and other surface damage which may have been concealed by the previous decorations, or even caused by their removal.

Finally, treat the wall and ceiling surfaces with a coat of size or diluted wallpaper paste, and leave this to dry before starting paperhanging. Size seals porous plaster, providing a surface with even absorption, and also makes it easier to slide the pasted lengths of wall covering into position on the wall.

PREPARING WALLS AND CEILINGS

1 Wash wall surfaces down with sugar soap (all-purpose cleaner) or detergent, working from the bottom up, then rinse them with clean water, working from the top down.

2 Wash ceilings with a floor mop or squeegee, after disconnecting and removing light fittings. Again, rinse off with clean water.

3 Fill cracks, holes and other defects in the wall and ceiling surfaces as appropriate, leave the filler to harden and then sand the repair down flush.

4 Apply a coat of size or diluted wallpaper paste to wall and ceiling surfaces that are to be papered, and leave them to dry before starting paperhanging.

CROSS-LINING

If the wall surface is in poor condition, has been previously decorated with gloss paint or is being decorated with a thin fabric wall covering, it is best to hang lining (liner) paper first. This is usually hung horizontally rather than vertically, with butt joints between lengths and with ends and edges trimmed just short of adjacent ceiling and wall surfaces. Use the same type of paste for the lining paper as for the subsequent wall covering.

MEASURING AND CUTTING TO LENGTH

1 For quick and easy calculations, mark the whole length of the pasting table at 300 mm (12 in) intervals with a pencil and metal straightedge.

2 Measure the length of wall covering needed for the drop, including trim allowances, and mark this on the paper. Cut the first piece to length.

PASTING WALL COVERINGS

1 Face the light to make it easy to spot any unpasted areas – they look dull, not shiny. Apply a generous band of paste down the centre of the length.

2 Align one edge of the wall covering with the edge of the pasting table, then brush the paste out towards that edge from the centre band.

3 Draw the length across to the other edge of the table, and apply paste out to that edge too. Check that there are no dry or thinly pasted areas.

4 Continue pasting until the end of the table is reached. Then lift the pasted end of the wall covering and fold it over on itself, pasted side to pasted side.

5 Slide the paper along the table so the folded section hangs down. Paste the rest of the length and fold the other end over on itself as before.

The first length of wall covering must be hung correctly if the decoration of the rest of the room is to go according to plan. Therefore the first thing to do is to decide on exactly where this is to be hung. The usual starting point is close to the door, just less than the wall covering's width away from the frame, so that the inevitable pattern discontinuity that will occur on returning to the starting point can be concealed on the short join above the door. If using a wall covering with a large design motif in a room which has a chimney breast (fireplace projection) it is preferable to start paperhanging on the chimney breast itself so that the design can be centred on it. When papering only part of a room, the starting point should be just less than the width of the wall covering from one corner of the room, to allow the edge of the covering to be trimmed accurately into the corner angle.

Next, use a roll of wall covering as a yardstick and mark off successive widths round the room walls with a pencil to check that there will not be any joins on external corners such as the sides of window reveals. If these occur, move the starting point along by about 50 mm (2 in) and recheck the join positions all round.

Finally, mark a true vertical line on the wall at the chosen starting point, using a pencil and a plumb bob and line. Failure to do this could result in the pattern running seriously out of true as successive lengths are hung.

1 At the chosen starting point, use a plumb bob and line to mark a vertical line on the wall surface. Join up the pencil marks with a straightedge.

2 Fetch the first length of pasted wall covering after leaving it to soak for the time recommended on the label. Carry it draped over the arm.

6 Peel the end of the length away from the wall so the excess can be trimmed with scissors. Brush the end back into place. Repeat at the bottom.

3 Unfold the upper flap and press the top edge of the length against the wall. Slide it across the wall until the edge lines up with the marked line.

4 Use a paperhanging brush (or a sponge for washables and vinyls) to smooth the wall covering into place. Work from the middle out towards the edges.

5 Use a pencil or the curved back of paperhanging scissors blades to mark the trimming line at ceiling level. Do the same at floor level.

7 Hang the next drop with the lengths exactly edge to edge. Brush the wall covering into the wall/ceiling angle and into the internal angle.

8 On flat wall coverings, run a seam roller down the join to ensure that it sticks securely. Never use a seam roller on embossed or relief wall coverings.

TIP

If a seam refuses to lie flat because it was inadequately pasted and has begun to dry out, brush a little extra paste underneath it and roll it again.

PAPERHANGING AROUND CORNERS

In a perfect world, rooms would have corners that were truly square and truly vertical, and it would be possible to hang wall covering all around the room in a continuous operation, simply turning the lengths that ran into the room corners straight onto the adjoining walls. In reality, corners are seldom square or true, and if the covering was hung in this way, lengths would be vertical on the first wall but could be running well off the vertical by the time they returned to the starting point. The effect can be visually disastrous, with vertical pattern elements clearly out of alignment at corners and horizontal pattern features sloping relative to the ceiling or skirting (baseboard).

The way to avoid these problems is to complete each wall with a cut-down strip that only just turns onto the next wall, to conceal the join in the corner angle. Then hang the remainder of the strip with its machine-cut edge against a newly drawn vertical line on the second wall, so that its other edge can be trimmed to follow the internal angle precisely. Any slight pattern discontinuity that results will not be noticeable except to the closest scrutiny, and the remaining lengths on the second wall will be hung truly vertically. A similar process is used when paperhanging around external corners, as at window reveals and on chimney breasts (fireplace projections).

PAPERING INTERNAL CORNERS

1 Hang the last full length before the corner of the room, then measure the distance to the corner from the edge of the length and add about 12 mm (½ in).

2 Use a pencil and straightedge to mark a strip of the required width, measured from the relevant edge (here, the left one), and cut it from the length.

3 Paste the strip and hang it in the usual way, allowing the hand-cut edge to lap onto the adjoining wall. Trim the top and bottom edges as usual.

4 Brush the tongue into the internal angle. If it will not lie flat because the corner is out of true, make small release cuts in the edge and brush it flat.

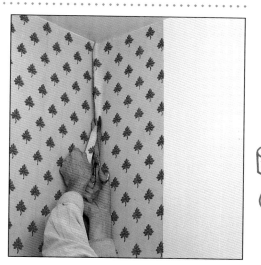

5 Measure the width of the remaining strip, subtract 12 mm (½ in) and mark a fresh vertical line on the adjoining wall at this distance from the corner.

6 Hang the strip to the marked line, brushing the wall covering into the angle so it just turns onto the surface of the first wall.

7 Use the back of the scissors blades to mark the line of the corner on the wall covering, then cut along the line and smooth the cut edge back into the angle. Use special overlap adhesive when using washables and vinyls on all lap joints.

PAPERING EXTERNAL CORNERS

1 Plan the starting point so that lengths turn external corners by about 25 mm (1 in). Brush the paper onto the next wall, making small cuts so it lies flat.

2 Carefully tear off a narrow strip of the wall covering along the turned edge to leave a 'feathered' edge that will not show through the next length.

3 Mark a vertical line on the next wall surface at a distance from the corner equal to the width of the wall covering plus about 6 mm (¼ in).

4 Hang the next full length to the marked line, with its other edge overlapping the feathered edge of the strip turned from the previous wall.

5 Brush this length into position, trim it at top and bottom as before, and run a seam roller down the overlap (not on embossed or textured wall coverings). Again, use a special overlap adhesive with washables and vinyls.

PAPERHANGING AROUND DOORS AND WINDOWS

Paperhanging on flat, uninterrupted walls is quite straightforward, calling only for the basic positioning and trimming techniques. Turning corners is only slightly more difficult. The trouble is that rooms also contain doors, windows and wall-mounted fittings and fixtures such as light switches and socket outlets (receptacles). Paperhanging around these obstacles can be tricky, but there are procedures for dealing with them.

Doors and window frames fitted flush with the internal wall surface present few problems; all that is necessary is to trim the wall covering so it finishes flush with the edge of the architrave (trim) or casing. Where the window or door is recessed, some careful patching-in of extra pieces is needed to cover all the surfaces of the reveal. It is also important to select the starting point to avoid joins between lengths falling on the external corners of such reveals; always check this point before beginning paperhanging, and adjust the starting point by about 50 mm (2 in) if it will occur.

Paperhanging round electrical fittings (fixtures) is not so difficult. The idea is to make diagonal cuts over the faceplate, cut away most of the resulting triangular tongues and tuck what is left behind the loosened faceplate. Always turn the power supply to the accessory off first. Do not do this with vinyl foils, which can conduct electricity; instead, simply trim the covering flush with the edges of the accessory faceplate. In the USA wall plates and socket outlets can be removed separately without disconnecting the wall receptacles or switches, which makes the task much simpler.

PAPERING AROUND FLUSH DOORS AND WINDOWS

1 On reaching a flush door or window frame, hang the previous length as normal. Then hang the next length to overlap the door or window frame.

2 Cut away the unwanted wall covering to within about 25 mm (1 in) of the edge of the architrave (trim) or window casing, and discard the waste strip.

3 Press the covering against the frame so that its corner is visible, and make a diagonal cut from the waste edge of the paper to the mark.

4 Use the paperhanging brush to press the tongues of paper well into the angles between the wall and the door architrave or window casing.

5 Peel back the tongues carefully and cut along the marked lines with paperhanging scissors. Then brush the trimmed edges back into position.

1 On reaching a recessed door or window frame, hang the previous length as normal. Then hang the next length, allowing it to overlap the recess.

2 Make a horizontal cut into the overlapping edge level with the underside of the reveal to allow the central portion of the length to cover the side wall.

PAPERING AROUND ELECTRICAL FITTINGS (FIXTURES)

Make diagonal cuts towards the corners, trim off the triangles and tuck the edges behind the loosened faceplate. The power must be turned off first.

3 On recessed windows, make a similar cut lower down the length, level with the top surface of the window sill. Then trim it to fit round the end of the sill.

4 Cut a patch to fit on the underside of the reveal, big enough to turn onto adjoining wall and frame surfaces. Press it well into the internal angles.

5 Tear along the edges of the patch that will be covered when the piece above the reveal and the tongue covering its side wall are brushed into place.

6 Trim the edges of the patch and tongue to meet the frame neatly. Then hang full widths when the other side of the reveal is reached, and repeat steps 1–6.

PAPERING STAIRWELLS

Paperhanging in stairwells is no different in principle from work in any other room. However, the job is made more difficult by the need to handle longer lengths of wall covering, and also because access to the higher reaches of the stairwell walls can be awkward. It is a job that requires careful planning, and is best tackled with the assistance of a second person.

First of all, work out the starting point. It is best to hang the longest drop – the one that reaches from landing ceiling to hall floor – first of all. Mark its position and check that other joins will not fall awkwardly round the rest of the stairwell, especially if it has a window opening onto it. Adjust the starting point if necessary.

The next thing to do is to work out how to gain access to the various wall surfaces involved without obstructing passage up and down the stairwell or blocking off the walls themselves. On a straight flight it may be possible to use components from a hired slot-together scaffold tower to make a suitable working platform. On flights with quarter or half-landings it will probably be necessary to tailor-make an assembly of ladder sections, stepladders, homemade supports and scaffold boards; two typical arrangements are shown in the illustrations. Nail scrap wood to stair treads to locate ladder feet securely, and lock scaffold boards together by drilling holes through them where they overlap and dropping a bolt through the holes (no need for a nut). Note that ladders or steps shown resting against wall surfaces will have to be repositioned as the work progresses.

ACCESS EQUIPMENT FOR STAIRWELLS

Use a selection of ladders, steps, scaffold boards and homemade supports to construct a platform that allows access to all the wall surfaces being decorated without obstructing the stairs themselves.

STARTING POINT

Aim to start work by hanging the longest drop first. Then work along the stairwell walls in sequence, turning corners and tackling obstacles as for other rooms.

1 Fold up long lengths of wall covering concertina-fashion with the top end of the length uppermost, and carry them to the stairs supported over the arm.

2 Get a helper to support the folds of wall covering while positioning the top end of the length on the stairwell wall against a vertical line.

3 When measuring lengths that will meet a dado (chair) rail or skirting (baseboard) at an angle, remember to measure the longer edge of the length.

4 Where the bottom edge of the length meets a shaped skirting, make small release cuts in the edge and trim it to follow the curve.

PAPERING AROUND OBSTACLES

Where the end of a handrail fits flush with the wall, cut the lower part of the length into two strips so their edges can be trimmed around the rail and joined edge to edge beneath it. Use a similar technique to fit the wall covering around a flush newel post.

PAPERING CEILINGS

Many people regard the papering of ceilings with horror. In reality they are easier to deal with than walls because they are flat, do not have any awkward angles (except in rooms with sloping ceilings and dormer windows), and have few obstacles attached to them apart from the occasional light fitting (fixture), which can in any case usually be removed quite easily.

The only thing that takes getting used to when papering ceilings is working on an upside-down surface, but the basic technique is no different from working on walls. The wall covering is simply positioned, brushed into place and then trimmed where it meets adjoining surfaces.

The most important thing to plan carefully is access equipment that will allow a complete length to be hung across the room. Nothing is more dangerous than attempting to step from chair to chair; proper access is a must. The best solution is to use scaffold boards or lengths of staging, supported by stepladders, trestles or homemade supports to create a flat, level walkway spanning the room from wall to wall at a height that allows the ceiling to be reached comfortably. It will take only a few seconds to reposition after hanging each length, ready for the next.

This is also a job where an additional pair of hands will be a big help, at least before gaining the knack of supporting a concertina of pasted wall covering with one hand while brushing it into position with the other. This can be done only with practice.

The first length should be hung to a guideline on the ceiling. The best way of marking this is with a chalked line, held against the ceiling at both ends and snapped against it. Use red chalk for a white ceiling.

1 Paste the wall covering in the usual way, but fold it up concertina-fashion with the starting end of the length folded over on itself. Lining (liner) paper has been used here.

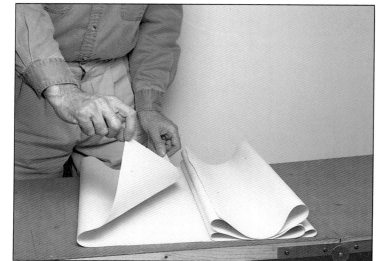

ACCESS EQUIPMENT FOR CEILINGS

Set up an access platform across the room, using scaffold boards supported on staging or stepladders, to create a walkway at a height that allows the ceiling to be comfortably reached.

2 Hang the first length to a chalked line just less than the width of the wall covering from the side wall. Support the folds on a spare roll of wall covering.

PAPERING ARCHES

The shape of an arch makes it impossible to get a pattern match along the curved join. It is best to choose a wall covering with a small design motif and a random pattern, to use different but complementary designs for the face walls and the arch surface, or to use lining (liner) paper inside the arch and paint it a plain colour.

To paper an arched recess, cover the face and back walls first, turning cut tongues of wall covering onto the arched surface. Then cover the arch surface as described below.

3 Trim the overlaps at the ends and along the side wall. Then hang the second length in the same way, butted up against the edge of the first length.

4 On meeting a pendant light fitting (fixture) pierce the wall covering over its centre and make a series of radial cuts outwards from the pierced point.

To paper a through archway, hang the wall covering on the two face walls and trim out the waste to leave an overlap of about 25 mm (1 in) all around. Make cuts in the edge so that the tongues can be turned onto the arch surface. Then cut a strip of wall covering a fraction narrower than the width of the arch surface and long enough to cover it in one piece, and brush this into place. Work from the bottom of one side upwards to the top of the arch, and then down the other side. Always use special overlap adhesive with washables and vinyls.

5 With the power turned off at the mains, unscrew the cover and trim the tongues off flush with the base of the fitting. Replace the cover to conceal the cut ends.

6 Where the ceiling runs into an alcove, cut the wall covering in line with the side wall of the recess and brush it into place. Trim off the waste section.

OTHER PAPERHANGING TECHNIQUES

Apart from the traditional method of pasting the wall covering on a pasting table and then hanging it on the wall, two other techniques may sometimes be needed. The first is hanging ready-pasted wall coverings, which are growing in popularity, while the second is hanging speciality wall coverings.

Hanging ready-pasted wall coverings could not be easier. The back of the wall covering – usually a washable or vinyl type, for obvious reasons – is coated during manufacture with an even layer of dried paste. To activate this, simply cut the length that is needed, roll it up with the top of the length on the outside of the roll, and immerse it in water. Special soaking troughs are sold by most wall covering suppliers, and are intended to be placed next to the skirting (baseboard) beneath the point where the length is to be hung. The trough is filled with cold (not hot) water, the length is immersed and drawn upwards onto the wall so that excess water drains back into the trough. It is then hung and trimmed in the usual way.

Many speciality wall coverings are designed to be hung by pasting the wall, not the wall covering. Some also have untrimmed edges, which need to be cut after overlapping adjoining lengths. The technique is, however, quite straightforward.

HANGING READY-PASTED WALL COVERINGS

1 Place the trough next to the wall, fill it with cold water and immerse the rolled-up length in it, top end outermost, for the recommended time.

2 At the end of the recommended soaking time, grasp the top end of the length and draw it upwards so that the excess water runs off it back into the trough.

3 Slide the top of the length into position on the wall, aligning it with a marked line or butting it up against its neighbour. Do not step in the trough.

4 Use a sponge rather than a paperhanging brush to smooth the length into place on the wall. This helps to absorb excess water from the surface.

1 Cut the wall covering to the length required, including a trim allowance, and roll it up face inwards around a broom handle or similar object.

2 Apply the recommended paste (usually a thick ready-mixed type) to the wall, and then unroll the wall covering onto the wet paste against a marked line.

3 Run a clean, dry paint roller backwards and forwards over the surface of the wall covering to bond it firmly to the wall.

4 Use a sharp utility knife – and a straightedge if needed – to trim the wall covering where it meets the ceiling and the skirting (baseboard).

5 To create neat joins, overlap adjoining lengths slightly and then cut through both layers with a sharp utility knife run along a straightedge.

6 Peel away the two waste strips and smooth the cut edges neatly back into place. Run a seam roller along the seam to ensure a good bond.

PUTTING UP FRIEZES AND BORDERS

Friezes and borders are narrow strips of printed paper or vinyl wall covering sold in rolls, and often come in colours and designs that complement wall coverings and fabrics manufactured by the same firm. A frieze is usually applied as a horizontal band running around the room, and can be positioned at ceiling level or next to a picture rail or dado (chair) rail. Borders, on the other hand, are used either to frame features of the room such as a door or window opening, or to create decorative panels on wall or ceiling surfaces – perhaps to frame a group of pictures, for example. They come in a range of widths.

Friezes and borders are available in plain and self-adhesive versions. The former is pasted in the same way as an ordinary wall covering, so this type is ideal for use on walls that have been painted or decorated with a plain printed wallpaper. If a border or frieze is to go over a washable or vinyl wall covering, use a special overlap adhesive or choose a self-adhesive type since ordinary wallpaper paste will not stick to the surface of the covering. Simply cut these to length, then peel off the backing paper bit by bit while positioning the length on the wall.

TIP

To gauge the effect a frieze or border will have, and to decide on the best position for it, stick lengths to the wall surface with masking tape before fixing them up permanently.

APPLYING A FRIEZE

1 Decide on the precise position of the frieze or border, then measure the distance from a nearby feature such as a ceiling or door frame.

2 Use a spirit level and pencil to draw true horizontal and vertical guidelines on the wall or ceiling surface at the marked position.

3 Cut the frieze or border to length and carefully apply paste to the length. Fold it up concertina fashion while working along it.

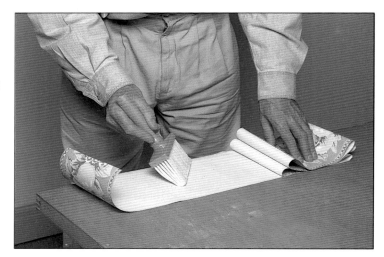

4 Offer the free end of the concertina up to the marked line and brush it into place. It will help to have an assistant when hanging long lengths.

5 Join successive lengths end to end when starting a new roll. If the pattern does not match, overlap the ends so it does and cut through both layers.

6 Finally, check that all horizontal edges and vertical joints are well bonded to the wall by running over them with a seam roller. Remove excess paste.

APPLYING A BORDER

1 Put up the individual lengths of a border in the same way as a frieze. To form corners, overlap the lengths at right angles and cut through both layers at 45°.

2 Peel away the two waste sections and press the neatly mitred ends back into place. Adjust their positions if necessary to get a perfect joint.

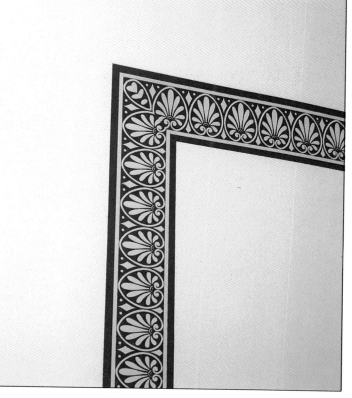

3 The finished corner joint shows how accurate alignment and careful cutting result in a neat joint with the pattern meeting along the mitred cuts.

TILING

Tiles have a long pedigree in the interior decoration business. Faience (glazed earthenware) plaques have been found in Cretan buildings dating from around 1800 BC, and a tradition of ceramic wall and floor decoration was established soon after this farther east in Syria and Persia (now Iran). Mosaic wall and floor decorations, incorporating stone (usually marble), glass and ceramic tesserae, were also a major feature of Roman interiors. The technique spread to North Africa and thence to Spain, and the Renaissance soon led to widespread use of decorative tiling all over Europe.

Probably the most important centre of ceramic tile making in Europe was Holland, where the creation of individually handpainted tiles in a unique blue-grey colour soon made Delft famous in the early seventeenth century. From there, the use of tiles spread rapidly, and it was not long before mass production was introduced. The end product is the familiar ceramic tile we use

today. The manufacturing and printing technology may have changed, and the adhesives and grouts used may have improved, but the result would be familiar to a seventeenth-century Dutchman.

The twentieth century has brought new kinds of tile, notably vinyl, lino and cork tiles which owe their existence to advances in plastics and resins technology. They offer a combination of properties that make them useful alternatives to ceramics in a wide range of situations, and are generally much less expensive.

This chapter concentrates on working with ceramic wall tiles, since they are the most popular of the types available. A wide range of situations is dealt with, from splashbacks to whole walls, including information on working around obstacles such as door and window openings and on creating special effects with tiled borders and feature panels. There are also sections on using other types of wall tiles, and on tiling floors.

OPPOSITE
Wall tiles have never been available in such a profusion of styles and designs, ranging from highly glazed plain types to more rustic versions with matt or textured surfaces and patterns that look as though they have been handpainted.

TYPES OF WALL AND FLOOR TILES

Ceramic tiles provide the most durable of all finishes in the home, whether for walls, floors or worktops, and there has never been a bigger choice of colours, designs, shapes and sizes. The main drawback with tiles is that they are comparatively expensive, so it is important to make the right choice of tiles at the start, and to make sure that they are expertly fixed in place.

Vinyl, lino and cork floor tiles offer an alternative floor finish to ceramics, and offer the same advantages of ease of laying small units combined with a surface finish that is warmer to the touch and also less noisy underfoot than ceramic tiles.

Ceramic tiles for walls

In today's homes, the surfaces that are tiled more often than any other are walls, especially in rooms such as kitchens and bathrooms where a hardwearing, water-resistant and easy-to-clean decorative finish is required. Often the tiling protects only the most vulnerable areas such as splashbacks above wash basins and shower cubicles; but sometimes the whole room is tiled from floor to ceiling.

Tiles used for wall decoration are generally fairly thin, measuring from 4 to 6 mm (³⁄₁₆ to ¼ in) thick, although some imported tiles (especially the larger sizes) may be rather thicker than

ABOVE One of the most striking tiling effects is the feature panel (**top**), a group of tiles that builds up into a complete picture and looks particularly effective when framed with a border. Tiles set at 45° and interspersed with triangular cut tiles (**above**) can also add interest to the finished design.

LEFT Many tile ranges include a variety of plain and patterned field tiles, teamed up with a complementary border tile, allowing the home decorator complete freedom to decide on the final design.

this. The commonest kinds are square, measuring 108 mm (4¼ in) or 150 mm (6 in) across, but rectangular tiles measuring 200 × 100 mm (8 × 4 in) and 200 × 150 mm (8 × 6 in) are becoming more popular.

Tile designs change with fashions in interior design, and current demand seems to be mainly for large areas of neutral or small-patterned tiles interspersed with individual motif tiles on a matching background. Plain tiles, often with a simple border frame, are also popular, as are tiles which create a frieze effect when laid alongside one another. Some sets of tiles build up into larger designs (known as feature panels), which can look quite striking when surrounded by an area of plain tiling. Some tile ranges still include what are known as *insert tiles* – tiles carrying moulded bathroom accessories

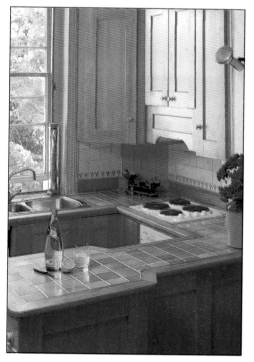

ABOVE Highly glazed tiles can make an unusual and durable surface for counter tops, but the grout lines need scrupulous cleaning to keep them hygienic.

such as soap dishes and toilet roll holders, though these are not as common or as popular as they were.

The surface of ceramic wall tiles is no longer always highly glazed, as it traditionally was. There are now semi-matt finishes, often with a slight surface texture that softens the somewhat harsh glare of a high-gloss surface.

Tile edges have changed over the years too. Once special round-edged tiles were used for the exposed edges of tiled areas, and plain ones with unglazed square edges (known as *field tiles*) elsewhere. Nowadays tiles are either the universal type or the standard square-edged variety. The former have angled edges so that when butted together they leave a gap for the grouting, which fills the spaces between them. The latter, as their name suggests, have square edges and so must be positioned with the aid of spacers.

Both types usually have two adjacent edges glazed so they can be used as perimeter tiles, and sometimes all four edges are glazed.

Tiles for floors and worktops

Although less widely used than wall tiles, ceramic floor tiles are a popular choice for heavy traffic areas such as porches and hallways. They are generally thicker and harder-fired than wall tiles, to enable them to stand up to heavy wear without cracking. Again, a wide range of plain colours, simple textures and more elaborate designs is available. Common sizes are 150 mm (6 in) and 200 mm (8 in) squares and 200 × 100 mm (8 × 4 in) rectangles; hexagons are also available in plain colours, and a popular variation is a plain octagonal tile which is laid with small square coloured or decorated inserts at the intersections.

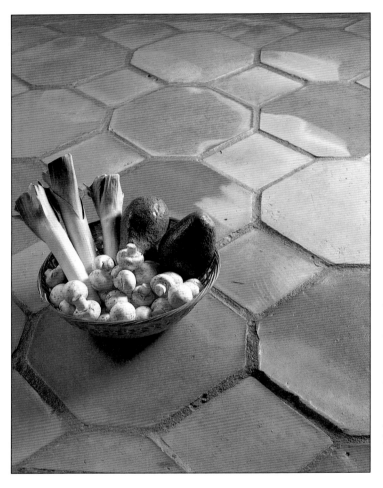

Quarry tiles are unglazed ceramic floor tiles with a brown, buff or reddish colour, and are a popular choice for hallways, conservatories and country-style kitchens. They are usually laid in a mortar bed, and after the joints have been grouted the tiles must be sealed with boiled linseed oil or a recommended proprietary sealer. Common sizes are 100 mm (4 in) and 150 mm (6 in) square. Special shaped tiles are also available for forming upstands at floor edges.

Terracotta tiles look similar to quarry tiles but are larger, and are fired at lower temperatures and so are more porous. They are sealed in the same way as quarry tiles. Squares, ranging in size between 200 and 400 mm (8 and 16 in), and rectangles are the commonest shapes, but octagons with small square infill tiles are also popular.

Mosaics

Mosaics are just tiny tiles – usually plain in colour, sometimes with a pattern –

BELOW Mosaic tiles are once more regaining the popularity they enjoyed in times past, but laying them is definitely a labour of love.

ABOVE Handmade terracotta tiles exhibit a subtle variety of shade and colour, but need sealing to keep them clean.

RIGHT Ceramic tiles provide a durable and waterproof floor surface for bathrooms. Here square coloured corner inserts set off the dazzling white octagonal tiles.

TILING

LEFT Lino tiles offer a warm, attractive and durable alternative to cork or vinyl floor coverings in rooms such as kitchens and hallways. Borders can be used to frame individual tiles.

Modern lino tiles, made from natural materials rather than the plastic resins used in vinyl tiles, offer far better performance than traditional linoleum. They come in a range of bright and subtle colours and interesting patterns, often with pre-cut borders.

All these types generally come in 300 mm (12 in) squares, although larger squares and rectangles are available in some of the more expensive ranges. They are generally sold in packs of nine, covering roughly 1 sq yd (0.84 sq m), although many kinds are often available singly.

ABOVE Cork is the warmest of tiled floor coverings underfoot, and when sealed is good-looking and durable too.

ABOVE The more expensive types of vinyl floor tile offer superb imitations of other materials such as wood, marble and terrazzo finishes.

which are sold made up in sheets on an open-weave cloth backing. These sheets are laid like larger tiles in a bed of adhesive, and all the gaps including those on the surface of the sheet are grouted afterwards. Square mosaics are the most common, but roundels, hexagons and other interlocking shapes are also available. Sheets are usually square and 300 mm (12 in) across, and are often sold in packs of five or ten. The best way of estimating quantities is to work out the area to be covered and to divide that by the coverage figure given on the pack to work out how many packs to buy. Note that wall and floor types are of different thicknesses, as with ordinary ceramic tiles.

Cork, vinyl and lino tiles

Cork tiles come in a small range of colours and textures. Their surface feels warm and relatively soft underfoot, and they also give some worthwhile heat and sound insulation – particularly

useful in bathrooms, kitchens, halls and even children's bedrooms. The cheapest types have to be sealed to protect the surface after they have been laid, but the more expensive vinyl-coated floor types can be walked on as soon as they have been stuck down. They need little more than an occasional wash and polish to keep them in good condition. However, even the best cork floor tiles are prone to damage from sharp heels and heavy furniture, for example.

Vinyl tiles come in a very wide range of plain and patterned types, and generally resist wear better than cork, so they can be used on floors subject to fairly heavy wear. However, they are a little less gentle on the feet. Some of the more expensive types give very passable imitations of luxury floor coverings such as marble and terrazzo. Most are made in self-adhesive form and very little maintenance is needed once they have been laid.

Tools for ceramic tiles

For almost any ceramic tiling job, large or small, the following are needed: tile adhesive; a notched adhesive spreader; some tile spacers; lengths of tile edge trim (optional); grout plus a flexible spreader; a steel tape measure; some lengths of 38 × 12 mm (1½ × ½ in) softwood battening (furring strips), plus masonry pins and a hammer for supporting the tiles on large wall areas; a spirit level; a tile cutter; a tile saw; a tile file; a piece of dowel for shaping the grout lines; a pencil and felt-tip pen; some sponges and cloths for wiping and polishing. Some silicone sealant or mastic (caulking) may also be needed for waterproofing joints where tiling abuts baths, basins and shower trays.

Tile cutters range from the basic – an angled cutting tip attached to a handle – to elaborate cutting jigs that guarantee perfectly accurate cuts every time. A tile saw is useful for making shaped cutouts to fit around obstacles such as pipework, and a tile file helps to smooth cut edges.

Both adhesive and grout for wall tiling are now usually sold ready-mixed in plastic tubs complete with a notched plastic spreader. For areas that will get the occasional splash or may suffer from condensation, a water-resistant adhesive and grout is perfectly adequate, but for surfaces such as shower cubicles which will have to withstand prolonged wetting it is essential to use both waterproof adhesive and waterproof grout. Always use waterproof grout on tiled worktops; ordinary grout will harbour germs.

Grout is generally white, but coloured grout is on sale and will make a feature of the grout lines (an effect that looks best with plain or fairly neutral patterned tiles).

TILING

TILING TOOLS, MATERIALS AND EQUIPMENT

These include a tile saw (**1**), adhesive (**2**), a polishing cloth (**3**), a spirit level (**4**), tile edge nippers (**5**), a tile cutter/snapper (**6**) or a tiling jig (**7**), a tile scriber (**8**), a tile cutter with width and angle jig (**9**), a heavy duty tile cutter (**10**), tile files (**11**) or a tile edge sander with abrasive strips (**12**), masking tape (**13**), masonry nails (**14**), a hammer (**15**), a homemade tile gauge (**16**), a retractable steel measure (**17**), a pencil (**18**), adhesive spreaders (**19** and **27**), a grout finisher (**20**) or dowel (**21**), tile edging trim (**22**), small and large tile spacers (**23**), a grout remover (**24**), a grout spreader (**25**), grout (**26**) and battens (furring strips) (**28**).

Ceramic floor tile adhesive is widely available in powder form as well as ready-mixed. It is best always to use a waterproof type (plus waterproof grout), even in theoretically dry areas.

Adhesive and grout are both sold in a range of sizes, sometimes labelled by weight, sometimes by volume; always check the coverage specified by the manufacturer on the packaging when buying, so as not to overbuy or run out halfway through the job.

Tools for cork, vinyl and lino tiles

Only a few simple tools are needed to lay cork and vinyl tiles, but, except for the self-adhesive type, special tile adhesive is required. This is sold ready-mixed in tubs, and usually comes complete with a notched spreader.

Special water-based adhesive is the type to choose for both cork and lino tiles; solvent-based contact adhesives were formerly the first choice, but their fumes are extremely unpleasant and also dangerously inflammable, and they are no longer recommended. For vinyl-coated cork tiles a special vinyl acrylic adhesive is needed. For vinyl tiles, an emulsion-type latex flooring adhesive is the best choice.

For unsealed cork tiles a sealer is required. Ordinary polyurethane varnish, as used for furniture, will do; there are also special floor sealers. Three coats will be needed.

Tools are simply a tape measure, a sharp utility knife and a steel straightedge for marking and cutting border tiles. A proprietary profile gauge with sliding steel or plastic needles makes it easy to cut tiles to fit round awkward obstacles such as architraves (trims) and pipework. But it is just as effective, and less costly, to cut a template from card or paper.

SETTING OUT TILED AREAS

The best way to practise tiling skills is to begin by covering just a small area such as a washbasin splashback, where setting out the tiles so that they are centred on the area concerned is a simple job and there is very little tile cutting to do.

For a larger area – a whole wall, or perhaps even a complete room – exactly the same techniques are used. The big difference is the sheer scale of the job, which makes the preliminary setting-out by far the most important part. The problem is that walls are seldom blank surfaces, and there may be a number of obstacles to tile around. Care must be taken to get the best fit around them with these inflexible tile squares, without needing to cut impossibly thin slivers to fill in gaps.

The most important thing to do is to plan precisely where the whole tiles will fall. On a flat, uninterrupted wall this is quite easy; simply find the centre line of the wall and plan the tiling to start from

there. However, there will probably be obstacles such as window reveals, door openings and built-in furniture in the room, all competing to be the centre of attention, and it will be necessary to work out the best 'centre point' while all the time trying to avoid having very thin cut tile borders and edges.

It is best to use a device called a *tiling gauge* – a batten (furring strip) marked out in tile widths – to work this out. The gauge is easy to make from a straight piece of timber about 1.2 m (4 ft) long, marked off with pencil lines to match the size of the tile. Use this to ensure that the tiles will be centred accurately on major features such as window reveals, with a border of cut tiles of equal width at the end of each row or column of tiles.

The next stage is the actual setting-out. With large areas of tiling, two things are vitally important. First, the tile rows must be exactly horizontal; if they are not, errors will accumulate as

the tiles extend across the wall, throwing the verticals out of alignment with disastrous results. When tiling right around a room, inaccurate levels mean that rows do not match up at the start and finish point. Second, the tiles need some support while the adhesive sets; without it, they may slump down the wall.

The solution is to fix a line of battens across the wall – or right around the room – just above the level of the skirting (baseboard), securing them with partly-driven masonry nails so that they can be removed later when the adhesive has set. The precise level will be dictated by setting-out with the tiling gauge, but will usually be between half and three-quarters of a tile width above the skirting. Do not rely on this being level; it may not be. Draw the line out in pencil first, using the spirit level, and then pin the battens up and check the level again. If everything is straight, it is time to start tiling.

TILING AROUND A DOOR

1 If the door is close to the room corner, start with whole tiles next to the frame. Use a vertical tile guide if the architrave (trim) is not truly vertical.

2 Tile the whole of the main wall area, adding cut tiles next to the room corner and at ceiling level. Remove the tile supports when the adhesive has set.

3 Fit a tile support above the door in line with the tile rows, and another between it and the other room corner, just above skirting (baseboard) level.

TILING

TILING AROUND A WINDOW

1 For tiling a wall with a window opening, first decide on where to centre the tiling. On a wall with one window, centre the tiling on a line drawn through its centre.

2 If there are two window openings on a wall, centre the tiles on a line drawn through the centre of each window, provided an exact number of whole tiles will fit between them.

3 Otherwise, centre the tiling on a line drawn midway between the windows. Always work across and up the wall, placing whole tiles up to window-sill level, then up the wall at either side of the window. Then, fit a tile support above the opening to support whole tiles there.

4 Remove the support strips and cut tiles to fit on the face wall at each side and across the top of the window. To tile a window reveal, place whole tiles so they overlap the edges of the tiles on the wall face. Then fill in between these and the frame with cut tiles.

4 Carry on placing whole tiles above the door opening, filling in with cut tiles at the room corner and at ceiling level as in step 2.

5 Remove the tile support above the door opening and fill in all around it with cut and whole tiles as required. Grout the tiles when the adhesive has set.

6 If the door opening is near or at the centre of the room wall, centre the tiling on it and fix tile supports and guide battens (furring strips) as required.

TILING

97

PREPARING THE WALL FOR TILING

The wall surface should be clean and dry. It is possible to tile over painted plaster or plasterboard (gypsum board), but old wall coverings should be removed and brick walls must be rendered. Note that modern tile adhesives allow tiling over existing tiles, so there is no need to remove these if they are securely bonded to the wall surface. There is also no need to fill minor cracks or holes; the tile adhesive will bridge these as it is applied to the wall surface.

When estimating quantities, first select the tile size. Then set out the area to be tiled on the wall and use the setting-out marks to count how many tiles are needed in each horizontal row and each vertical column. Count cut tiles as whole tiles, and then multiply the two figures together to reach the total required. Always add a further 5 per cent to the total to allow for breakages and miscalculations.

MAKING AND USING A TILING GAUGE

1 Use a pencil and one of the chosen tiles to mark up a length of wood for use as a tiling gauge. Allow for the width of tile spacers if using them.

2 Hold the tiling gauge horizontally against the wall to see how many tiles each row will take, and also to centre the tiling on a wall feature or window opening.

3 Similarly, hold the gauge vertically to assess how many tiles will fill each column, and where best to position any cut tiles that may be needed.

MARKING OUT A SPLASHBACK

1 When tiling a small area with rows of whole tiles, use the tiling gauge to mark the extent of the tiled area on the wall. Here each row will have five tiles.

2 Next, use a spirit level to mark a true horizontal base line above which the first row of whole tiles will be fixed. Cut tiles will fit below it.

3 Then use the spirit level again to complete a grid of horizontal and vertical guidelines on the wall surface, ready for a tile support to be fixed.

FITTING TILE SUPPORTS

1 Use masonry pins (tacks) to fix the support to the wall, aligned with the guide line. Drive the pins in only part of the way so that they can be removed later.

2 When tiling large areas or whole walls, pin a vertical guide batten (furring strip) to the wall as well to help keep the tile columns truly vertical.

POSITIONING CUT TILES FOR PANELS

ABOVE If the height of a tiled splashback is determined by a feature such as a mirror or window, position a row of cut tiles along the top of the panel.

ABOVE If the width of the tiling is defined, as with a bath panel, always position cut tiles of equal size at either side.

ESTIMATING QUANTITIES

Tile size	No/sq m	No/sq yd
106 × 106 mm (4¼ × 4¼ in)	86	71
200 × 100 mm (8 × 4 in)	48	41
150 × 150 mm (6 × 6 in)	43	36

TILING PLAIN WALLS

Once all the necessary setting-out work has been done, the actual technique of fixing tiles to walls is quite simple: spread the adhesive and press the tiles into place. However, there must be an adhesive bed of even thickness to ensure that neighbouring tiles sit flush with one another. To obtain this, use a toothed spreader (usually supplied with the tile adhesive; buy one otherwise). Scoop some adhesive from the tub with the spreader, and draw it across the wall with the teeth pressed hard against the plaster to leave ridges of a standard height on the wall. Apply enough adhesive to fix about ten or twelve tiles at a time.

Bed the tiles into the adhesive with a pressing and twisting motion, aligning the first tile with the vertical guideline or batten (furring strip). If using tile spacers, press one into the adhesive next to the top corner of the first tile, and place the second one in the row. Carry on placing spacers and tiles until the end of the row is reached.

Add subsequent rows in the same way until all the whole tiles are in place. It is now time to tackle any cut tiles that are needed at the ends of the rows, and along the base of the tiled area beneath the horizontal tile support. Remove this, and the tile spacers, only when the adhesive has set; allow 24 hours.

FIXING WHOLE TILES

1 Use a notched spreader to scoop some adhesive from the tub and spread it on the wall. Press the teeth against the wall to leave ridges of even height.

2 Place the first tile on the tile support, with its side edge against the pencilled guideline or vertical guide batten (furring strip) as appropriate.

3 Add a tile spacer against the tile corner and place the second tile. Add more tiles to complete the row, then build up succeeding rows in the same way.

CUTTING TILES

1 Use a pencil-type tile cutter and a straightedge to make straight cuts. Measure and mark the tile width needed and score a line across the glaze.

2 Place a nail or matchstick (wooden match) under the scored line at each side of the tile, and break it with downward hand pressure on each half of the tile.

USING A TILE-CUTTING JIG

1 For making angled cuts as well as straight ones, a tile-cutting jig is invaluable. To set it up, first fix the side fence to the angle required.

2 Then draw the slide-mounted cutting point across the tile while holding it firmly in place with the other hand. Take care to score the tile only once.

3 Finally snap the tile along the scored line by holding the tile against the guide bars and lowering the cutter handle with its tip under the tile.

COMPLETING THE WALL

1 Measure, mark and cut the sections of tile needed to complete each row of tiling. Spread a little adhesive over their backs and press them into place.

2 When tiling adjacent walls, place all the cut pieces on the first wall. Repeat the operation on the second wall, overlapping the original cut pieces.

3 When tiling external corners, always set out the tiles so that whole tiles meet on the corner. Overlap the tiles as shown.

---

3 Use a cutting guide or tiling jig if preferred, especially for cutting narrow strips. This type holds the tile securely and also guides the tile cutter accurately.

4 The traditional way of making a cutout in a tile is to score its outline on the tile and then to gradually nibble away the waste material with pincers.

5 An alternative is to use a special abrasive-coated tile saw. This is indispensable for making internal cutouts – to fit around pipes, for example.

FINISHING OFF TILED AREAS

When all the tiles are in place, including any cut tiles that are required, it is time to tackle the final stage of the job – filling in the joint lines between the tiles with grout. This can be bought in powder form or ready-mixed; the latter is more convenient to use, but a little more expensive. Use a flexible spreader (usually supplied with the grout) to force it into the gaps, a damp sponge or cloth to remove excess grout from the face of the tiles, and a short length of wooden dowel or similar material to smooth the grout lines. A clean, dry cloth is needed to polish the tiles afterwards.

Alternative edging techniques

Most ceramic wall tiles have two glazed edges, making it possible to finish off an area of tiling or an external corner with a glazed edge exposed. However, there are alternative ways of finishing off tiling. It can be edged with wooden mouldings or plastic trim strips.

Wooden mouldings can be bedded into the tile adhesive on walls; to edge worktops they can be pinned (tacked) or screwed to the worktop edge.

Plastic edge and corner mouldings (nosings) have a perforated flange which is bedded in the tile adhesive before the tiles are placed. These mouldings come in a range of pastel and bright primary colours to complement or contrast with the tiling.

GROUTING THE TILES

1 Apply the grout to the tile joints by drawing the loaded spreader across them at right angles to the joint lines. Scrape off excess grout and reuse it.

2 Use a damp sponge or cloth to wipe the surface of the tiles before the grout dries out. Rinse it out in clean water from time to time.

3 Then use a short length of wooden dowel or a similar implement to smooth the grout lines to a gently concave cross section.

4 Allow the grout to harden completely, then polish the tiles with a dry cloth to remove any slight remaining bloom and leave them clean and shiny.

USING EDGE TRIMS

1 Bed plastic edge or corner trim into the adhesive, then position the tiles so that they fit flush against the curved edge of the trim strip.

2 As an alternative to plastic, use wooden mouldings bedded in the tile adhesive. Here an L-shaped moulding forms a neat external corner trim.

3 When tiling over existing tiles, some way of disguising the double thickness along exposed edges will be needed. A quadrant (quarter-round) moulding is ideal.

4 Wood can be used to edge a tiled counter top. Start by attaching the moulding to the edge of the worktop so it will fit flush with the tiled surface.

5 Spread the tile adhesive and bed the tiles in place, checking that they lie level with the top edge of the moulding and flush with each other.

6 Plug the counterbored screw holes by gluing in short lengths of dowel and chiselling them off flush with the moulding. Finally, grout the tile joints.

DECORATIVE TILE EFFECTS

The preceding pages have dealt with tiling walls in the technical sense of planning the layout and fixing the tiles. However, tiles are more than just wall covering units; they come in a range of sizes and designs which can also be used creatively in a variety of ways.

The first involves finishing off a part-tiled wall with a band of narrow tiles in a colour or design that complements or contrasts with the main tiled area, to form a decorative border. These tiles are available in lengths that match standard tile widths, and are usually 50–75 mm (2–3 in) wide. They are cut and fixed just like any other tile.

The second method is to incorporate a group of patterned tiles as a feature panel within a larger area of plain tiling. The group may just be contrasting patterned tiles, or may be a multi-tile motif – a group of four, six or more tiles that fit together to form one large design when they are fixed in position. Tile manufacturers offer a range of mass-produced designs you can choose from, or a motif panel can be commissioned from a specialist tile supplier. Plan the motif's position on the wall carefully, and build it in the usual way as tiling progresses.

CREATING A DECORATIVE PANEL

1 Start by making up a tiling gauge to suit the tiles you are working with, and use it to mark the position of the first row of tiles on the wall surface.

2 Put up a support batten (furring strip) if necessary, then spread some tile adhesive on the wall, and place any plain tiles that will be below the decorative panel.

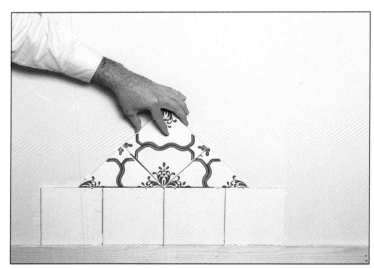

3 Start placing the first tiles that will form the decorative panel. Here the tiles are being laid at an angle of 45°, so half tiles are placed first.

4 Continue adding whole and half tiles to build up the pattern, checking as you work that the edges of the panel are truly horizontal and vertical.

5 Here the panel is being surrounded by slim border tiles. Add whole tiles to the top of the panel first, working from the centre line outwards.

6 At the corners of the panel, fit an over-long horizontal tile and hold another vertically over it so you can mark a 45° cutting line on each tile.

7 Make the 45° cuts on the end of each corner tile, then bed the horizontal tile in place. Check that the cut end is precisely aligned with the panel corner.

8 Repeat the process at the other end of the horizontal section of the border. Both end pieces should be the same length, as the border is centred.

9 Fit the border tiles up each side of the decorative panel, then mark the position of the mitre cut on the last tiles, cut them and fit them in place.

RIGHT The finished panel, neatly centred as a decorative splashback above a washbasin.

Small mosaic tiles are an attractive alternative to square or rectangular tiles, especially for small areas of tiling where their size will look particularly appropriate. Modern mosaic tiles come in a range of shapes and sizes, from simple squares and roundels to interlocking shapes such as hexagons. They are generally sold in sheets backed with an open-mesh cloth that holds the individual mosaic pieces at the correct spacing and greatly speeds up the installation process, since the entire sheet is stuck to the wall in one go. If cut pieces are needed to fill in the perimeter of the tiled area, simply cut individual mosaic tiles from the sheet with scissors, trim them to size with a tile cutter and position them one by one. Mosaic tiles are fixed and grouted with ordinary tiling products.

One other type of wall tile is popular as a wall covering. Cork tiles are made by compressing the bark of the cork tree into blocks, and then slicing them up into squares – 300 mm (12 in) is the commonest size – or rectangles. They come in a range of natural shades, and may also be stained or printed with surface designs during manufacture. They are stuck to the wall surface with a special water-based contact adhesive, and since they are virtually impossible to remove once placed, they should be regarded as a long-term decorative option and their use carefully planned beforehand.

TIP

If using cork tiles on walls, change the faceplate screws on light switches and socket outlets (receptacles) for longer ones; the originals will be too short to reach the lugs in the mounting box.

USING MOSAIC TILES

1 Start by putting up a horizontal tile support and a vertical tiling guide, as for ordinary tiling. Then apply an area of tile adhesive to the wall.

2 Position the first sheet of mosaic tiles on the wall, in the angle between the tiling support and the tiling guide, and press it firmly into place.

USING CORK TILES

1 To ensure that the tile rows and columns build up correctly, draw horizontal and vertical pencil guidelines on the wall. Place the first tile.

2 If border tiles are to be cut, hold a whole tile over the last whole tile fixed, butt another against the frame and mark its edge on the tile underneath it.

3 After placing several sheets, use a mallet and a piece of plywood to tamp the mosaics down evenly. Use a towel or a thin carpet offcut as a cushion. Ensure the grouting spaces between each sheet are equal.

4 To fill in the perimeter of the area, snip individual mosaic tiles from the sheet, cut them to the size required and bed them in the adhesive.

5 Spread grout over the tiled area, working it well into the gaps between the individual mosaics. Wipe off excess grout, and polish the surface when dry.

3 Place the marked tile on a board and cut it with a sharp utility knife. The exposed part of the sandwiched tile in step 2 will fit the border gap precisely.

4 Fit the cut piece of border tile in place on the wall. Shave or sand its cut edge down a fraction if it is a tight fit. Cut and fit others in the same way.

5 To fit a tile around an obstacle such as a light switch, make a paper or card template and test its fit before cutting the actual tile.

6 Run a rolling pin or a length of broom handle over the completed surface to ensure that all the tiles are well bonded to the wall.

SETTING OUT TILED FLOORS

Like tiled walls, tiled floors need careful setting-out if the end result is to look neat and professional. This is especially important with glazed ceramic and quarry tiles and also patterned vinyl and lino tiles, but matters rather less with plain vinyl or cork tiles where the finished effect is of uniform colour and the joints between the tiles are practically invisible.

Fortunately the necessary setting-out is much easier with floor tiles than wall tiles, since the tiles can be dry-laid on the floor surface and moved around until a starting point is found that gives the best arrangement, with cut border tiles of approximately equal size all around the perimeter of the room.

In a regular-shaped room, start by finding the actual centre point of the floor, by linking the midpoints of opposite pairs of walls with string lines. In an irregularly-shaped room, place string lines as shown in the illustration so that they avoid obstructions, and then link the midpoints of opposite pairs of strings to find the room's centre. Now dry-lay rows of tiles out towards the walls in each direction, remembering to allow for the joint thickness if appropriate, to see how many whole tiles will fit in and to check whether this starting point results in over-narrow border tiles or awkward cuts against obstacles. Move the rows slightly to improve the fit if necessary, then chalk the string lines and snap them against the floor surface to mark the starting point.

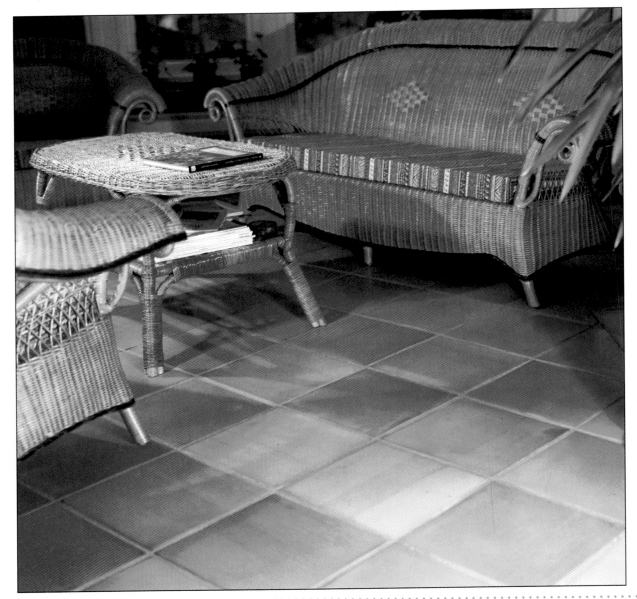

LEFT Quarry and terracotta tiles provide a durable and attractive floor covering and are especially suited to kitchens and conservatories. To ensure that the tiles are correctly aligned with equal borders around the perimeter of the room, it is essential to follow the correct setting-out procedures.

1 In a regular-shaped room, find the room's centre by linking the midpoints of opposite pairs of walls with string lines.

2 In an irregularly shaped room, use string lines that avoid obstacles, and link the midpoints of these as shown to find the centre point.

3 To ensure that tiles will be laid square to the door threshold if the walls are out of square, place a string line at right angles to it across the room to the opposite wall.

4 Place a second string line at right angles to the first so that it passes through the room's centre point.

5 Place a third string line at right angles to the second, again passing through the centre point, to complete the laying guide.

6 Dry-lay rows of tiles out from the centre of the room towards the walls, allowing for the joint width as appropriate to check the width of the border tiles and the fit around any obstacles.

7 Adjust the string lines to get the best possible fit, chalk them and snap them against the floor to mark the laying guidelines.

LAYING CERAMIC FLOOR TILES

Both glazed ceramic and quarry tiles can be laid directly over a concrete floor, as long as it is sound and dry. They can also be laid on a suspended timber floor if it is strong enough to support the not inconsiderable extra weight (check this with a building surveyor). In this case cover the floorboards with exterior-grade plywood, screwed down or secured with annular nails (spiral flooring nails) to prevent it from lifting; this will provide a stable, level base for the tiles.

Glazed ceramic floor tiles are laid with specially formulated adhesive, which should be a waterproof type in bathrooms and a flexible type if tiling on a suspended floor. Quarry and terracotta tiles are laid on mortar over a solid concrete floor, and in thick-bed tile adhesive over plywood.

Old floor coverings should be lifted before laying ceramic or quarry tiles, but if a solid floor is covered with well-bonded vinyl or cork tiles, these can be left in place and tiled over, using tile adhesive. First remove any wax polish used on them.

Set out the floor as described previously, but transfer the starting point to the corner of the room farthest from the door once the setting-out has been completed.

TIP

Remember to take off and shorten room doors before laying floor tiles, and remove enough to allow the door to clear both the plywood underlay and the new tiles.

LAYING CERAMIC FLOOR TILES

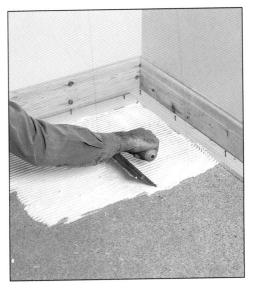

1 Pin tiling guides to the floor in the corner of the room at right angles to each other, then spread some adhesive on the floor with a notched-edge trowel.

2 Place the first tile in the angle between the tiling guides, butting it tightly against them and pressing it down firmly into the adhesive bed.

3 As the tiles are laid, use tile spacers to ensure an even gap between them. Use a straightedge to check that all the tiles are horizontal and level.

4 To cut border tiles, lay a whole tile over the last whole tile laid, butt another against the skirting (baseboard) and mark its edge on the tile underneath.

TILING

5 Cut the tile and use the exposed part of the sandwiched tile in step 4 to fill the border gap. Use the offcut to fill the next border gap if it is wider than the gap.

6 Use a squeegee to spread grout over the tiles and fill all the joint lines. Wipe excess adhesive from the surface of the tiles with a damp cloth.

7 Use a piece of dowel or a similar rounded implement to smooth the grout lines. Then polish the tile surface with a clean, dry cloth.

LAYING QUARRY TILES

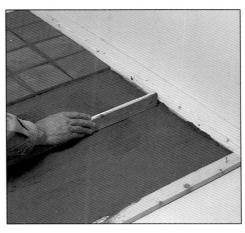

1 Add a third tiling guide to form a bay four tiles wide. Put down a thin mortar bed and place the first row of tiles, using a tiling gauge to space them.

2 Complete four rows of four tiles, then check that they are level. Tamp down any that are proud and lift and rebed any that are lying low.

3 Complete the first bay, then remove the third tiling guide and reposition it another four tile widths away. Fill the second bay with mortar and tamp it down.

4 Complete the second bay in the same way as the first. Continue in this fashion across the room until all the whole tiles are laid.

5 If installing a tiled upstand, place this next, aligning individual units with the floor tiling. Then cut and fit the border tiles.

6 Mix up a fairly dry mortar mix and use a stiff-bristled brush to work it well into the joints between the tiles. Brush away excess mortar while working.

LAYING VINYL, LINO AND CORK FLOOR TILES

Vinyl, lino and cork floor tiles are available in both plain and self-adhesive types. Cork tiles may be unsealed or vinyl-coated. For plain vinyl tiles an emulsion-type latex flooring adhesive is used, while plain cork tiles and lino tiles are best stuck with a water-based contact adhesive; solvent-based types give off fumes that are most unpleasant and are also dangerously flammable. For vinyl-coated cork tiles, use a special vinyl acrylic adhesive.

Since these tiles are comparatively thin, any unevenness in the subfloor will show through the tiles. Cover timber floors with a hardboard underlay first. Concrete floors may need localized repairs or treatment with a self-smoothing compound to give them a smooth finish.

If laying patterned tiles, set the floor out carefully. With plain tiles, setting-out may not appear to be so important, but nevertheless the floor should still be set out carefully to ensure that the tile rows run out at right angles from the room door.

1 If using self-adhesive tiles, simply peel the backing paper off and place the tile in position on the subfloor against the marked guidelines.

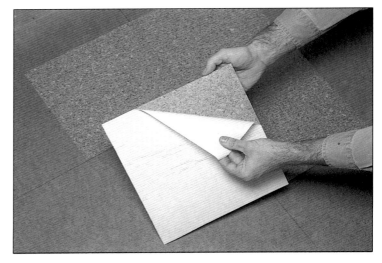

2 Align self-adhesive tiles carefully with their neighbours before sticking them down; the adhesive grabs positively and repositioning may be difficult.

3 If using non-adhesive tiles, spread the appropriate type of adhesive on the subfloor, using a notched spreader to ensure an even thickness.

4 After placing an area of tiles, use a smooth block of wood to work along the joints. This will ensure that they are all well bedded in the adhesive.

TILING

5 To cut border tiles, lay a whole tile over the last whole tile laid, butt another against the skirting (baseboard) and mark its edge on the tile underneath.

6 Place the marked tile on a board and cut it with a sharp utility knife. The exposed part of the sandwiched tile in step 5 will fit the border gap perfectly.

7 Fit the cut piece of border tile in place. Trim its edge slightly if it is a tight fit. Mark, cut and fit the other border tiles in exactly the same way.

8 To cut a tile at an external corner, lay a whole tile over the last whole tile in one adjacent row, butt another against the wall and draw along its edge.

9 Move the sandwiched tile to the other side of the corner, again butt the second whole tile against the wall and mark its edge on the sandwiched tile.

10 Use the utility knife to cut out the square waste section along the marked lines, and offer up the L-shaped border tile to check its fit before fixing it.

SEALING CORK TILES

When laying unsealed cork tiles, take care not to get adhesive on the faces of the tiles, and seal the surface with three coats of polyurethane varnish or a proprietary cork sealer to protect the surface from dirt and moisture. If access to the room is necessary while the floor is being sealed, do half the floor one day and the other half the next day.

LAYING FLOOR COVERINGS

The wide range of floor coverings includes carpets, sheet vinyl, and decorative wood panels and strips.

Carpets laid loose have been used on floors for millennia, but it is only a few decades ago that wall-to-wall fitted carpeting became popular. Traditional woven carpets made from natural fibres have been challenged by carpets made from synthetic fibres and by alternative methods of manufacture. There is now a huge choice of colours and patterns in types to suit all locations and wear conditions, available in various widths.

Sheet vinyl floor coverings come in a huge range of colours and patterns, and may also have a surface embossed along the lines of the design to give plausible imitations of other floor coverings such as tiles, marble, wood and cork. Some more expensive types have a cushioned underside formed by incorporating small air bubbles during manufacture, which makes them warmer and softer underfoot than their solid counterparts.

There are two main types of wooden floor covering, wood-block, sometimes called wood mosaic, and wood-strip. The former consists of small slivers of wood (usually a hardwood) laid in groups and stuck to strong cloth to form wooden 'tiles', while the latter is just what its name implies: narrow hardwood planks laid over an existing floor.

OPPOSITE
Fitted carpet is still the most popular choice for living rooms, and the combination of hardwearing fibres and stunning designs now available makes it possible to complement and enhance any style of interior.

TYPES OF FLOOR COVERING

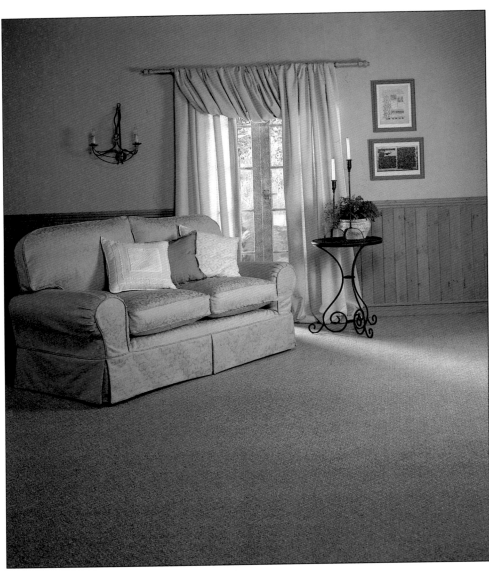

When choosing new floor coverings, remember that there is more to it than simply ordering wall-to-wall carpet throughout, and mistakes can be expensive. Floor coverings have to withstand a great deal of wear and tear in certain areas of the average home, especially if there are children or animals in the family, so choosing what to put where is very important.

There is a wide choice of materials on the market, and laying them is well within the capability of most people. Shopping for floor coverings has never been easier either. All the major do-it-yourself suppliers stock a huge range of materials – plus all the tools and accessories needed to lay them. If they do not stock exactly what is required, there are also specialist flooring and carpet suppliers.

Carpets

Carpets consist of fibre tufts or loops woven or stuck to a durable backing. *Woven* carpets are generally the most expensive. Modern types are made by either the Axminster or the Wilton method, which differ in technical details but both produce a durable product which can be patterned or plain. *Tufted* carpets are made by stitching tufts of fibre into a woven backing, where they are secured by attaching a second backing under the first with adhesive. Some of the less expensive types have a foam underlay bonded directly to the backing; others require a separate underlay.

A wide range of fibre types is used in carpet construction today, including wool, nylon, acrylic, polypropylene and viscose rayon. Fibre blends can improve carpet performance; a mixture of 80 per cent wool and 20 per cent nylon is particularly popular for providing a combination of warmth, resilience, wear, low flammability and resistance to soiling.

Pile length and density affect the carpet's performance as well as its looks, and most carpets are classified to indicate the sort of wear they can be expected to withstand. The pile can be *cut*, often to different lengths, giving a sculptured effect; *looped* (shag), that is, uncut and left long; *corded*, which means uncut and pulled tight to the backing; or *twisted*, which gives a tufty effect. A dense pile wears better than a loosely woven one which can be parted to reveal the backing.

Carpet widths are described as *broadloom*, more than 1.8 m (6 ft) wide; or *body* (stair carpet), usually up to 900 mm (3 ft) wide. The former are intended for large areas, the latter for corridors and stairs. Broadloom carpet is available in various imperial and metric widths.

Carpet tiles

These are small squares of carpet of various types, designed to be loose-laid.

LAYING FLOOR COVERINGS

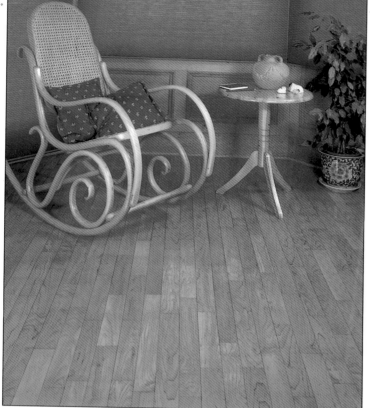

LEFT Sheet vinyl can offer excellent imitations of a wide range of other floor coverings, including wood, tiles and even marble or terrazzo.

BELOW Carpet tiles have a long commercial pedigree, and can be a clever choice in the home too since they can be lifted for cleaning and rotated to even out wear.

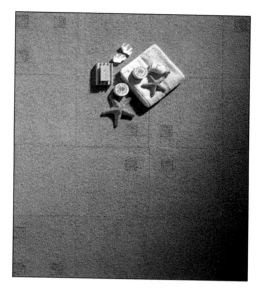

Cheaper tiles resemble cord and felt carpets, while more expensive ones may have a short or long cut pile. Common sizes are 300, 450, 500 and 600 mm (12, 18, 20 and 24 in) square.

Sheet vinyl flooring

This is a relatively thin material which provides a smooth, hygienic and easy-to-clean floor covering that is widely used in rooms such as kitchens, bathrooms and hallways. It is made from layers of plastic resins, with a clear wear layer protecting the printed design and frequently with an air cushion layer between this and the backing for extra comfort and warmth underfoot. It is fairly flexible and easy to cut for an exact fit; it is generally loose-laid, with double-sided adhesive tape used only at seams and edges.

Sheet linoleum (lino) is also becoming popular again for domestic use, and is available in some stylish designs and colourways with optional contrasting border designs. Lino is more difficult for the amateur to lay,

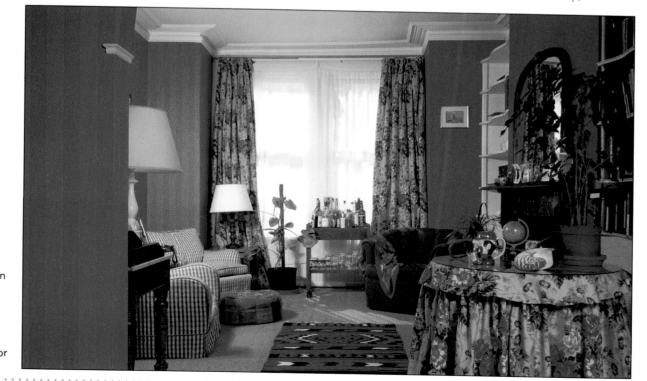

RIGHT Natural mattings in coir or sisal provide a hardwearing floor covering. Available in a wide range of neutral shades and textures, as well as striped and check designs, they are at home in traditional or modern interiors.

TYPES OF FLOOR
COVERING (continued)

however, being heavier, less flexible and harder to cut than sheet vinyl.

Vinyl flooring is available in a wide range of designs, including realistic imitations of ceramic tiles, wood, cork and stone. It is sold by the linear metre (or yard) from rolls 2, 3 or 4 m (6 ft 6 in, 10 ft or 13 ft) wide; the larger width enables seamfree floors to be laid in most medium-sized rooms.

ABOVE Modern sheet linoleum has taken on a new lease of life, offering a range of sophisticated colourways teamed with stylish borders that are perfect for kitchens, utility rooms and hallways.

LEFT Sealed cork flooring offers a unique combination of warmth and resilience underfoot, coupled with an easy-clean surface that looks attractive too.

BELOW Solid wood-strip flooring, shown here in beech, provides a luxury floor covering that looks stunning and will also last a lifetime.

Wood floor coverings

These come in two main forms: as square wood-block panels made up of individual fingers of wood stuck to a cloth or felt backing for ease of handling and laying; or as wood-strip flooring – interlocking planks, often of veneer on a plywood backing. They are laid over the existing floor surface; most are tongued-and-grooved, so only occasional nailing or clipping is required to hold them in place.

Wood-block panels are usually 300 or 450 mm (12 or 18 in) square, while planks are generally 75 or 100 mm (3 or 4 in) wide and come in a range of lengths to allow the end joints to be staggered from one row to the next.

LEFT Wood is an excellent choice for entrance halls too, where a durable yet good-looking floor surface is essential.

are extremely hardwearing kitchen carpets available, with a specially treated short nylon pile that is easy to keep clean, and also water-resistant bathroom carpets that give a touch of luxury underfoot without turning into a swamp at bathtime.

Leisure areas – living rooms, dining rooms and bedrooms – are commonly carpeted wall to wall. Do not be tempted to skimp on quality in living rooms, which get the most wear and tend to develop distinct traffic routes. However, it is reasonable to choose light-duty types for bedrooms.

Alternatives to carpets depend simply on taste in home decor. Options include sanded and sealed floorboards teamed with scatter rugs, or a parquet perimeter to a fine specimen carpet. Sheet vinyl or cork tiles may also be worth considering for children's rooms.

Room-by-room choices

In principle it is possible to lay any floor covering in any room of a home. However, custom and the practicalities of life tend to divide the home into three broad areas.

Access areas such as halls, landings and stairs need a floor covering that is able to cope with heavy traffic and muddy shoes. Ideal choices for hallways are materials with a water-repellent and easy-clean surface – for example, sheet vinyl, vinyl tiles, a wood-strip or wood-block floor, sanded and sealed floorboards, or glazed ceramic or quarry tiles. For stairs, where safety is paramount, the best material to choose is a heavy-duty carpet with a short pile, which can also be used on landings.

Work areas such as kitchens and bathrooms also need durable floor coverings that are easy to clean and, especially in the case of bathrooms, water-resistant as well. Sheet vinyl is a popular choice for both rooms, but tiles of various types can also provide an excellent surface – sealed cork, with its warm feel underfoot, is particularly suitable in bathrooms. However, if carpet is preferred for these rooms there

BELOW Sanded floorboards can be further enhanced with a delicate stencilled border design. Always seal floorboards with several coats of good quality varnish for a hard-wearing finish.

For laying *carpet* the basic essentials are a tape measure and a sharp utility knife with a good supply of extra blades for cutting and trimming the carpet to fit. As an alternative, special carpet shears can be used.

For a *woven carpet* a carpet stretcher is invaluable. This is a device with a horizontal pad of metal spikes at one end which is locked into the carpet, and a cushioned pad at the other end which is nudged with the knee to stretch the carpet into place. It is probably best to hire this relatively expensive tool, which will not be needed very often.

Also needed are some carpet gripper strips to hold the carpet in position around the perimeter of the room. Gripper strips are thin strips of plywood fitted with angled nails that grip the underside of the carpet, and they are themselves nailed to the floor about 10 mm (⅜ in) from the skirting (baseboard) all around the room. The edge of the carpet is then tucked down into the gap, usually with a carpet fitter's bolster. A wide brick bolster (stonecutter's) chisel may be used instead, as long as it is clean.

A range of tools for laying carpet, vinyl and wooden floorings include: gripper rods (**1**), a single-sided brass threshold (saddle) strip (**2**), an aluminium carpet-to-vinyl strip (**3**), a threshold cover strip (**4**), a carpet-to-carpet strip (**5**), right-handed (**6**) or left-handed (**7**) carpet shears, a carpet knife with spare blades (**8**), staples (**9**) and a staple hammer (**10**), a recess scriber (**11**), a tack hammer (**12**), a carpet fitter's bolster (**13**), dividers (**14**), an adjustable straightedge (**15**), hessian (burlap) carpet tape (**16**), liquid adhesive (**17**), double-sided tape (**18**), a retractable steel tape measure (**19**), a carpet stretcher (**20**), a tenon saw (**21**), a pad saw (**22**), a coping saw (**23**) and an electric jigsaw (saber saw) (**24**).

Foam-backed carpet does not need gripper strips. It may be stapled to the floor with a staple gun, or stuck down with double-sided adhesive tape. For both woven and foam-backed types, adhesive seaming tape may also be needed to join sections of carpet together and threshold (saddle) strips to neatly finish the carpeted edge off at door openings.

For laying *sheet vinyl*, again a tape measure and a sharp utility knife are needed. A long steel straightedge will also be invaluable. For bonding the lengths to the floor along edges and seams, use either double-sided tape or bands of liquid adhesive, spread with a toothed spreader. Lastly, a pair of compasses or a scribing block and pencil, plus a shape tracer, are needed to transfer onto the sheet the outlines of the various floor-level obstacles around the edge of the room.

For laying *wood-block* and *wood-strip* floor coverings, the requirements are general woodworking tools, some adhesive and a spreader for wood-block floors, and pins (tacks) or fixing clips for wood-strip floors, plus varnish or sealer if laying an unsealed type.

UNDERLAYS

Lining paper or cloth underlay is recommended for foam-backed carpets as it prevents the foam from sticking to the floor surface. For woven carpets use either a foam or felt underlay: they are available in various grades and should be matched to the carpet being laid. Heavy-duty underlays are recommended for heavy wear areas such as hallways, or where extra insulation is required.

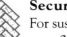

Securing loose boards

For suspended wood floors – boards laid over floor joists – start by lifting the old floor covering and checking that all the boards are securely fixed to their joists, and that they are reasonably flat and level. Loose boards will creak annoyingly when walked on, and raised edges or pronounced warping may show as lines through the new floor covering.

Use either cut nails or large oval-headed nails to secure loose boards. When driving them near known pipe or cable runs, take care not to pierce them; it is best to drive the new nails as close to existing nail positions as possible for safety.

Laying hardboard

Covering the existing boards with a hardboard underlay is an alternative to floor sanding as a way of ensuring a smooth, flat surface ideal for thin sheet floor coverings. Lay the boards in rows with the joints staggered from row to row, and pin them down with hardboard pins driven in at 150 mm

(6 in) spacings. Lay separate strips above known pipe runs.

If preparing to lay glazed ceramic or quarry tiles on a suspended wood floor, put down exterior-grade plywood.

Sanding floors

Where old floorboards are very uneven, or it is planned to leave them exposed but they are badly stained and marked, hire a floor sanding machine. This resembles a cylinder (reel) lawnmower, with a drum to which sheets of abrasive paper are fitted. A bag at the rear collects the sawdust; however, always wear a face mask when sanding floors. Also hire a smaller disc or belt sander for finishing off the room edges.

If necessary, drive any visible nail heads below the surface. Start sanding with coarse abrasive paper, running the machine at 45° to the board direction, then use medium and fine paper in turn with the machine running parallel to the boards. Use the disc or belt sander to tackle the perimeter of the room where the large sander cannot reach.

SECURING FLOORBOARDS

1 Drive in any nails that have lifted due to warping or twisting of the floorboards, and then recess their heads slightly using a nail punch.

2 If nails will not hold the floorboard flat against the joist, drill pilot and clearance holes and use wood screws to secure the board firmly in place.

TIP

When sanding floorboards, always raise the drum at the end of each pass to prevent the abrasives from damaging the boards while the machine is stationary.

LAYING HARDBOARD

1 If hardboard sheets are used as an underlay for a new floor covering, start by punching in any raised nail heads all over the floor.

2 Nail the hardboard sheets to the floorboards at 150 mm (6 in) intervals along the edges and also 300 mm (12 in) apart across the face of each sheet.

1 Use a floor sander to smooth and strip old floorboards. Drape the flex (cord) over one shoulder and raise the drum before starting the machine up.

2 Run the machine at 45° to the board direction to start with, first in one direction and then in the other at right angles to the original passes.

3 Then switch to a medium-grade abrasive and run the sander back and forth parallel with the board direction. Finish off with fine-grade abrasive.

4 Use a smaller disc or belt sander to strip areas close to the skirtings (baseboards) and door thresholds, where the larger drum sander cannot reach.

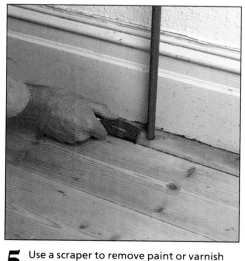

5 Use a scraper to remove paint or varnish from inaccessible areas such as around pipework, then sand the stripped wood smooth by hand.

Ground floors of solid concrete are prone to two main problems: cracking or potholing of the surface, and rising damp caused by a failure in the damp-proof membrane within the floor structure. Cracks and depressions may show through new floor coverings, especially thinner types such as sheet vinyl, while dampness will encourage mould growth beneath the covering.

Relatively narrow cracks can be patched with a repair mortar of 1 part cement to 3 parts sand, or an exterior-quality masonry filler.

If the floor surface is uneven or pitted, it can be covered with a thin layer of self-smoothing compound. There are two types available; both are powders and are mixed with either water or with a special latex emulsion. The mixture is made up in a bucket and poured onto the floor surface, trowelling it out to a thickness of about 3 mm (⅛ in). The liquid finds its own level and dries to give a hard, smooth surface which can be walked on in about 1 hour. Leave it to dry for 24 hours before laying a floor covering over it.

An alternative approach is to cover the concrete with a floating floor of chipboard (particle board), if raising the floor level will not cause problems at door thresholds. The boards can be laid directly on the concrete over heavy-duty polythene (polyethylene) sheeting, which acts as a vapour barrier. If additional insulation is required, put down polystyrene boards first and then lay the new flooring over them.

Treat damp floors immediately with one or two coats of a proprietary damp-proofing liquid.

LAYING A SELF-SMOOTHING COMPOUND

1 Start by sweeping the floor clear of dust and debris. Then scrub away any patches of grease from the surface with strong detergent solution.

2 Key the surface of vinyl floor tiles by sanding it before laying the compound. Wipe away the dust with a damp cloth.

3 If the concrete surface is very dusty or appears unduly porous, seal it by brushing on a generous coat of diluted PVA building adhesive (white general-purpose adhesive).

4 Mix up the self-smoothing compound in a bucket, following the manufacturer's instructions carefully to ensure that the mix is the right consistency and free from lumps.

5 Starting in the corner farthest from the room door, pour the compound out onto the floor surface to cover an area of about 1 sq m (11 sq ft).

6 Use a plasterer's trowel to smooth the compound out to a thickness of about 3 mm (⅛ in). Mix, pour and level further batches as required.

LAYING A CHIPBOARD FLOOR

1 You can level and insulate a concrete floor by laying a floating floor of chipboard (particle board) over it. Put down heavy-duty polythene (polyethylene) sheets first.

2 Tape the sheet to the walls; it will be hidden behind the new skirting (baseboard) later. Then butt-joint 25 mm (1 in) polystyrene insulation boards.

3 Cover the insulation with tongued-and-grooved flooring-grade boards. Use cut pieces as necessary, and add a tapered threshold (saddle) strip at the door.

REMOVING OLD FLOOR COVERINGS

Generally speaking, old floor coverings should always be lifted before laying new ones. This also provides an opportunity to inspect the floor itself and to carry out any repairs that may be necessary. However, there are some situations where it may not be practical or necessary to lift an existing floor covering – for example, where vinyl tiles have been laid over a concrete floor and they are firmly stuck to it. Stripping such a large area will be an extremely time-consuming job unless a professional floor tile stripping machine is hired.

1 The backing of old foam-backed carpets may remain stuck to the floor surface. Brush it up, and also remove any remaining staples or seaming tape.

2 To lift vinyl tiles or sheet vinyl that has been stuck along edges and seams, use a heat gun to soften the adhesive and quickly pull up the flooring.

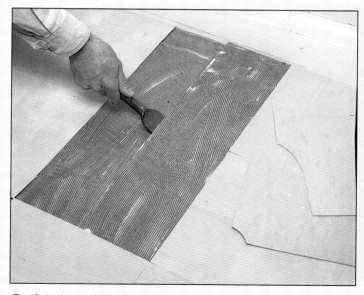

3 If vinyl or cork tiles have been stuck onto a hardboard underlay, lift a few tiles to expose the board edges and then lever the boards up in one piece.

4 Lift wood-block or wood-strip floors if they are damaged or show signs of lifting. Otherwise cover them by pinning on a hardboard overlay.

PAINTING AND VARNISHING FLOORS

Rather than being replaced, floors can simply be brightened up with paint or varnish. This is not only economical, but can create some effects that an off-the-shelf material cannot provide. This technique can be used directly on both solid and wooden floors as long as the surface is in good condition. If it is not, cover floorboards with a hardboard overlay, or treat solid floors with a self-smoothing compound.

Concrete floors can be given a smooth, washable and durable finish by using special floor paint. Make sure the surface is clean, dry and free from oil or grease. Then apply the first coat thinned with white spirit (paint thinner) to act as a sealer, and add two further full-strength coats.

Varnishing bare floorboards, especially after they have been stripped with a floor sander, can create a stunning floor that will contrast beautifully with loose-laid rugs. A stain can be applied before the varnish if wanted. Simply prepare the floor in the same way as any other indoor woodwork, repairing any major surface defects and checking that nail heads are well punched down. If using stain, apply sparingly with a cloth along the grain direction and leave it to dry. Apply three coats of clear varnish to seal the surface. Alternatively, use a coloured sealer to do both jobs with one product. Paint can also be used if it is preferred to hide the grain of the wood.

Stencils or other patterns can be applied either direct to the boards or to a hardboard overlay. A tiled effect can be created by putting down hardboard squares that have been decorated with a special paint effect such as marbling. At least three coats of varnish should be applied over any painted effect, or it will soon wear away.

PAINTING CONCRETE FLOORS Seal and decorate concrete floors in areas such as utility rooms by applying a proprietary floor paint with a paint roller on an extension pole.

STAIN EFFECTS Stain and varnish new or stripped floorboards after sanding them smooth and filling any defects. Use a cardboard mask if applying more than one shade.

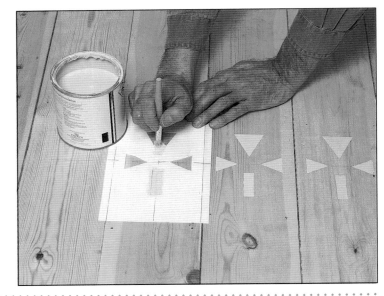

STENCIL DESIGNS Effects such as stencils can be applied to a stained or painted floor. Mark out the line of the pattern on the floor and stencil on the design.

LAYING FLOOR COVERINGS

1 **PAINTING HARDBOARD** Cover poor-quality floorboards with hardboard, laid with the smooth side uppermost, then paint on the chosen design. Use a strip of wood as a guide.

2 Alternatively, use masking tape to outline the design, apply the paint, and remove the tape when the paint is just touch-dry.

3 With any painted effect, allow the paint to dry hard, then seal the floor surface with three coats of clear varnish or floor sealer.

ABOVE Here plain floorboards have been enhanced with a two-colour painted diamond design, an effect that tones well with the simple painted decor.

LAYING FOAM-BACKED CARPET

Laying traditional woven carpet can be difficult for the amateur, because it has to be correctly tensioned across the room by using gripper strips and a carpet stretcher if it is to wear well. Because of the cost of such carpet, it may be considered best to leave the job to professionals. However, there is no reason why the do-it-yourselfer should not get some practice by laying less expensive foam-backed carpet in, for example, a spare bedroom. It is possible to disguise any slight inaccuracies that creep into the cutting and fitting process more easily here than with smooth sheet floor coverings such as vinyl, so the job is a good introduction to the general technique of laying roll floor coverings.

Start by putting down a paper or cloth underlay on the floor, taping the joins and stapling the underlay down so that it cannot creep as work continues. Unroll the carpet across the room, with the excess lapping up the walls. Roughly trim the excess all around the room, leaving 50 mm (2 in) for final trimming. Make small cuts at external corners such as around chimney breasts (fireplace projections), and let the tongues fall back into alcoves, then trim off the waste across the face of the chimney breast. Next, press the carpet into internal corners and mark the corner point with a finger. Make cuts to remove the triangle of carpet from the internal angle. Finally, trim the perimeter with a knife drawn along the angle between skirting (baseboard) and wall, and secure the edges with double-sided adhesive tape. Fit a threshold (saddle) strip across door openings.

1 Before laying a foam-backed carpet, put down a paper or cloth underlay to keep the foam from sticking to the floor. Tape joins and staple it in place.

2 Put double-sided adhesive tape all around the perimeter of the room, then unroll the carpet and position it so that it laps up the room walls.

3 Butt the edge of the carpet up against the longest straight wall in the room. Peel the backing paper off the tape and bed the edge into place.

4 Work the carpet across the floor to the opposite wall to ensure that it is lying flat. Then trim that edge against the skirting (baseboard) and tape it down too.

5 Make cuts at internal and external corners in order to bed the carpet onto the tape. Trim excess carpet by drawing a knife along the angle. Take care not to over-trim.

6 Use adhesive seaming tape to join pieces of carpet together where necessary in particularly large rooms. Pressure from a wallpaper seam roller ensures a good bond.

LAYING CARPET TILES

Carpet tiles are among the simplest floor coverings to lay, because they are highly tolerant of any slight inaccuracy in cutting to fit. The cheapest types are usually plain in colour and have a very short pile or a corded appearance, while more expensive tiles may have a longer pile and are available in patterns as well as plain colours. Most are designed to be loose-laid, with just the edges and door thresholds (saddles) secured with bands of adhesive or double-sided tape. This makes it easy to lift individual tiles for cleaning or to even out wear.

Most carpet tiles are marked on the back with an arrow to indicate the pile direction. Align these for a plain effect, or lay them at right angles to create a chequerboard effect. When satisfied with the layout, lift perimeter tiles and put down double-sided tape all around the room. Peel the backing paper off the top of the tape and press the tiles into place. Finish doorways with a threshold (saddle) strip.

CUTTING CARPET TILES

1 Cut carpet tiles from the back on a cutting board, using a sharp utility knife and a steel straightedge, after measuring the size of the cut tile required and marking the tile back.

2 After cutting cleanly through the backing, separate the two halves and lay the cut tile in place. Trim any frayed pile off with scissors.

LAYING WOVEN CARPET

The laying and trimming technique used for laying woven carpets is broadly similar to that described for foam-backed carpets, with two main exceptions: the edges are secured on toothed gripper strips instead of by double-sided adhesive tape, and the carpet must be tensioned across the room to ensure that it wears evenly and cannot ruck up in use.

Start by nailing the gripper strips to the floor all around the room, using a hardboard or cardboard spacer to set them about 10 mm (⅜ in) away from the skirtings (baseboards). Then put down a good-quality foam underlay, paper side up, cutting it to fit just inside the gripper strips. Tape any joins and staple the underlay to the floor at regular intervals.

Now unroll the carpet, trim it roughly and make small diagonal cuts at internal and external corners. Use a carpet fitter's bolster or a clean brick bolster (stonecutter's chisel) to press one edge of the carpet down onto the gripper strips, then trim off excess carpet and use the bolster to tuck the carpet edge into the gap between the strips and the wall.

Use the carpet stretcher to tension the carpet along the adjacent walls and across the room, hooking it onto the gripper strips as each section is stretched. Trim the other walls too, and finally fit the carpet neatly into the doorway, securing it with a threshold (saddle) strip.

1 Nail gripper strips all around the perimeter of the room, using a spacer to set them slightly away from the skirting (baseboard).

2 Lay underlay, trimmed to butt up to the gripper strips. Tape pieces together as necessary, then staple the underlay to the floor at intervals.

3 Unroll the carpet and trim it roughly all around. Then make cuts at external corners so that tongues of carpet will fit around them.

4 Press one edge of the carpet onto the gripper strips with a carpet fitter's bolster to ensure that the angled teeth grip the carpet backing securely.

5 Cut off the excess carpet along this edge by running a sharp utility knife along the angle between the gripper strip and the skirting, as shown.

6 Use the blade of the bolster to tuck the trimmed edge of the carpet into the angle between strip and the skirting. Then tension the carpet along adjacent walls.

7 Make release cuts at internal corners too, then trim the waste along the other walls of the room as before and tuck the cut edges into the perimeter gap.

8 At door frames and similar obstacles, trim the carpet to follow the contours of the obstacle as closely as possible, and press it onto the gripper strip.

STRETCHING CARPET

Stretch a carpet along two adjacent walls of the room, hooking it onto the gripper strips. Then stretch it across the room first in one direction, then in the other.

9 Complete the installation by fitting a door threshold (saddle) strip. Different types are available for linking carpet to carpet and carpet to smooth floor coverings.

LAYING STAIR CARPET

The technique of carpeting a flight of stairs is similar in principle to that used for carpeting a room, with gripper strips being used to hold the carpet to the treads. The job is easiest on a straight flight, but it is not too difficult to cope with winding flights or projecting bullnose steps because cuts can be made across the carpet at any point on the flight and the joins hidden neatly at the back of the tread.

Start by nailing on the gripper strips just above the bottom edge of each riser and just in front of the rear edge of each tread. The space between them should be about the same as the thickness of a single fold of the carpet. Instead of two lengths of the normal plywood-based strip, special one-piece L-section metal grippers can be used here. Add short lengths of ordinary gripper strip to the sides of the treads, the thickness of the carpet away from the sides of the flight. Next, cut pieces of underlay to cover each tread and the face of the riser below, and fix them in position with a staple gun or carpet tacks.

Start laying the carpet at the top of the flight. If the same carpet is being used on the landing, this should be brought over the edge of the top step and down the face of the first riser. Therefore the top edge of the stair carpet should be tucked into the gripper strips at the bottom of the first riser. Trim the edges of the carpet on the first tread, then on the next riser, and tuck them in before locking the fold of carpet into the gripper strips at the back of the next tread with a carpet fitter's bolster. Continue in this way to the bottom of the flight, where the stair carpet finishes at the base of the first riser whether or not the floor below uses the same carpet.

1 Cut lengths of gripper strip to fit across the width of the flight, and nail them in position at the foot of each riser and also at the back of each tread.

2 Next, cut and fit a short length of gripper strip to the side of each tread. Position them just less than the carpet thickness away from the sides of the flight.

3 Cut pieces of underlay to fit between each tread/riser angle, and staple or tack them in place so they fit smoothly over the nosing at the front of the tread.

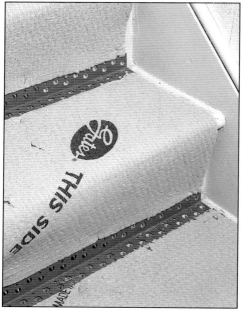

4 As an alternative to using two lengths of plywood gripper strip in the tread/riser angle, fit a one-piece L-section metal strip there instead.

5 Start fitting the carpet at the top of the flight, trimming each tread and riser in turn and then forcing a fold of carpet into the angled gripper strips.

6 On an open-string staircase, either trim the carpet to fit around each baluster or fold over the edge and tack it to fit against the baluster as shown here.

1 When fitting a stair runner rather than a full-width carpet, paint or stain the stair treads and anchor the carpet with stair rods.

7 On winder (curved) stairs, cut a piece of carpet to cover each tread and the riser beneath it. Align it so that the weave is at right angles to the riser.

8 Secure each piece of carpet to the gripper strip at the rear of the tread first, then stretch it over the tread and down to the next gripper strip.

2 If you are using foam-backed carpet on your stairs, fit special gripper strips for foam-backed carpet into the angles between treads and risers.

9 Trim off the waste from the bottom edge of the riser, then repeat the cutting and fitting sequence for any other winder steps on the flight.

10 If the flight finishes with a projecting bullnose step, trim and tack the carpet to the riser as shown and cover the riser with a separate strip.

LAYING SHEET VINYL

Sheet vinyl flooring can be difficult to lay because it is wide and comparatively stiff to handle, and edge cutting must be done accurately if gaps are not to be noticeable against skirtings (baseboards). Lengths of quadrant beading (a base shoe) can be pinned (tacked) around the perimeter of the room to disguise any serious mistakes.

Most rooms contain at least one long straight wall, and it is often easiest to butt one edge of the vinyl up against this first of all. Use a block of wood and a pencil to scribe the wall profile onto the vinyl and cut along this line for a perfect fit. Alternatively, simply press the vinyl into the angle between wall and floor and cut along it with the knife held at a 45° angle. Then press the ends of the length neatly against the walls at right angles to the first wall, make small diagonal cuts at internal and external angles, and trim the edges to fit there. Finally stick down the edges and any seams with double-sided adhesive tape. Finish off doorways with proprietary threshold (saddle) strips.

1 Unless the wall is perfectly straight, make a cut at the corner and trim the adjacent edges of the sheet with a sharp knife along the angle of wall and floor.

2 At door architraves (trims), make cuts into the edge of the sheet down to floor level so the sheet will lie flat, and trim off the tongues.

3 Use a similar technique for trimming the sheet around larger obstacles such as washbasin pedestals.

4 To join sheet vinyl edge to edge, overlap the two sheets so that the pattern matches and cut through both layers against a steel straightedge. Discard the waste strips.

5 Place a strip of double-sided tape underneath the joint line, peel off the backing paper and press the two cut edges firmly down onto the tape.

6 To fit the sheet around plumbing pipework, make a cut into it at the pipe position and then trim out a circle of the material to fit around it.

7 At door openings, fit a threshold (saddle) strip to anchor the edge of the sheet. Here an existing strip has been prised up and is being hammered down again.

Sheet vinyl flooring is ideal for kitchens with its easy-to-clean surface. The cushioned types also offer extra warmth and softness underfoot.

MAKING TEMPLATES FOR SHEET VINYL

Where sheet vinyl flooring is being laid around unusually shaped obstacles such as washbasin pedestals and piping, the best way of getting an accurate fit is to make a template of the obstacle so that its shape can be transferred onto the vinyl. Use taped-together sheets of paper cut to roughly the outline of the room and the obstacle. Tape the template to the floor, and use a block of wood and a pencil (or a pair of compasses) to draw a line on the template parallel with the outline of the obstacle.

Next, transfer the template to the vinyl, and use the same block of wood or compass setting to scribe lines back onto the vinyl itself. These lines will accurately represent the shape of the room and the obstacle. Cut along them and remove the waste, then stick down edges and seams as before.

PREPARING THE TEMPLATE

To make a cutting template for a room full of obstacles, such as a bathroom, tape sheets of paper together with their edges about 50 mm (2 in) from the room walls all around. Tear in from the edges to fit the template around the obstacles as shown, ready for the outline of the room and the obstacles to be scribed onto the template.

1 Use a block and pencil to scribe the wall outline onto the paper.

2 Tape the template over the sheet vinyl and use the same block with a pencil to scribe a copy of the room outline back onto the vinyl.

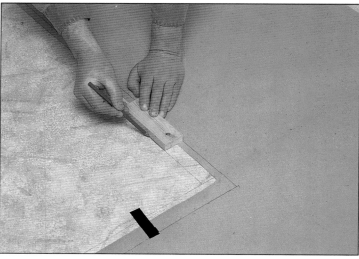

3 Use the same scribing technique as in step 1 to draw the outline of obstacles such as washbasin pedestals onto the paper template.

4 Repeat step 2 to scribe the outline of the obstacle onto the vinyl. Fix the pencil to the block with tape or a rubber band if that makes it easier to use.

5 Using a sharp utility knife, cut carefully around the outline of the obstacle. Make a cut into the waste area, test the cutout for fit, and trim it slightly if necessary.

6 To make cutouts around pipes, use a slim block and a pencil to scribe the pipe position onto the template as four lines at right angles to each other.

7 Place the template over the vinyl at the pipe position, and use the same block and pencil to mark the cutout on the vinyl as a small square.

8 Use compasses or a pipe offcut to draw a circle inside the square, then cut carefully round the circle and cut into the waste area from the edge.

LAYING WOOD MOSAIC FLOORING

The least expensive way of getting a decorative timber floor finish is by laying mosaic floor tiles, which are square tiles made up from a number of small fingers of decorative hardwood mounted on a cloth or felt backing sheet. This acts as an underlay as well as bonding the fingers together; the result is a sheet that will bend along the joint lines, and so can be easily cut to size if required. Alternatively, the fingers may be wired or stuck together to produce a rigid tile. In either case, tiles are generally either 300 mm (12 in) or 450 mm (18 in) square.

The fingers themselves may be solid wood or veneer on a cheaper softwood backing, and are usually arranged in a basketweave pattern; however, other patterns are also available. A wide range of wood types is used, including mahogany, teak, oak, iroko and merbau. Some tiles are supplied sealed, while others have to be varnished or sealed after being laid.

Laying wood-block floor tiles is a comparatively straightforward job, similar to any other floor tiling project in terms of preparation and setting-out. Store the panels unpacked in the room where they will be laid for at least seven days, to allow them to acclimatize to indoor temperature and humidity levels. This will help to reduce shrinkage or expansion after the tiles are laid. However, an expansion gap should always be left around the perimeter of the room.

1 Find the starting point in the same way as for other kinds of tile. Mark tiling guidelines on the floor and spread some adhesive in the first quarter.

2 Align the first tile carefully with the tiling guidelines and press it firmly down into the adhesive. Bed it down with a hammer and a wood offcut.

3 Lay the next panel in the same way, butting it up against its neighbour. Wipe off any adhesive from the tile faces immediately.

4 To cut edge pieces, lay a whole tile over the last whole tile laid and butt another on top against the skirting (baseboard). Draw along its edge on the middle tile.

5 The tile can be bent along the main joint lines, and then sections can be separated by cutting through the backing fabric with a sharp utility knife.

6 More complicated cuts running across the fingers of wood can be made with a tenon saw, using very light pressure to avoid splitting or tearing the thin strips.

7 At door architraves (trims) and other similar obstacles, make a paper template or use a proprietary shape tracer to mark the tile. Cut the outline with a coping saw.

8 Cover the cut edges of the tiles by pinning lengths of quadrant beading (a base shoe) to the skirtings. Alternatively, use cork expansion strips along the edges.

9 On new work, do not fix the skirtings until the flooring has been laid. They will then hide the expansion gap.

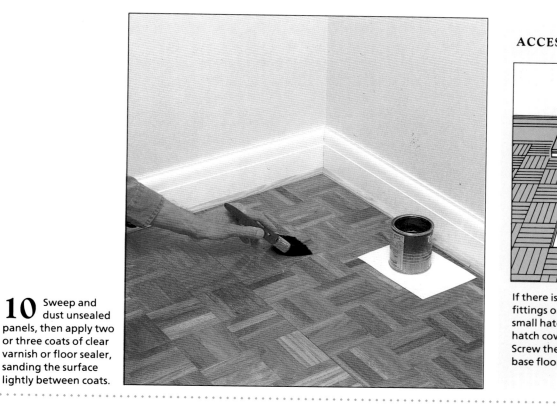

10 Sweep and dust unsealed panels, then apply two or three coats of clear varnish or floor sealer, sanding the surface lightly between coats.

ACCESS HATCHES

If there is a need for access to electrical fittings or pipe runs below the floor, make small hatches so that a whole tile plus the hatch cover can be lifted if necessary. Screw the tile and cover down onto the base floor with wood screws.

LAYING FLOOR COVERINGS

LAYING WOOD-STRIP FLOORING

Wood-strip flooring is available in two main types: as solid planks, and as laminated strips (rather like plywood) with a decorative surface veneer. Lengths range from as little as 400 mm (16 in) up to 1800 mm (6 ft), and widths from 70 mm (2¾ in) up to around 200 mm (8 in). Solid planks are usually about 15 mm (⅝ in) thick; laminated types are a little thinner.

Both types are generally tongued-and-grooved on their long edges for easy fitting. Some are designed to be fixed to a wooden subfloor by secret nailing; others are loose-laid, using ingenious metal clips to hold adjacent strips together.

A wide range of wood varieties is available in each type. Laminated types are generally pre-finished; solid types may also be, but some need sealing once they have been laid.

All the hard work involved in putting down wood-strip flooring lies in the preparation; the actual laying, like so many decorating jobs, is simple and proceeds gratifyingly quickly.

Always unpack the strips and leave them in the room where they will be laid for about a week to acclimatize to the temperature and humidity levels in the home. This will help to avoid buckling due to expansion, or shrinkage due to contraction, when laid.

If the manufacturer recommends the use of a special underlay – which may be polythene (polyethylene) sheeting, glass fibre matting or foam – put this down next, and tape or staple the joins together so they do not ruck up while the floor is laid.

1 Make sure that the subfloor is clean, dry and level. Then unroll the special cushioned underlay across the floor, taping one end to keep it in place.

2 Prepare all the lengths of board by hammering the special metal joint clips into the groove on the underside of the boards, next to the tongued edge.

3 Lay the first length, clips outwards, against the wall, using spacers to create an expansion gap next to the wall. Glue the ends of butt-jointed lengths.

4 Position the second row of boards, tapping them together with a hammer and an offcut so the clips on the first row engage in the groove of the second.

5 The last board is fitted without clips. Cut it to width, allowing for the spacers as in step 3, and apply adhesive along its grooved edge.

6 Insert some protective packing against the wall before levering the strip into place. Tamp it down level with a hammer and protect the floor with a board offcut.

LAYING FLOOR COVERINGS

7 Replace skirtings (baseboards) or pin (tack) on lengths of quadrant beading (a base shoe) to hide the expansion gap. Weight the board down so it fits tightly against the floor.

8 To fit a board around a pipe, mark its position and drill a suitably sized hole. Then cut out a tapered wedge which can be glued back after fitting the board.

ABOVE Hardwearing and elegant, wood-strip flooring is a practical choice for living rooms, especially if teamed with scatter rugs.

FEATURES AND FITTINGS

A bare room with its areas of flat and featureless plasterwork is a blank canvas which can be embellished in many different ways. Paint and wall coverings obviously play their part, but there is also a wide range of other features which can be added to the room to give it its own personality. Some are purely decorative, but the majority are practical as well.

In the purely decorative department come features such as cornices (crown moldings) which run around the angle between wall and ceiling, friezes and panel mouldings used to frame door and window openings or groups of pictures, and even such things as recessed ornamental niches for displaying treasures.

In the more practical group come wooden mouldings fitted to protect the fragile plaster surfaces. These include skirtings (baseboards) fitted around the walls at floor level, architraves (trims) around flush door and window openings, and dado (chair) rails to prevent

furniture – especially chairs – from damaging the walls. Picture rails belong in this group too, allowing pictures and mirrors to be hung anywhere without having to make new fixings.

On a larger scale are add-on features such as wall panelling, which can be fixed to wall and ceiling surfaces as an alternative to more usual wall coverings, and replacement doors and ornamental fire surrounds. These can set off a chimney breast (fireplace projection) to excellent effect even if the fireplace is not in use.

The scheme is completed with the right choice of fittings – handles, catches and so on – for the doors and windows, and also with the selection of hardware to support curtains and drapes, whether this is an unobtrusive track or a more decorative pole. There is a huge range of products to choose from in all of these categories.

The walls and ceilings of your rooms can be enhanced in many ways: for example, with decorative wood or plaster mouldings, fire surrounds, wall panelling, replacement doors, new door and window furniture, and curtain (drapery) tracks and poles. Pictures and mirrors provide the finishing touches.

Plaster mouldings

Perhaps the simplest type of ornamental plasterwork is the panel moulding. This is a relatively narrow and shallow decorative strip used, as its name suggests, to outline areas on walls or ceilings which will be treated in a different way to the rest of the room, especially as a way of highlighting pictures, mirrors or alcoves.

Panel mouldings are made in a wide range of profiles, from plain fluted and reeded effects to more elaborate versions such as egg-and-dart, flower-and-husk, Roman vine and Greek key. They are made in standard lengths which vary according to the complexity of the design, and these are simply butt-jointed to make up the panel size required. Corners can be mitred to create square and rectangular panels, or can be formed with matching corner blocks or special re-entrant curves.

Cornices (crown moldings)

Cornices have always been one of the most impressive decorative plaster features. They were originally used externally in classical architecture at

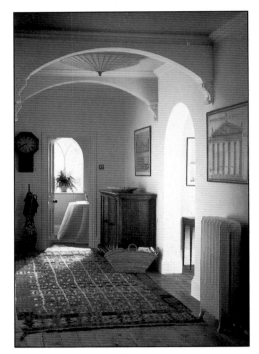

ABOVE Ornamental plasterwork, such as cornices (crown moldings) and corbels supporting delicate arches, add a flourish to any decor, especially in period homes.

LEFT Decorative mouldings are very much in vogue as a means of breaking up large expanses of wall and displaying picture groups. The choice of paint colours is important in balancing the different, defined areas of wall.

LEFT Open fires, whether real or gas-powered, need a fire surround to frame them. Softwood mouldings with marble inserts look particularly effective.

BELOW Even the simplest colour schemes gain a three-dimensional element from the use of wall panelling and mouldings.

the edges of roofs, but were soon also used inside on the perimeter of ceilings. As with panel mouldings, a huge range of profiles is available, from authentic Greek and Roman forms through eighteenth- and nineteenth-century styles, and featuring such classic motifs as acanthus, dentil, swag-and-drop and egg-and-dart. Wall and ceiling projections range from a delicate 32 mm (1¼ in) for single ogee (or cyma) types up to the massive 400 × 100 mm (16 × 4 in) of an ornate Adam-style frieze. Cornices are made in standard lengths, usually 2 or 3 metres or yards. Corners are formed by cutting mitres with a tenon or fine-toothed panel saw.

Plain concave mouldings – known as coving – are also available, made either as a paper-faced moulding with a plaster core, or machined from wood.

Ceiling roses

A ceiling rose is the perfect complement to a room with a cornice (crown molding) or ceiling panelling. It is a circular or elliptical moulding which can be used with or without a pendant light at its centre. A wide range of patterns is available, from classic designs to plainer modern versions. Sizes start at around 300 mm (12 in) in diameter and range up to a massive 1.5 × 1.2 m (5 × 4 ft) for the largest decorative ovals.

Wooden mouldings

The term 'moulding' is really a misnomer, better applied to decorative plasterwork which is, literally, moulded into shape. Timber mouldings are machined with shaped cutters and routers, to produce a wide range of cross sections.

Most everyday mouldings are machined either from softwood or from

LEFT In high-ceilinged rooms, deeper skirtings (baseboards) and cornices (crown moldings) can help to make the ceiling appear lower. They can be picked out with contrasting shades of paint or matched to the wall colour.

a cheap hardwood. As a general guideline, the larger mouldings – architraves (door and window trims), skirtings (baseboards) and the like – are cut from softwood, while mouldings with smaller and more intricate profiles are made from hardwood. Mouldings can be given a coloured finish, or other woods can be imitated, by staining and varnishing them.

Skirtings (baseboards)

These boards are fitted to plastered walls at ground level to protect the plaster surface from damage by careless feet or furniture – and incidentally to allow floor cleaning implements to be used right up to the floor edge without wetting or marking the walls. Until recently, the fashion was for fairly low, plain skirtings with either a pencil-rounded or splayed-and-rounded cross section; these were usually painted. However, in many new homes there is now a switch back to deeper, more ornate skirtings with traditional profiles, often stained and varnished.

Architraves (trims)

These perform a similar job to skirtings (baseboards), being fitted around flush door and window openings to create a decorative and protective border. They are available in styles to match both plain and ornate skirtings, and are either run down to floor level, with the skirting abutting their outer edges, or rest on a small floor-level plinth block.

Dado (chair) and picture rails

These are horizontal mouldings fixed to wall surfaces, the former about 900 mm (3 ft) from the floor and the latter a short way below ceiling level. They were both popular until the 1930s, and are now making a comeback.

The dado rail was designed to protect the plaster from damage by the backs of chairs, and also provided a natural break in the wall's colour scheme. Traditionally the area below the rail – the whole surface was known as the dado (wainscot) – was panelled or finished in a relief wall covering, while that above it was papered or painted.

The picture rail allowed pictures to be hung – and moved about – at will, and also provided a visual break in rooms with high ceilings.

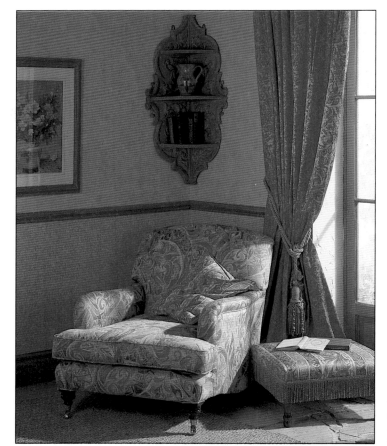

LEFT Dado (chair) rails allow the use of different but complementary wall coverings above and below the rail. Picture-frame mouldings in a similar style and finish integrate the decorating scheme.

BELOW Window dressing adds the finishing touch to any room. Here an attractive festoon blind is suspended from a wooden pole.

BOTTOM Wood panelling below dado (chair) rail level is a durable alternative to wall coverings. The natural divide can be highlighted with attractive stencil borders.

Curtain (drapery) tracks and poles

One last fixture that deserves some attention is the hardware that supports the curtains (drapes). Curtain tracks and poles may be wall- or ceiling-mounted, and can be made of metal, wood or plastic in a range of styles and finishes. The simplest types of curtain track are slim and unobtrusive; more complex versions include cords or motor drives to move the curtains. Ornamental poles are a distinctive feature in their own right.

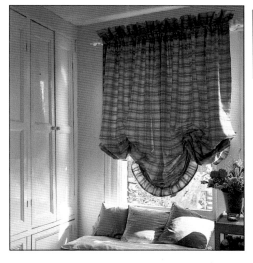

Wall panelling

This is formed by fixing tongued-and-grooved or overlapping 'shiplap' boards to wall surfaces. It is often used between the skirting (baseboard) and dado (chair) rail, but floor to ceiling panelling is another option. It can also be fixed to ceiling surfaces, and can be painted or stained and varnished, as wished, once installed.

Doors and windows

Replacing room doors is one way of giving a room a dramatic facelift, especially if the existing doors are out of keeping with the look of the room. There is a huge range of panelled and glazed doors now available, and installing one may be as simple as removing the old door and hanging the new door in its place.

New doors deserve new fittings, and again there is a wide range of handles, knobs and latches to choose from, including various metallic finishes, wood, plastic and even glass and ceramics. The same applies to windows. Changing these is a bigger job than replacing a door, but simply fitting new stays and catches can give an old window frame a new lease of life.

PUTTING UP A CORNICE (CROWN MOLDING)

Three types of decorative cornice are commonly used in today's homes. The first is coving, a relative of sheet plasterboard (gypsum board), which consists of a concave hollow-backed plaster core sheathed in a strong paper envelope. It is fixed in place with adhesive. The second is the moulded cornice, made either from traditional fibrous plaster or from modern foamed plastics to imitate the ornate decorative cornices often found in older buildings. This comes in a range of profiles, and plaster types must generally be secured in place with screws because of their weight. Plastic types are stuck in position with adhesive. The third type is a machined wooden trim with a similar profile to plasterboard cornice, and is either nailed direct to the wall framing or to a nailing strip or batten (furring strip) in the angle of the wall and ceiling.

Apart from its decorative appearance in framing the ceiling, a cornice can also help to conceal unsightly cracks which often open up around the ceiling perimeter as the ceiling expands and contracts with changes in temperature and humidity, or the building settles.

FITTING A CORNICE (CROWN MOLDING)

1 Hold a length of cornice squarely in the wall/ceiling angle and draw out two parallel pencil guidelines on the wall and ceiling surfaces.

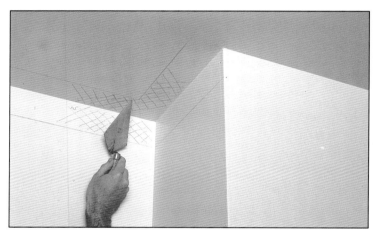

2 Remove any old wall coverings from between the guidelines by dry-scraping them. Cross-hatch painted or bare plaster to key the surface.

3 Either mix up powder adhesive or use a ready-mixed type. With plasterboard (gypsum board) or plastic types, butter adhesive onto both edges of the rear of the cornice.

4 Press the length into place between the guidelines, supporting it if necessary with partly-driven masonry nails. These are removed once the adhesive has set. Cut any mitres first.

5 Fit the adjacent corner piece next. Here the next section also incorporates an external mitre; measure and cut this carefully before fitting the length.

6 Complete the external corner with a further length of cornice, butting the cut ends closely together and ensuring that the length fits between the lines.

7 Fill any slight gaps at external and internal angles with a little cellulose filler (spackle), applied with a filling knife (putty knife) to leave a crisp, clean joint. Sand the filler smooth once hardened.

8 Before the adhesive sets hard, use a damp sponge to remove any excess from wall and ceiling surfaces and also to smooth over the filled joints.

CUTTING A CORNICE (CROWN MOLDING)

1 Make up a large mitre block big enough to hold the cornice, and use this and a tenon saw to make accurate 45° cuts for internal and external corners.

2 Some cornice manufacturers supply a paper template which enables cutting lines to be marked accurately for internal and external corners.

3 When using cut pieces to complete a wall, mark off the length required directly, square a line across the cornice with a pencil and cut it to length.

FEATURES AND FITTINGS

PUTTING UP A DADO (CHAIR) RAIL

A dado rail is a flat-backed wooden moulding that runs around the room about one-third of the way up from the floor. Its primary purpose is to protect the wall surfaces from damage caused by furniture – especially chair backs – knocking against them. Once fitted, it can be painted, varnished or stained to complement or contrast with the room's colour scheme. It also serves as a visual break in the surface of the wall, since different treatments can be used above and below the rail – wallpaper above, for example, and wood panelling below. The rail can be nailed to wood-framed walls after using a stud finder to locate the vertical members of the frame. On masonry walls, do not use masonry nails, as the rail may need to be removed in the future; use screws and wall plugs instead.

A picture rail is, as its name implies, used to support pictures. It is fixed to the wall a short distance below the ceiling, and has a curved upper edge designed to accept S-shaped picture hooks, from which the pictures hang on wire, cord or chain. Since large pictures (and also large mirrors) can be heavy, the rail must be securely fixed – with screws rather than nails. As with dado rails, a picture rail can be decorated to complement or contrast with the wall covering. Its presence also allows the ceiling decoration to be carried down to rail level, a useful trick for making a high ceiling appear lower.

1 Start by deciding on the precise height at which to fix the rail, and draw a horizontal line around the room with a spirit level and pencil.

2 Alternatively, use a chalked string line pinned to the wall to mark the horizontal guideline on each wall of the room in turn.

3 Drill clearance and countersink holes in the moulding at roughly 600 mm (2 ft) intervals. Alternatively, counter-bore holes for wooden plugs instead.

4 Hold the first length of rail up to the guideline and use a bradawl or similar tool to mark the fixing positions on the wall through the screw holes.

5 On masonry walls, drill holes for wall plugs. On wood-framed walls, use cavity fixings or locate the studs so that nails can go directly into them.

6 Drive the first screw at one end of the length, then the next at the other end before driving intermediate screws. This keeps the rail exactly on line.

MAKING ANGLED JOINS

1 If planning to fit a dado (chair) rail down a staircase, draw guidelines parallel with the flight on the staircase wall and mark the two meeting rails.

7 If lengths need joining along the length of a wall, make 45° mitre cuts on the mating ends so that any shrinkage which occurs will not open up a visible gap.

8 Always use butt joints at internal angles. Scribe the rail profile onto the rear face of the length that will go on the second wall.

2 Cut the ends of the two rail sections so that they will form a neat joint line; it should exactly bisect the angle between the two sections.

9 Cut carefully along the marked line with a coping saw, then fit the cut end so it butts tightly against the face of the dado rail on the first wall.

10 Use mitred joints at external corners, cutting at just under 45° so that there is no chance of an ugly gap at the corner.

FEATURES AND FITTINGS

Panel mouldings, made in fibrous plaster, plastic or resin compound, can be used to form a range of decorative panels on wall and ceiling surfaces. These can frame features such as a group of pictures, a large mirror, or simply an area decorated in a different way to bring visual contrast to the wall or ceiling surface. Panels can also be used in conjunction with a dado (chair) rail of a matching moulding, decorating the wall below the rail in the same way as the wall surface within the panels, to help make high walls appear lower than they really are.

Panels can be joined with simple mitred joints at the corners or with matching corner pieces which come in a range of styles, from ornate square corner blocks to elegant re-entrant quadrant (quarter-round) shapes.

It is a good idea to plan the shape, size and effect a panel will have by simply forming its outline on the wall or ceiling surface with masking tape. Reposition the tape as necessary until the proportions look right, then mark up, cut and fit the mouldings.

Other moulded embellishments that can be added with the minimum of effort include corbels, which give arches and mantel shelves some visible if non-structural support, and decorative niches which appear to be recessed into the wall surface.

Moulded plaster or foamed plastic ceiling roses can be bought in styles to match the more decorative cornice (crown molding) styles. These can be used to great effect either on their own or in conjunction with pendant light fittings. The heavier plaster types must be screwed to ceiling joists, but light plaster and plastic ones can simply be stuck in place.

USING PANEL MOULDINGS

1 Once the size, shape and position of the panel are fixed, use a spirit level and pencil to mark the panel outline on the wall surface.

3 Press the moulding into place on the wall, aligning it carefully with the pencil lines. If necessary, part-drive thin pins (tacks) through it for extra support.

5 Square the cutting line across the back of the moulding and saw through it carefully with a fine-toothed tenon saw. Sand the cut end smooth.

2 Spread the adhesive smoothly onto the back of the moulding with a flexible filling knife (putty knife). Remove excess adhesive along the edges.

4 Before fitting the corner pieces, check that the patterns will match at the joints. Mark the overlap and cut down the moulding if necessary.

6 Cut and fix all the horizontal and vertical components first, working to the guidelines, then position and align the corner pieces to complete the panel.

FITTING A NICHE

1 To fit an ornamental niche, spread a generous bed of adhesive all around the perimeter of the flat back, and add one or two blobs in the centre.

2 Press the niche into place on the wall, checking that it is truly vertical with a spirit level. Provide some temporary support if necessary.

3 Use a damp sponge to remove any adhesive that has been squeezed out around the perimeter of the niche. Do not disturb the niche while doing this.

ABOVE RIGHT The niche installed, with its clever proportions making the recess appear deeper than it really is. Leave the adhesive to harden completely before putting anything on display.

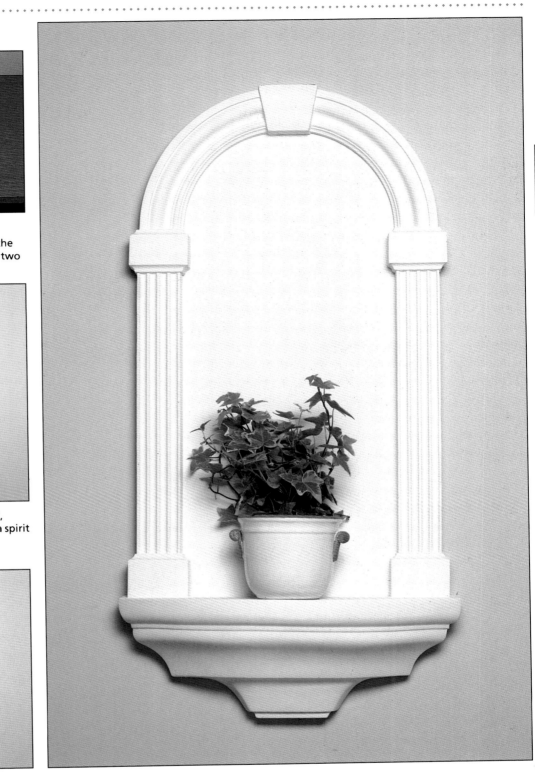

CEILING ROSES

To add a ceiling rose, mark its position carefully, then apply adhesive to its rear face and press it into place. Wipe off excess adhesive. Heavy plaster types should be screwed to ceiling joists for security and the screw holes filled.

REPLACING TRIM MOULDINGS

Trim mouldings are both practical and decorative. They are used as skirtings (baseboards) to protect wall surfaces at floor level from accidental damage, and around door and window openings as architraves (trims) which frame the opening and disguise the joint between the frame and the wall surface. Both can be plain or ornate, and can be painted, stained or varnished. They may need replacing if they are damaged or simply look unfashionable.

Skirtings are often fixed directly to masonry walls with large cut nails in older homes, or with masonry nails in more recent ones. Alternatively, they may be nailed to rough timber fixing blocks or grounds (furrings) which are themselves nailed to the masonry. Boards fixed to blocks are much easier to remove than those nailed direct to the wall, since both cut and masonry nails can have a ferocious grip. In the latter situation it is often easier to

punch the nails through the boards and into the walls than to try to prise them out. Boards on wood-framed walls are simply nailed to the frame, and so are easy to remove.

Architraves are pinned (tacked) in place to the edges of the door or window frame. It is an easy job to prise the trims away with a bolster (stonecutter's) chisel without causing undue damage to the frame or the surrounding wall surface.

REPLACING SKIRTINGS (BASEBOARDS)

1 To replace a small area of damaged board, prise it away from the wall slightly, wedge it and use a tenon saw and mitre box to cut out a section.

2 Nail small support blocks behind the cut ends of the board, using masonry nails on solid walls, and then nail the cut ends to the support blocks.

3 Cut a piece of replacement board to fit, with its ends mitred to match the cutout section. Use plain wood if the skirting profile cannot be matched.

4 Nail the replacement board to the support blocks. If using plain wood, pin (tack) on decorative mouldings to build up a close match to the existing board.

5 When replacing whole lengths, use mitre joints at external corners. Fix the first length, then mark the inside of the mitre on the back of the next board.

6 Cut the mitre joints with a power saw with an adjustable sole plate. Set the cutting angle to just under 45° to ensure that the joint will fit well.

7 At internal corners, fit the first length right into the corner. Then scribe its profile onto the second board; cut this with a coping saw, and fit it.

REPLACING ARCHITRAVES (TRIMS)

1 Prise off the old mouldings. They should come away easily. If necessary, lever against a block to avoid damaging the surface of the wall.

2 Hold an upright against the frame so that the inside of the mitre joint can be marked on it. Repeat for the other upright.

3 Cut the end of the moulding, using a mitre block or box. Alternatively, mark the line across the moulding with a protractor or combination square.

4 Fix the uprights to the frame by driving in nails at 300 mm (12 in) intervals. Recess the heads with a nail punch and fill the holes later.

5 Hold the top piece above the two uprights to mark the position for the mitre cut at each end. Make the cuts as before and test the piece for fit.

6 Nail the top piece to the frame, checking that the mitre joints are accurately aligned. Then drive a nail through each corner to secure the joint.

CREATING FIRE SURROUNDS

For those who are bored with the minimalist look of a simple hole-in-the-wall fireplace, a traditional fire surround and mantelshelf is just the thing. Complete fire surrounds are made in various types of wood or stone (and sometimes in a combination of the two), but they are relatively expensive and may not be precisely what is wanted. But it is possible to create the ideal effect, and save money into the bargain, by creating a custom-built surround from off-the-shelf planed timber (dressed lumber) and a range of decorative mouldings.

This simple design illustrates the basic principles of creating a tailor-made surround. Start by deciding on the overall height and width, and mark this on the wall around the fireplace opening. Then screw a series of vertical and horizontal support strips to the wall to act as fixing grounds for the various components of the surround.

The surround shown here is made from wood measuring 150 × 25 mm (6 × 1 in) and 50 × 25 mm (2 × 1 in). The mantelshelf and the crosspiece below it are full width, while the vertical side members are cut down in width by the wood's thickness (see step 2). This means that the angled joint between the sides and the crosspiece is not 45°, although it appears so in the pictures (see steps 7 and 8).

The completed surround can be finished with paint, stain or varnish; or it could be given a special paint effect such as marbling or graining.

1 Start by deciding on the precise size and location of the surround. Mark this on the face of the chimney breast (fireplace projection), using a spirit level.

2 Mark the wood thickness on the face of the two uprights. Cut them down in width, using a power saw with a fence or a clamped-on guide.

3 Make up the mantelshelf by nailing lengths of 50 × 25 mm (2 × 1 in) wood to its underside and then pinning on scotia (cove) mouldings as shown.

4 Screw a length of 50 × 25 mm (2 × 1 in) wood on edge to the underside of the mantelshelf. Its length is the width of the surround minus twice the width of the wood.

5 **RIGHT** Fix the support strips. The side strip spacing matches the width of the uprights. The cross strip is placed to match the width of the crosspiece.

6 Fix the mantelshelf in place with screws as shown. Check that the cross strip spacing is correct by holding the crosspiece against the two strips.

7 Lay an upright and the crosspiece at right angles to each other, and set a sliding bevel to the angle of the corner mitre. Cut the mitres as required.

8 Cut the uprights to length and screw both uprights to the supports. Then fix the crosspiece in place, checking that the mitres are a close fit.

9 Cut a corner block to match the dimensions of the uprights and crosspiece. Nail it in place as shown. Punch in the nail heads.

10 Make up each pedestal by nailing the full-width facing piece to a short length of 50 × 25 mm (2 × 1 in) wood. Support the facing piece with an offcut.

11 Nail the pedestals in place and punch in the nail heads. Complete the surround by nailing two mitred lengths of scotia moulding as shown.

ABOVE The fire surround in position. Add decorative wood mouldings to the uprights, crosspiece and/or corner blocks and plinths, if wished. The surround can be painted or stained and varnished to complement the decor.

Wood has many attractions as a surface covering for walls and ceilings – apart from its price. The natural variety of the wood grain can look highly attractive when varnished or stained, and the material both looks and feels warm and welcoming.

The commonest types of wood used are softwoods, but if money is no object hardwoods can be used instead. The individual planks should have tongued-and-grooved edges; square-edged boards will shrink slightly once installed, and unsightly gaps will open up between the boards as a result.

When estimating how much wood will be needed, remember to use the width of the exposed face, not the overall board width. To avoid visible butt joints between lengths, order lengths that are long enough to reach from floor to ceiling (or across the room if cladding a ceiling surface). When the wood arrives, stack it in the room where it will be installed for several days to allow it to dry out and acclimatize to the ambient temperature and humidity; this will minimize any subsequent shrinkage or expansion.

Nail 50 × 25 mm (2 × 1 in) support strips to the walls about 600 mm (2 ft) apart to provide a true fixing ground for the panel boards. These will run horizontally for vertical boards and vice versa. Add extra support strips at ceiling level, and at floor level if removing and repositioning the existing skirting (baseboard). Otherwise leave it to serve as the base support strip, and fit a new skirting when all the panelling is in place.

1 Tap fixing nails into each support strip at about 300 mm (12 in) intervals and hold the strip to the wall. Check that it is level and drive in the nails.

2 If the walls are uneven or out of true, insert slim packing pieces between the strips and the wall to keep the faces of the strips vertical.

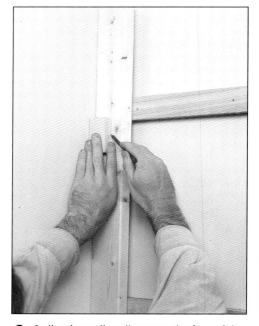

3 Scribe the wall outline onto the face of the first board by holding its grooved edge against the wall and running a block and pencil down it as shown.

4 Fix the boards to the support strips by interlocking their tongued-and-grooved edges and then driving nails through the exposed tongue of each board.

5 When fixing subsequent boards, close up the joints by tapping the board edge with a hammer. Use an offcut of wood to protect the board edge.

6 Saw or plane the final board down to the required width and 'spring' the last two boards into place. Secure the last board by nailing through its face.

7 Neaten internal corners by pinning or gluing a length of scotia (cove) moulding into the angle. Use this at ceiling level too.

8 Butt-join the two boards that form an external corner, and then conceal the joint with a length of birdsmouth (corner bead) moulding.

DEALING WITH OBSTACLES

1 To fit panelling round a flush socket outlet (receptacle), replace the old flush mounting box with a surface-mounted one and then fix battens (furring strips) round the box to support the edges of the panelling.

2 Cut boards to length as necessary to fit beneath projecting window sills, and make cutouts in individual boards so they will fit neatly round socket outlets.

HANGING A NEW DOOR

Fitting new internal doors can go a long way towards giving the home a completely new look. A new door may be fitted for purely cosmetic reasons – because the existing one is out of style with the room's decor – or because the old one is warped or damaged. Whatever the reason, there is a huge selection of replacement doors available, made from hardwood or softwood in styles ranging from plain flush doors to highly ornate ones with solid or glazed panels. Glazed doors are ideal for admitting extra light to dark rooms or passageways, but national building regulations or local building code requirements must be followed in the choice of glass – reinforced (safety) glass may be required if there is any danger of an accident.

When replacing a door, it is generally advisable to fit new hardware – hinges and latches especially. Door handles and knobs can be removed and replaced if they must match others in the room. In countries where wood-frame construction is the norm, pre-hung doors complete with frame and architrave (trim) are widely available. To fit them, all that is necessary is to set the unit in the opening, using wood shims to get it plumb, and then nail it into position ready for the trim mouldings to be attached. The door is even pre-bored to accept the new lock or latch.

1 Remove the old door and use it as a guide to marking the hinge positions on the edge of the new door. Square the lines across it with a try square.

2 Set a marking gauge to match the width of the hinge, and scribe a line parallel to the door edge between those made in step 1.

3 Use a chisel and mallet to cut into the door along the marked lines and then to chop out a shallow recess to match the thickness of the hinge leaf.

4 Hold the hinge in position in the recess, and mark the positions of all the screw holes on the door edge with a pencil or bradawl.

5 Drill pilot holes into the door edge at each of the marks. Check that they are at right angles to the door edge. If not, the screws will be crooked.

6 Screw the hinge to the door with matching screws. Drive them fully home and check that the screw heads sit square and flush in the countersinks.

DOOR SIZES

Doors are made in a range of standard sizes. If the old door is a standard size, buying the correct replacement is simple; but if it is not, a door in the next largest size will need to be sawn or planed down as required. Bear this in mind when deciding on the style of door. Panelled doors can be reduced in size more easily (and by more) than flush ones. However, doors cannot be cut down excessively or they come apart: do not cut away the tenon joints in the corners, nor remove too much of the edge wood on a flush door.

7 If re-using the old hinge recesses, screw the door to the frame using screws one size up from the originals. If cutting new recesses, hold the door in the opening and mark the hinge positions.

8 Square lines across the frame at the marks, then measure the width of the hinge leaf and mark the width of the recess required on the frame.

9 Cut along the marked lines with a sharp chisel, then carefully cut out the recess to the required depth. Take care not to let the chisel slip.

10 Prop the door back in position and mark the hinge screw positions. Drill pilot holes, then drive in the screws to secure the hinges to the frame.

TIP

If the door binds on the hinge side and will not close properly, the hinge recesses are too deep. Unscrew the hinges and insert cardboard packing pieces.

Door and window fittings can be ornamental as well as practical and secure. The simplest type of door catch is a spring-loaded ball which is recessed into the door edge. The ball engages in a recess in the door frame as the door is pushed closed, and retracts as the door is pulled open.

A more positive action is provided by a mortise latch; this is also recessed into the door edge and has a projecting bolt which is flat on one face and curved on the other. As the door is pushed shut, the curved face hits the striking plate on the door frame and pushes the bolt back into the latch body. When the door is fully closed the bolt springs out into the recess in the striking plate, with its flat face providing a positive latching action. Turning the door handle rotates a spindle, withdrawing the bolt from the striking plate and allowing the door to open again. A mortise lock combines the same latch mechanism with a lockable bolt.

The commonest items of hardware used on hinged windows are a rotating cockspur handle that is used simply to fasten the window, and a casement stay which props it open in one of several different positions. On sliding sash windows, the basic hardware is a catch that locks the two sashes together when they are closed.

TIP

If fitting lockable window catches and stays, do not leave the keys in the locks in case they fall out as the window is opened and closed. Instead, hang them on a pin driven into the window frame. This also ensures that they are readily available if the window has to be opened in an emergency.

FITTING A MORTISE LATCH

1 To fit a mortise latch to a new door, use the latch body to mark the mortise position on the door edge, in line with the centre rail or lock block.

2 Set a mortise gauge to a setting just wider than the thickness of the latch body, and scribe the outline of the mortise centred on the door edge.

3 Use a flat wood bit in a power drill to make a series of holes between the guidelines, a little deeper than the length of the latch body.

4 Chop out the waste with a chisel and mallet, then pare down the sides of the mortise and clean out the recess. Try the latch for fit in the mortise.

5 Draw around the latch faceplate on the edge of the door, then cut around the lines with a chisel and make a series of parallel cuts across the grain.

6 Carefully chisel out the waste wood between the marked guidelines, taking care not to let the chisel slip and cut beyond the ends of the recess.

7 Hold the latch body against the face of the door in line with the mortise and with its faceplate flush with the door edge. Mark the spindle position.

8 Clamp a piece of scrap wood to the other side of the door. Drill a hole big enough to accept the spindle through the door into the scrap wood.

9 Slide the latch into place in its mortise and make pilot holes through the faceplate with a bradawl. Then drive in the faceplate fixing screws.

10 Insert the spindle and fit a handle onto each end of it. Check that the spindle rotates freely, then screw both the handles to the door.

11 Close the door in order to mark where the latch bolt meets the frame. Then chisel out the recesses for the bolt and striking plate, and screw on the plate.

FITTING A WINDOW HANDLE AND STAY

1 Decide where the cockspur handle should go on the casement and make pilot holes through it with a bradawl. Then screw the handle to the casement.

2 Fit the striking plate to the frame so the cockspur will engage in it. Drill out the frame to a depth of about 20 mm (¾ in) through the slot in the plate.

3 Fit the casement stay by screwing its baseplate to the bottom rail of the casement about one-third of the way along from the hinged edge.

4 Open the window to find the right position for the pins on the frame. Attach the pins, then fit the stay rest on the casement rail.

FITTING CURTAIN (DRAPERY) TRACKS AND POLES

There are many different methods of hanging curtains and drapes, ranging from simple rings on a wooden pole to complex tracks which are often cord-operated and which may even be motor-driven. Poles may be wood or metal, while tracks are either metal or plastic. Some are designed to be unobtrusive, others to be a definite design feature. The choice depends on the style of decor, and also to some extent on the curtains themselves, since some heading styles work better with one type than another. Choose the curtain style first, then check with the supplier to see which track styles will work best.

Fixing curtain track can be tricky on a masonry wall. The top of the window opening may be bridged by a reinforced concrete or a galvanized steel beam, concealed behind the plaster. The problem lies in making firm fixings into this beam, since drilling concrete at a precise spot to take a wall plug and screw can be difficult, and a cavity fixing such as a spring toggle is needed for a steel beam. It is often easier either to fit the track above the beam, or to put up a wood support strip first and then attach the track to that. If the worst comes to the worst, a ceiling-mounted track could be used instead. Fixing track to wood-framed walls, by contrast, could not be easier. The brackets can be fixed anywhere on the wooden beam over the opening.

PUTTING UP A CURTAIN (DRAPERY) POLE

1 Draw a pencil guideline on the wall, and mark the bracket positions along it. Attach the bracket bases after drilling and/or plugging the holes.

2 Slot in the bracket extensions and tighten the locking screws. Slide in the pole, fit the rings and finial, and screw through the brackets into the pole.

PUTTING UP A ROLLER BLIND (SHADE)

Roller blinds, as their name implies, consist of a length of material – usually fabric – wound onto a roller that is mounted in brackets close to the window. They can be used instead of curtains and drapes for a simple, uncluttered effect, or in conjunction with them – for example if extra shade is required in sunny windows.

1 Screw the roller brackets to the frame close to the top corners, with the fixing flanges facing inwards so there is room to use a screwdriver.

2 Cut the roller and fabric to the required width, and insert the pin caps at each end to match the brackets – one is round, the other rectangular.

3 Hang the roller on its brackets, then pull it down to check the tension. If it will not retract, lift off the ratchet end, roll up the blind and replace it.

FEATURES AND FITTINGS

PUTTING UP CURTAIN (DRAPERY) TRACK

1 Decide at what level to fit the track, and use a pencil and spirit level to draw a guideline on the wall surface. Extend the line at the sides.

2 Drill holes for wall plugs in masonry walls, or make pilot holes in wood-framed ones, at the spacings recommended in the instructions. Fit the brackets.

3 If a ceiling-mounted track is needed, locate the joist or joists and screw a support strip into place. Then attach the track brackets to the support strip.

4 If lengths of track must be fitted together to cope with wide windows, use special connectors which do not interfere with the runners.

5 Mount the track on the brackets. Here this is done by rotating a locking cam via a small lever; on other types there is a locking screw.

6 Fit the curtain hooks to the heading tape, then clip the hooks to the track. Some types have hooks on the track already; simply hook the curtains on.

TIP

If a curtain overlap is required, form an S-bend on one length of track so that it overlaps the track behind. Clip the special extension bracket to the tracks and screw the bracket to the wall.

HANGING PICTURES AND MIRRORS

However beautifully walls are decorated, they will still look rather featureless unless they are brightened up by hanging some pictures, and perhaps a mirror or too as well. Apart from their obvious function, mirrors can make a room seem brighter by reflecting light from the window.

For hanging pictures there is a choice of using individual supports for each picture, or hanging them from a picture rail. Individual supports range from small plastic or metal picture hooks, which are simply nailed to the wall, to heavy-duty fixings attached with screws – and wall plugs on masonry walls. The choice depends solely on the weight of the picture. Use single-pin picture hooks for pictures with a slimline frame up to around 600 mm (2 ft) in either dimension, and a two-pin hook for anything of similar size in a heavy frame. Use two hooks, one at each side of the frame, for pictures up to about 900 mm (3 ft) across, and switch to a screw-in hook for anything larger. With picture rails, the standard S-shaped hooks will support reasonable weights.

Mirrors can be hung like pictures as long as the fixing is strong enough to take the weight. Otherwise they can be secured directly to the wall with special mirror clips. If they have pre-drilled holes at the corners they can be fixed with screws – ideally, mirror screws with special domes or clip-on covers (rosette fastenings).

MIRROR FIXINGS

1 Mirrors can be fixed with pre-drilled holes, using screws plus special washers and spacers that cushion the mirror and allow air circulation.

2 Mark and drill the fixing holes, then thread the screw through the washer, the mirror and the rear spacer before driving the screw. Do not overtighten it.

3 The screw head should just start to compress the washer. Cover it with a screw-on dome (rosette fastening) if using mirror screws, or with a plastic cover otherwise.

4 If using mirror clips, first draw a guideline on the wall where the bottom of the mirror will go, and fit the fixed bottom clips at each end.

5 Set the bottom edge of the mirror in the bottom clips, checking that it is truly level, and mark the wall to indicate where its top edge will be.

6 Screw the slotted top clips to the wall so their top edges are just above the line. Raise them, set the mirror in place, and press the top clips down.

For a more attractive finish, choose special screws with screw-on domes (rosette fastenings) for fixing mirrors.

PICTURE FIXINGS

1 Traditional brass picture hooks come in one-pin and two-pin versions. The holes in the hook guide the pin in at an angle to the wall for a firmer fixing.

2 Small plastic picture hooks have three or four short pins to help locate the hook, and are secured by a longer pin driven through the centre hole.

3 A picture rail allows pictures to be hung in any position and at any height. Simply place the hook over the rail and hang the picture wire over it.

SOFT FURNISHINGS

Most items of soft furnishing are expensive to buy ready-made but they can be made just as successfully at home and much more cheaply. Curtains and drapes, cushion covers, bed linen and table linen require the minimum of sewing skills and little equipment beyond a sewing machine and iron.

The choice of fabric plays a major part in setting the style of a room, creating accents of colour to enliven a neutral decor or providing a means of coordinating different elements effectively in a room. Colour is an important consideration when furnishing a room – light shades tend to open it out, while dark and vivid shades tend to enclose it. Many people tend to play safe by choosing neutral or pastel shades which, although easy to live with, can look rather boring and impersonal.

Making soft furnishings at home is the perfect way to experiment with colour and make a visual statement. Most items require a few metres (yards) of fabric at the most. A good point to bear in mind when selecting fabric is that there are no hard-and-fast rules, apart from trying not to mix too many different colours and

patterns in one setting. Most good stores will supply swatches of furnishing fabrics without charge for colour matching at home.

Another consideration is that the chosen fabric should be suitable for the intended purpose – for example, heavyweight cloths will make up into good curtains and cushion covers but will be too stiff and unyielding to make a successful tablecloth or bed valance. A lot of these details are primarily common sense but, when in doubt, be guided by the sales assistant's specialist knowledge.

This section contains information about the types of fabric and curtain heading tapes, tools and equipment required as well as comprehensive instructions showing how to make a variety of soft furnishings from lined curtains to tablemats. When making any of the projects in this section, read through the instructions carefully before starting, especially those which refer to calculating the amount of fabric required. Finally, make sure each stage is understood before starting to cut out the fabric.

OPPOSITE
Soft furnishings in stunning fabric designs can transform a room. Curtains and drapes, tie-backs, piped and frilled scatter cushions and stylish box cushions for benches and window seats are just some of the projects featured in this section.

1   2   3   4

TYPES OF FABRIC

Fabrics are made from different types of fibres which can be used singly or in combinations of two, three or more. The fibres can be natural, such as cotton, wool and linen, or man-made, such as acrylic and acetate. Fabric is formed by weaving, knitting or netting threads made from these fibres. When selecting fabrics for different items of soft furnishing, always choose the appropriate weight and a suitable fibre composition.

Cotton is the most common type of fabric, often with small amounts of synthetic fibres added for strength and to improve the crease-resistance of the finished item. Linen is extremely strong, although expensive and inclined to crease badly; the addition of both cotton for economy and synthetics to help prevent creasing is usual. Both

cotton and linen shrink when laundered and this should be taken into account when estimating the amounts required. Some furnishing fabrics are pre-shrunk during manufacture and this point should always be checked when purchasing.

Man-made fibres have different properties, depending on their composition, but the majority resist creases and shrinking. Their most common use for soft furnishings, apart from being added to cotton and linen blends, is for making easy-care nets and sheer curtains (drapes) which are lightweight, launder well and keep their colour through countless washes.

BROCADE
Cotton, cotton/synthetic blend or acetate with a woven self-pattern

created by areas of different weaves. Used for making formal curtains and drapes and cushion covers.

CALICO
Inexpensive, medium-weight woven cotton either dyed or printed, also sold unbleached. Used for curtains and blinds (shades), in particular.

CHINTZ
Glazed, medium-weight furnishing cotton, traditionally printed with patterns of roses and other flowers, birds and animals.

DAMASK
Similar to brocade, but with a satin weave giving a flatter finish. Made in cotton, cotton/synthetic blends and linen and used for tablecloths and napkins.

DOWN-PROOF CAMBRIC
Medium-weight plain cotton fabric

10   11   12   13

5 6 7 8 9

specially treated to prevent feathers and down from working their way through the weave. Used for making feather cushion pads and pillows.

GINGHAM

Checked fabric woven from cotton or cotton/polyester blends often used to make soft furnishings for kitchens.

HAND-WOVEN FABRIC

Heavyweight or medium-weight cotton with an irregular, rather rough weave used for curtains, cushion covers and bedspreads.

LACE

An openwork cotton or synthetic fabric, usually with a strong pattern applied to a mesh background, used for curtains, tablecloths and bedspreads.

LAWN

A light, delicate cotton, often with a woven stripe pattern.

LINEN UNION

Hardwearing, heavyweight fabric made from linen with some added cotton suitable for curtains and upholstery. Often printed with floral designs.

MADRAS

Hand-woven pure cotton originating from Madras, India. Usually dyed in brilliant colours, often with a woven pattern of checks, plaids and stripes.

POPLIN

A lightweight or medium-weight cotton either plain or printed.

PVC

Sturdy cotton treated with a wipe-clean plastic coating (polyvinylchloride). Used for kitchen tablecloths.

SATEEN

Cotton or cotton/synthetic fabric with a slight sheen. Curtain lining is usually lightweight cotton sateen.

SHEETING

Extra-wide fabric for making bed linen, usually woven from 50 per cent cotton and 50 per cent polyester or other man-made fibre so it is easy-care.

TICKING

Heavy woven cloth with narrow stripes. Originally used for covering pillows, mattresses and bolsters but today used as a decorative fabric in its own right.

VELVET

Heavy fabric made from cotton or cotton/synthetic blends with a cut pile used for formal curtains and cushion covers. Corduroy (needlecord) is similar, but here the cut pile forms regular ridges down the cloth.

VOILE

Light, semi-transparent cotton or synthetic fabric used for sheer curtains and bed drapes.

14 15 16 17 18

TOOLS AND EQUIPMENT FOR SOFT FURNISHINGS

The most expensive piece of equipment needed for making soft furnishings is a sewing machine. Although a modern swing-needle machine is preferable because of its zigzag stitching, an ordinary straight stitch machine, either hand or electric, is perfectly adequate. Always work a small piece of practice stitching on a fabric sample before starting a project, adjusting the stitch length and tension as necessary. Fit a new needle whenever necessary;

machine needles become blunt very quickly, especially when sewing on synthetic blends, and a blunt needle can cause uneven stitches and puckering. Have the machine serviced by a professional repairer at regular intervals and put it away after each sewing session to prevent it from becoming covered with dust.

A steam iron is also essential. Choose a fairly heavyweight one and keep the sole plate spotlessly clean at all

times. Fill the iron with distilled water (available from a pharmacy or motor accessory shop) when using the steam facility to avoid limescale forming inside the water reservoir and clogging the steam jets. A sturdy ironing board with a well-padded surface or slip-on cover is also needed.

Sewing needles come in various shapes and sizes; choose a type of needle which feels comfortable when stitching. As a general guide, *betweens*

S O F T   F U R N I S H I N G S

172

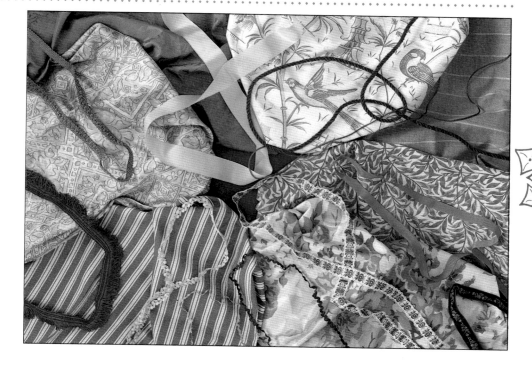

RIGHT Choose fabrics from a wide range of plain, woven and printed patterns, accessorizing with ribbons, cords and braid in complementary or contrasting colours.

are short needles, *sharps* are slightly longer and used when tacking (basting) or gathering, *straws* or *milliner's needles* are very long and useful when sewing through several layers of fabric.

STORING EQUIPMENT

Try to keep the necessary equipment in good order, clean and tidily stored so it is always easy to find immediately. A plastic tool box with divided trays is useful for this purpose.

Fabric, threads and trimmings should be stored in a cool, dust-free place. Keep offcuts of fabric in self-seal plastic bags with the appropriate threads and label the bags with the date and the name of the project. This is useful in case the stitching needs to be repaired or a patch added to conceal a damaged area.

TOOLS AND EQUIPMENT

OPPOSITE This selection of useful sewing aids includes: looped vertical tape for Austrian and Roman blinds (shades) (**1**), curtain (drapery) heading tape (**2 & 19**), woven curtain tape (**3**), pins (**4**), magnet (**5**), tape measure (**6**), sewing threads (**7**), dressmaker's pencil (**8**), needle threader (**9**), thimbles (**10**), sewing needles (**11**), furnishing braid and fringe (**12**), three sizes of scissors (**13**), zip fastener (**14**), piping cord (**15**), toggle for blind or curtain pull cords (**16**), curtain rings and hooks (**17**) and blind cord (**18**).

There are different types of needle threader available and these can be helpful when using fine, hard-to-thread needles. Whether or not a thimble is used when hand sewing is largely a matter of personal preference, but using one will protect the fingers.

Glass-headed pins are easy to see and handle. If the ordinary type of pin is preferred, choose a brand which is stainless and rustproof to avoid marking the fabric. Store pins in a dry place. A small horseshoe magnet is useful to retrieve pins and needles from the floor after a sewing session.

There are several types of sewing threads for both hand and machine use. Use mercerized cotton thread when sewing pure cotton and linen; core-spun thread (thread with a coating of cotton around a polyester core) for general purpose stitching; spun polyester thread on synthetic fabrics. Use tacking thread for tacking in preference to sewing thread as it breaks easily and tacking stitches can be removed without damaging the fabric.

Good quality scissors are a real investment as they will cut accurately and stay sharp longer than cheaper ones. Drop-forged scissors are heavy, but the blades can be sharpened repeatedly over many years while the

lightweight type with plastic handles are very comfortable to use. Buy a large pair with 28 cm (11 in) blades for cutting out fabric, a medium-sized pair with 10 to 12.5 cm (4 to 5 in) blades for trimming seams and cutting small pieces of fabric and a small pair of needlework scissors for unpicking or snipping thread ends.

Choose a fibreglass tape measure marked with both metric and imperial measurements as fabric and plastic tape measures will eventually stretch and become inaccurate. A wooden metre ruler (yard stick) is also useful. A dressmaker's pencil is more convenient for marking fabric than tailor's chalk as it can be sharpened to a fine point. Choose white or yellow for marking dark fabrics and blue for light ones.

NOTE

The metric and imperial measurements quoted in the following projects are not exact equivalents. Always follow just one set of measures, either centimetres or inches, to ensure perfect results. Note also that contrasting thread has been used for the stitching for clarity only; it is normal to match the colour of the thread with the dominant shade of the furnishing fabric.

CURTAIN AND DRAPERY HEADINGS

Curtains and drapes can remain drawn across a window at all times, serving either as a purely decorative feature in the room, or a means of disguising a less than desirable outlook. In other rooms, curtains will need to be pulled back during the day to let in light and air and then be drawn across the window at night to provide privacy and keep out the evening chill. Curtains can be made in a variety of fabrics and styles, but they all need some means of attaching them to a pole or rail fixed above the window.

There is a wide range of ready-made heading tapes available in the stores which will help to create a number of different window treatments, giving effects from a narrow ruched band (standard tape) to an intricately pleated border (smocked tape). The tapes are stitched along the top of the fabric, usually with two parallel rows of stitching, then the fabric is gathered or pleated by means of integral cords in the tape. A series of pockets suspends the curtain from rings or hooks attached to the curtain (drapery) track or pole.

The choice of heading tape is largely a matter of personal preference, but keep in mind that the weight of the curtain fabric should be suitable for the style to be created – a very fluid, lightweight cloth, for example, is not suitable for forming cartridge pleats as this requires a more substantial fabric. With all these tapes, follow the manufacturer's instructions to calculate the exact amount of fabric required and how to stitch the tapes in position.

ABOVE An elegant metal pole with ornate finials enhances a curtain with a smart triple pleated heading.

STANDARD TAPE

Suitable for all types of fabric, standard tape produces a narrow, ruched band at the top of the curtain (drape). This type is particularly useful for unlined curtains in the kitchen or bathroom. Between 1½ and 2 times the track width of fabric will be needed.

HEAVYWEIGHT PENCIL PLEAT TAPE

Pencil pleat tapes are probably the most popular type available, especially for floor-length curtains. Use this tape to create narrow, regular pleats on heavy fabrics. Between 2¼ and 2½ times the track width of fabric will be needed with this heading.

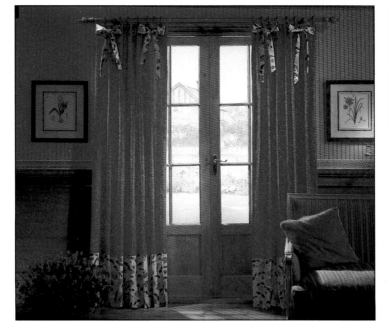

RIGHT **RIGHT** Make a dramatic feature of floor length curtains by adding contrasting bows and a deep border. The wooden pole blends well with other woodwork features.

OTHER TYPES OF HEADINGS

In addition to other tapes specifically designed for making valances and attaching separate curtain (drapery) linings, one of the most useful types is the lightweight curtain tape for use with net, lace, voile and other semi-transparent fabrics. This type of tape will gather the cloth evenly, but is light enough not to show through sheer fabric and make a heavy distracting line across the curtain top.

Lightweight tapes are made from synthetic materials, so be careful to set the iron at a moderate temperature when giving the curtains a final press before hanging them.

MEDIUM-WEIGHT PENCIL PLEAT TAPE

Similar to the heavyweight version, this tape is narrower and ideal for medium-weight printed and woven cottons. Between 2¼ and 2½ times the track width of fabric will be needed.

TRIPLE PLEAT TAPE

This type of tape creates elegant, fanned pinch pleats in groups of three at intervals across the curtain. Double the track width of fabric will be needed, plus special triple pleat hooks to hold the fanned pleats in position when the curtain is hanging.

CARTRIDGE PLEAT TAPE

Cartridge tape creates formal, cylindrical pleats spaced at regular intervals across the curtain. Use a medium-weight or heavyweight fabric to show the pleats to best effect. Double the track width of fabric will be needed.

BOX PLEAT TAPE

Crisply tailored box pleats are simple to achieve with this tape, which is suitable for curtains, valances and dressing table drapes. About 2½ times the track width of fabric will be needed.

GOBLET TAPE

A stylish effect creating neat, goblet-shaped pleats. This tape requires three rows of stitching instead of the usual two rows and about 2½ times the track width in fabric. This tape can also be used to make valances.

SMOCKED TAPE

This creates an unusual smocked effect, once strictly the preserve of the professional curtain-maker. This tape requires four rows of stitching instead of the usual two rows and about 2½ times the track width in cloth. This tape can also be used to make valances.

LINED CURTAINS AND DRAPES

Curtains are the largest item of soft furnishing to make and although they may appear difficult, they in fact require only the minimum of sewing skills. The secret of successful curtain-making lies in accurate measuring, estimating and cutting out. Choose one of the curtain heading tapes illustrated on the previous two pages, depending on the required effect and the weight of the fabric, and always consult the manufacturer's instructions when stitching the tape in position.

Lined curtains are suitable for most windows, but for the kitchen and bathroom unlined ones may be preferable, as these are easier to launder. To make unlined curtains, simply omit the lining steps shown below and turn and stitch a narrow double hem along the side edges before attaching the heading tape.

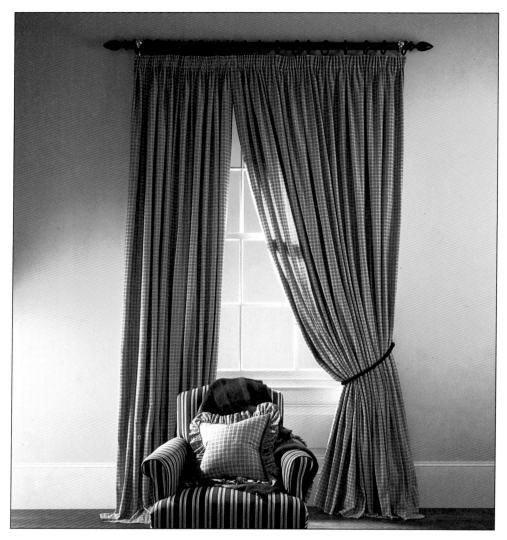

RIGHT Lined curtains and drapes hang well and the lining also acts as a barrier to sunlight, preventing fabric colours from fading.

1 Place the lining on the fabric chosen for the curtain (drape) with the right sides together and the lower raw edges aligning. Mark the centre point of the curtain on both the fabric and the lining, using a dressmaker's pencil.

2 With the right sides of the fabric and lining still facing, pin them together along the side edges taking care that the lower edges of both the fabric and lining are still aligned. At the top of the curtain, the lining should be 4 cm (1½ in) shorter than the fabric.

3 Mark the finished length of the curtain and the sewing line for the hem on the lining with a dressmaker's pencil, taking into account the 15 cm (6 in) hem allowance. Stitch along the side edges 1 cm (⅜ in) from the raw edge, stitching from the top of the lining to about 10 cm (4 in) from the hem sewing line.

4 Turn to the right side. Press the side edges making sure that the fabric pulls over to the wrong side by 2.5 cm (1 in). Matching the marked points at the top of both fabric and lining, fold 4 cm (1½ in) of fabric over onto the wrong side and press in place.

5 Tucking under the raw edges, pin the heading tape in position just below the top of the fabric. Following the manufacturer's instructions, machine stitch the tape to the curtain, taking care to stitch each long side in the same direction to avoid puckering.

6 Fold over a double 7.5 cm (3 in) hem along the lower edge of the fabric and press in place. If using heavyweight fabric, fold the corners over to form a mitre, trimming away the surplus cloth. Tack (baste) along the hem.

7 Turn up and pin a double hem along the lower edge of the lining so the hem edge will hang about 2 cm (¾ in) above the finished fabric hem. Trim away any surplus lining and tack along the hem.

Floor length curtains can add the illusion of height to square windows. Accentuate the effect by holding the curtains back at window sill level with tie-backs.

8 Pull up the cords on the heading tape until the curtain is the correct width, pulling from the centre of the tape. Knot the cords loosely at the centre of the curtain. Hang the curtain for a few days to allow the fabric to settle, then slip stitch both the cloth and lining hems. Finally, slip stitch the lining to the fabric down the remainder of the side.

To add width to a narrow window, extend the curtain (drapery) track or pole at each side so that, when pulled back, the curtains do not obscure the window.

CALCULATING FABRIC REQUIREMENTS

To calculate the amount of fabric and lining required, follow these guidelines.

To calculate the *width*, multiply the width of the curtain (drapery) track or pole by the amount of fullness needed for the chosen heading tape (usually between 1½ and 2½ times the width of the window) and allow 3.5 cm (1⅜ in) for each side hem. Divide the curtain width required by the width of the fabric, rounding up as necessary. Allow 3 cm (1¼ in) for each join that is necessary.

To calculate the *length*, measure downwards from the track or pole to the required curtain length, then add on 4 cm (1½ in) to accommodate the heading tape and 15 cm (6 in) for the bottom hem.

To calculate the *total* amount of fabric required, multiply the length by the number of widths needed.

Almost the same amount of *lining* as curtain fabric is needed, with just 5 cm (2 in) less in the width and 4 cm (1½ in) less in the length.

LIGHTWEIGHT CURTAINS AND DRAPES

Lightweight curtains can be made from fine cottons and sheer fabrics, such as net, lace and voile. Shears are used to make curtains for windows where privacy is needed from the outside world, but light is still required to filter through into the room. This type of curtain is often used as a permanent feature, together with heavier, lined curtains which are drawn at night. Lightweight cotton curtains also add a decorative touch to windows and glazed doors and cupboards.

A simple method is shown in the first set of steps, where the curtain is supported with lengths of curtain wire threaded through casings at the top and bottom. The wires are held in place by small hooks attached to the top and bottom of the window or door frame. The other two treatments are less formal and the curtains can be drawn back where permanent privacy is not essential. These styles look best hung from a narrow wooden or brass pole.

The curtain with ribbon bows is softly gathered and is suitable for floor-length curtains made about 1 m (39 in) longer than usual to allow the fabric to settle into graceful folds when it reaches the floor. The eyelet heading requires less fabric as the curtain is not gathered.

CURTAINS AND DRAPES ON WIRES

1 Cut out the fabric, allowing 2 or 3 times the window width and 2 cm (¾ in) for each side hem, 6.5 cm (2½ in) for the top hem and 6.5 cm (2½ in) for the bottom one. Turn, pin and machine stitch double 1 cm (⅜ in) side hems. Along the top of the fabric, turn under 1 cm (⅜ in) and press. Turn under a further 5.5 cm (2¼ in), pin and tack (baste) in place. Repeat to make the bottom hem.

2 Measure 3 cm (1¼ in) from the outer fold along the top of the curtain (drape) and mark the point with a pin. Machine stitch along the hem from this point, parallel with the folded edge. Repeat along the bottom hem.

3 Machine stitch 5 mm (¼ in) from the inner fold along the top hem to complete the top casing. Repeat along the bottom hem to make the second casing. (A plain hem instead of a casing can be used at the bottom of the curtain, if wished.)

4 Thread a piece of curtain wire through the top casing and another piece through the bottom casing (if using). The screw eyes at either end of the wires are held in place with small hooks screwed into the window frame in the required positions.

ABOVE Lightweight curtains gathered on wires at the top and bottom of the doors enhance a country-style cupboard (closet) as well as hiding its contents.

SOFT FURNISHINGS

EYELET HEADING

1 Cut out the fabric, allowing 2.5 cm (1 in) for each side hem, 6.5 cm (2½ in) for the top hem and 5 cm (2 in) for the bottom one. Turn, pin and machine stitch double side and bottom hems. Along the top of the fabric, turn under 1 cm (⅜ in) and press. Turn under a further 5.5 cm (2¼ in), pin and tack (baste) in place. Machine stitch 5 mm (¼ in) from the inner and outer folds.

2 Mark the positions for the eyelets on the wrong side of the hem approximately 10 cm (4 in) apart using a sharp pencil. Position the hem over a scrap piece of thick cardboard or wood and, following the manufacturer's instructions carefully, use the eyelet tool and a hammer to make a hole in the fabric at one of the pencil marks.

3 Following the manufacturer's instructions, assemble both parts of the eyelet around the hole. Position the other end of the eyelet tool over the top and hit sharply with the hammer. Repeat steps 2 and 3 until all the eyelets are attached. Attach the curtain (drapes) to the pole by looping thick piping cord through the eyelets and over the pole.

BOW HEADING

1 Cut out the fabric in the same way as an ordinary unlined curtain (drape), allowing extra on the length if floor-length folds are required. Turn the side and bottom hems in the same way, then attach a suitable heading tape along the top of the curtain.

2 Divide the top of the curtain into 15–20 cm (6–8 in) sections and mark with a pin on the right side. (It may be necessary to adjust the size of the sections slightly to suit the width of the curtain, but make sure that the ribbons will be evenly spaced.)
Cut 2 cm (¾ in) wide satin ribbon into 1 m (39 in) lengths, fold in half and mark the centre with a pin. Stitch a ribbon to the curtain at every marked position. Pull up the cords until the curtains are the correct width, then attach to the pole by tying the ribbons in a reef knot over the pole. Tie the ends into bows and trim.

LEFT The light and airy feel of this bedroom is in part due to the lightweight cotton curtains, held in place with ribbon bows, which allow the sunlight to filter into the room.

WORKING WITH SHEERS

When working with sheers, try to avoid joining fabric widths as this can look unattractive. Instead, make separate curtains or drapes and hang them together on the same wire or curtain pole.

Take care when pressing sheer fabrics as many contain a high proportion of synthetic fibres which melt when in contact with high heat. Test by pressing a spare piece of fabric with the iron set to 'low' or 'synthetics' and then adjust the temperature as required.

PELMETS (VALANCES) AND TIE-BACKS

Fabric-covered pelmets are quick and simple to make with a special PVC material which is self-adhesive on one side and lined with velour on the other. The adhesive is covered with backing paper, which is printed with ready-to-cut pelmet patterns to suit most styles of decoration. Attach the finished pelmet to a batten (furring strip) with the returns secured to the wall above the curtain (drapery) track with angle irons. The batten should be 5 cm (2 in) longer than the curtain track at each side of the window.

Plain shaped tie-backs are made with the help of buckram shapes coated with a special iron-on adhesive. The buckram is available in kit form, precut in several sizes to suit the width of the curtains. Tie-backs are attached to the wall with rings and hooks. Experiment with the position of the hooks, before fixing, to assess the most pleasing effect.

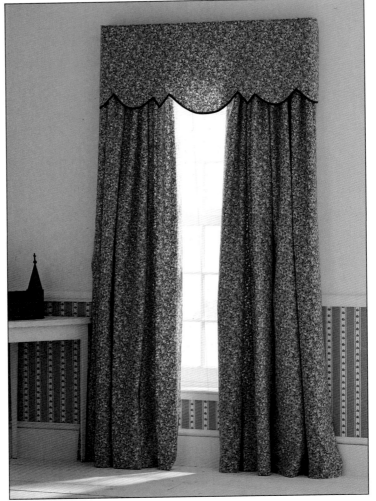

LEFT A fabric-covered pelmet (valance) provides the perfect finishing touch to this window treatment and echoes the shape of the wallpaper border.

PELMET (VALANCE)

1 Measure the batten (furring strip) and the returns. Cut out the PVC pelmet material to this length, taking care to centre the chosen pattern. Cut out the shaped edge of the pelmet material along the correct line for the required shape. Cut out a piece of fabric about 3 cm (1¼ in) larger all around than the pelmet material.

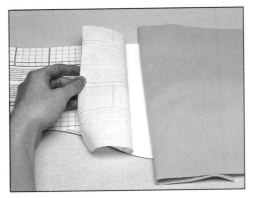

2 Lift the backing paper at the centre of the pelmet material, cut across and peel back a small amount on either side. Matching centre of the fabric with the centre of the pelmet material, press the fabric onto the exposed adhesive. Keeping the fabric taut, peel away the backing and smooth the fabric onto the adhesive using the palm of the hand.

3 Turn the pelmet material so the velour backing is facing upwards. Using a sharp pair of scissors, cut the surplus fabric away around the edge of the pelmet material.

SOFT FURNISHINGS

PELMET (VALANCE) STYLES

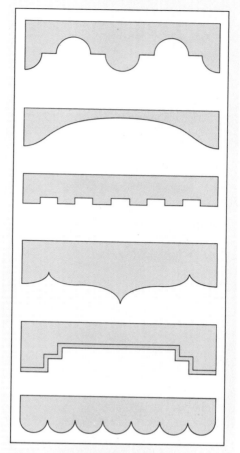

Pelmet styles can be plain or fancy, scalloped or stepped. Choose a style to suit the chosen fabric and the general decor of the room. Always make the shape perfectly symmetrical.

4 For a neat finish, glue a length of braid around the edge of the pelmet using a suitable craft adhesive. Attach strips of touch-and-close fastener to the batten with staples or tacks – use the hooked part only as the velour backing of the pelmet material acts as the looped part of the fastener. Press the finished pelmet in position on the batten.

SHAPED TIE-BACK

1 To make the back of the tie-back, pin the buckram shape onto the fabric and cut out around the edge of the shape. Lay this on the wrong side of the fabric to make the front and mark a line on the fabric with a dressmaker's pencil 1.5 cm (½ in) outside the buckram shape all around. Cut out the larger front piece.

3 Snip into the edge of the surplus fabric all around the tie-back. This will help the fabric to lie neatly without puckering when it is turned over to the wrong side.

2 Sandwich the buckram between the front and back pieces (wrong sides together) and press with a hot dry iron to secure all the layers together, taking care not to scorch the fabric.

4 Fold the surplus fabric over to the wrong side of the tie-back and turn under the raw snipped edge. Using matching sewing thread, stitch the folded edge neatly in place taking care that the stitches do not go through onto the right side of the tie-back. Stitch a brass ring onto each end of the tie-back.

TIE-BACK VARIATIONS

It is easy to vary the look of plain tie-backs by adding a narrow frill or by binding the edge with a bias strip of contrasting fabric.

A strip of wide, fancy ribbon or braid makes an unusual tie-back – simply apply iron-on interfacing on the wrong side to stiffen the ribbon and cover the back with a strip of lining fabric. Turn the raw edges under, and slip stitch together around the edge.

RIGHT Position tie-backs about two-thirds of the way down a short curtain for maximum effect, but do experiment with the positioning before making the final fixing.

BLINDS AND SHADES

Blinds are becoming a popular alternative window dressing to a pair of curtains (drapes). The two styles described here, although made using very similar techniques, create very different effects – choose the softly ruched Austrian blind for a pretty, feminine window treatment and the smartly pleated Roman blind for a room with a modern decor.

Use a light- or medium-weight fabric to make an Austrian blind – anything from lightweight voile or sheer to standard cotton curtain fabric is fine. Heavy brocades and handwoven cottons are unsuitable as they are much too thick to drape well. A special type of track is needed to hang and mount the blind; known as Austrian blind track, it is now widely available.

Roman blinds, on the other hand, benefit from being made in a reasonably substantial fabric and can be lined to add body to the horizontal pleats and also to retain the warmth of a room. A batten (furring strip) and angle irons will be needed to mount the blind to the top of the window. Use strips of touch-and-close fastener to hold the blind in place on the batten.

ROMAN BLIND (SHADE)

1 Cut out the fabric. Turn, pin and stitch double 1.5 cm (½ in) side hems. Turn, pin and stitch a double 2.5 cm (1 in) hem along the top of the fabric. Press all the hems.

2 Pin and stitch a strip of Roman blind tape close to the side edge, turning under 1 cm (⅜ in) at the top to neaten. Stitch another strip along the remaining edge, then attach further strips at regular intervals across the blind, approximately 25–30 cm (10–12 in) apart.

3 At the bottom of the blind, turn over 1 cm (⅜ in) and press, then turn over a further 5 cm (2 in) to enclose the ends of the tape. Pin and stitch the hem close to the inner fold, leaving the sides open.

4 Stitch narrow tucks across the width of the blind to correspond with alternate rows of loops or rings on the tape. Make the first tuck level with the second row of loops or rings from the bottom of the blind. To make the tucks, fold the fabric with the wrong sides facing and stitch 3 mm (⅛ in) from the fold.

LEFT Tailored Roman blinds (shades) are the perfect answer for windows and decors which demand a simple treatment.

1 Cut out the fabric. Turn, pin, tack (baste) and stitch double 2 cm (¾ in) side hems. Turn, pin, tack and stitch a double 2 cm (¾ in) hem along the bottom of the fabric. Press all the hems.

2 Fold the fabric, right sides together, vertically like a concertina at approximately 60 cm (24 in) evenly spaced intervals and press thoroughly. The resulting folds mark the positions of the vertical tapes.

3 Pin and stitch a strip of Austrian blind tape close to one of the side hems, turning under 1 cm (⅜ in) at the bottom to neaten. Stitch another strip along the remaining side hem, then attach further strips vertically at regular intervals across the blind, aligning one edge of the tape with the pressed folds.

4 Turn 2 cm (¾ in) over at the top of the blind and press. Pin the heading tape in position, folding under the raw edges, and stitch in place.

CALCULATING FABRIC REQUIREMENTS

Austrian blind (shade)

To calculate the *length*, measure the window drop and add 11 cm (2¼ in) for hem allowances.

For the *width*, measure the width of the window and multiply by 2 to 2½ depending on the type of heading tape used. Add 8 cm (3 in) for side hems.

For the two types of *tape*, enough heading tape to extend across the width of the fabric is needed, plus extra for turnings. Sufficient strips of Austrian blind tape to position at 60 cm (24 in) intervals across the width of the blind are also needed. Each strip should be the length of the blind plus 1 cm (⅜ in); make sure there is a loop or ring 1 cm (⅜ in) up from the bottom of each strip so they will line up across the blind.

Roman blind (shade)

To calculate the *length*, measure the window drop, add 14 cm (4½ in) for hem allowances and a little extra for the horizontal tucks.

For the *width*, measure the window and add 6 cm (2 in) for side hems.

For the *tape*, sufficient strips of Roman blind tape to position at 25–30 cm (10–12 in) intervals across the width of the blind are needed. Each strip should be the length of the blind plus 1 cm (⅜ in); make sure there is a loop or ring 1 cm (⅜ in) up from the bottom of each strip so they will match across the blind.

TO MOUNT A ROMAN BLIND (SHADE)

Attach the blind to the top of the batten with touch-and-close fastener. Cut each length of cord twice the length of the blind plus the distance of the right-hand edge. Lay the blind on a flat surface and thread each cord through the loops in the tape. Knot each length securely on the bottom loop and thread the other end through the corresponding screw eyes on the batten, ending with all the cord ends on the right-hand side of the blind. Knot the cords together at the top, cut the ends off level and knot again.

Austrian blinds are mounted in much the same way, with the cords threaded through rings attached to the track.

LEFT Austrian blinds, although made in much the same way as Roman blinds, offer a totally different window treatment – pretty, feminine and very decorative.

SQUARE AND ROUND CUSHION COVERS

Cushions add comfort and a stylish touch to most rooms. Newly covered cushions are a relatively inexpensive way of enlivening a monotone colour scheme as they require little fabric compared to curtains (drapes) or blinds (shades). Simple shapes like squares and circles show off strong colours and patterns to best advantage and both shapes can be decorated with frills or piping or both combined.

Both types of cushion shown on this page have a zip inserted in the back seam – a neater method than making the opening in a side seam. Although a zip is the most convenient method of fastening a cushion cover, making it easy to remove for laundering, the opening may be closed with a row of slip stitches which need to be replaced whenever the cover is removed.

SQUARE CUSHION COVER

1 Measure the cushion pad, adding 1.5 cm (½ in) all around for ease, plus 1.5 cm (½ in) for seam allowances. Do not forget to allow an extra 3 cm (1 in) for the centre back seam. Cut out the front and two back pieces. Pin and stitch the centre back seam 1.5 cm (½ in) from the raw edges, making sure to leave an opening to accommodate the zip fastener. Press the seam open.

BELOW Frills and piping in matching or contrasting fabric add a special touch to round and square cushion covers.

2 Pin and tack (baste) the zip in position along the opening, as shown, allowing the fabric to meet centrally over the zip teeth. Machine stitch the zip in place using a zip foot on the machine.

3 Press the seam allowances around the zip. Open the zip, making sure the fabric does not catch in the teeth and the ends are stitched securely. With the zip still open, place the front and back pieces together so that the right sides are facing.

4 Pin and machine stitch twice around the edge about 1.5 cm (½ in) from the raw edge. Clip the surplus fabric away close to the stitching at the corners to reduce the bulk. Press the seams and turn the cover to the right side through the zipped opening. Press the seams, insert the cushion pad and close the zip.

FRILLS

To make a frill, a piece of fabric is needed which is twice the depth of the finished frill plus 3 cm (1¼ in), and between 1½ and 2 times the outside measurement of the cover. You may need to join several strips together to achieve the right length.

1 Join the ends of the strips together with a flat seam. Fold the strip in half lengthways with the wrong sides facing. Make one or two rows of running stitches along the raw edges of the strip, taking the stitches through both layers and leaving a long end of thread at one end of each row.

2 Gather the frill by pulling up the long threads until the frill is the right size to fit around the cushion front. Wind the long threads around a pin to secure them and even out the gather with the fingers.

To add a frill to either a square or round cushion, align the raw edge of the frill with the raw edge of the front cover, right sides together. Tack and sew the frill in place, then continue making up the cover in the usual way.

RIGHT Choose sumptuous fabrics for cushion covers to complement curtains and wall coverings for a harmonious decorating scheme.

ROUND CUSHION COVER

1 Measure the diameter of the cushion pad and add 1.5 cm (½ in) all around for ease, plus 1.5 cm (½ in) for seam allowances. Make a paper pattern to this size using dressmaker's pattern paper. Pin onto the fabric and cut out one piece for the front of the cover.

2 Rule a line across the paper pattern to mark the position of the back seam. The line should measure approximately 12.5 cm (5 in) longer than the zip. Cut the paper pattern in two along this line.

3 Pin both pattern pieces onto the fabric and cut out, remembering to allow an extra 1.5 cm (½ in) for the seam allowance on the straight edge of each piece.

4 Pin and stitch the back seam, making sure to leave an opening which is long enough to accommodate the zip fastener. Finish off the cover in the same way as the square cover.

BOX AND BOLSTER CUSHIONS

Box cushion covers are often made to fit a particular chair or window seat as they can accommodate a thick cushion pad or piece of foam block. The covers should look neatly tailored and are best made in a crisp, cotton furnishing fabric. The seams can be enhanced with piping made from matching or contrasting fabric – plain piping looks particularly effective with patterned cushion fabric. Always pre-shrink cotton piping cord by washing it in hot water before use.

Circular bolster cushions look attractive on most types of furniture and make a good visual contrast against the more usual rectangular cushions. This shape of cushion works particularly well with striped, check and tartan cloth, especially when a contrasting tassel, ribbon bow or pompon is used as a trim.

BOX CUSHION

1 Cut out the fabric. Cut the back gusset in half lengthways and place together with the right sides facing. Pin and stitch the seam 1.5 cm (½ in) from the raw edges, leaving an opening for the zip. Press the seam open.

2 Pin and tack the zip in position along the opening, as shown, allowing the fabric to meet centrally over the zip teeth. Stitch the zip in place using a zip foot on the machine.

3 With the right sides facing, join the four gusset pieces together along the short ends, taking a 1.5 cm (½ in) seam allowance and leaving 1.5 cm (½ in) unstitched at each end of the seams. Press the seams open.

4 With the right sides facing, pin and stitch the top edge of one gusset section to one edge of the top cover piece, taking a 1.5 cm (½ in) seam allowance. At the gusset seam, leave the needle in the fabric, raise the machine foot and pivot the fabric so the next section of gusset aligns with the next side of the top cover piece. Continue pinning and stitching each section around the top in this way. Open the zip, then repeat the procedure to attach the bottom cover piece to the remaining side of the gusset. Trim away the surplus cloth at the corners and then turn the cover right side out through the zip opening.

FRENCH SEAMS

A French seam encloses the raw edges of fabric and prevents them fraying. It is worked in two stages: first stitch with the pieces wrong sides facing (**TOP**). Trim down the raw edges close to the first row of stitching. Then stitch with the right sides facing (**ABOVE**).

BELOW A box cushion adds comfort and style to an attractive bench. The seams have been piped in a contrasting fabric to accentuate the boxy shape.

BOLSTER CUSHION

1 Cut out the fabric. Pin and stitch the length of the bolster cover with a French seam (see illustrations). Turn the resulting tube right side out and press the seam.

2 Turn under a double 1.5 cm (½ in) hem at each end of the tube. Pin and tack (baste) the hem in place using a contrasting coloured thread so the stitches are easy to detect.

3 Machine stitch along the hems, keeping the stitching close to the inner folds. Remove the tacking stitches and press thoroughly.

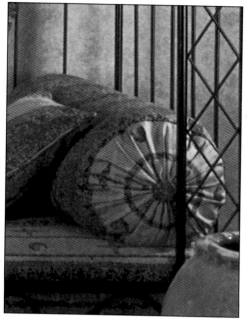

ABOVE Gathered bolsters contrast well with the more usual rectangular cushion shapes.

4 Using double thread run a row of gathering stitches along each end of the tube, close to the outer fold of the hem and leaving a long thread end. Insert the bolster pad in the tube, then tighten the gathering threads to close the cover. Secure the thread ends, then cover the small hole left at each end by attaching a furnishing tassel, ribbon bow or a covered button.

CALCULATING FABRIC REQUIREMENTS

Box cushion

Measure the length and width of the top of the pad and add 1.5 cm (½ in) all around for seam allowances. Two pieces of fabric this size are needed, one for the top and one for the bottom of the cover. The gusset is made from four pieces of fabric joined together. Measure the depth and width of the pad and add 1.5 cm (½ in) all around for seam allowances. Cut out three pieces of fabric to this size. Add an extra 3 cm (1 in) to the depth of the fourth piece for the zip seam in the back gusset.

Bolster cushion

To calculate the *length*, measure the bolster from the centre point of one end, along the length and around to the centre point of the opposite end, adding a total of 6 cm (2 in) for hem allowances.

To calculate the *width*, measure the circumference of the pad and add 3 cm (1 in) for seam allowances.

PIPING

1 Fold a piece of fabric in half diagonally and press the fold. Open out the fabric and using a ruler and pencil, mark out strips parallel to the fold about 4–5 cm (1½–2 in) apart, depending on the thickness of the piping cord. Cut out the strips.

2 Join the strips together with a flat seam to make the required length. Place the piping cord along the centre of the strip, fold it over with wrong sides facing and pin together. Tack (baste) and stitch close to the cord.

3 Lay the covered cord on the right side of the fabric with raw edges aligning and tack in place. Cover with a second piece of fabric, right side downwards and raw edges matching. Stitch the layers together along the seamline using a zip foot on the machine. Remove the tacking stitches.

TABLECLOTHS

Both square and round tablecloths are quick to make. For practical uses choose a washable fabric, either plain or patterned, in a shade which matches or coordinates with the general colour scheme of the room as well as any favourite tableware.

Cotton and synthetic blends are easy to sew, require practically no ironing and so make a good choice for everyday tablecloths in the kitchen or dining room. Plain, heavy cotton and linen look better for more formal occasions, but they require more hard work to keep them looking good over the years. Always treat stains on table linen immediately and launder as soon afterwards as possible.

SQUARE TABLECLOTH

1 Measure the sides of the table top, adding twice the required drop from the edge of the table and 3 cm (1 in) all around for hem allowances. Cut out the fabric. Turn and press a double 1.5 cm (½ in) hem around the sides.

BELOW Choose a pretty printed fabric to make a covering for a rectangular kitchen table.

2 Unfold both hems and cut across each corner diagonally, as shown, within 5 mm (¼ in) of the corner point at the inner fold.

3 Pin the diagonal edges together, with the right sides facing, and stitch a narrow seam 5 mm (¼ in) from the raw edge. Stitch from the inner corner point and make the seam 1.5 cm (½ in) long. Press each seam and turn the corners out to the right side.

4 Re-fold the double hem along the pressed lines. The diagonal seams at each corner make a neat mitre. Pin, tack (baste) and stitch around the edge of the tablecloth, close to the inner fold. Press the hem.

RIGHT Cover a round occasional table with a floor-length plain undercloth, then top it with a small square cloth made of coordinating fabric.

JOINING FABRIC

When joining fabric to make either a square or round tablecloth, avoid making a seam down the centre as this can look rather unsightly. Instead, cut out two pieces of fabric to the correct width and use one as the central panel. Cut the second piece in half lengthways and join to either side of the panel, matching the pattern if necessary. Use an ordinary flat seam and neaten the raw edges.

ROUND TABLECLOTH

1 Measure the diameter of the table top and add twice the depth of the drop plus 3 cm (1 in) for hem allowances. Make a pattern from dressmaker's pattern paper using a pencil tied to a piece of string measuring half your final measurement. Hold one end of the string down on the paper, pull the string taut and draw a quarter circle on the paper with the pencil. Cut out the pattern.

2 Fold the fabric into four and pin on the quarter circle pattern, aligning the folded edges of the fabric with the straight edges of the paper. Cut out using sharp scissors.

3 Stitch around the outside of the fabric 1.5 cm (½ in) from the raw edge. This line of stitching marks the hem edge. Press the edge over onto the wrong side of the fabric along the stitched line without stretching the fabric.

4 Carefully turn under the raw edge to make a double hem, then pin and tack (baste) the hem in place. Stitch around the edge of the tablecloth close to the inner fold of the hem. Press the hem well.

TABLEMATS AND NAPKINS

Tablemats and napkins make the perfect table setting for an informal meal. They are simple to make and can be a good way of using offcuts and remnants of fabric.

Tablemats can be made from plain or patterned fabric and are most effective when machine quilted with a layer of wadding (batting) sandwiched between the top and bottom pieces of fabric. The layers help to protect the table surface beneath the plates. Bind the edges with matching or contrasting fabric or ready-made bias binding. Alternatively, choose ready-quilted fabric and follow the instructions for binding given here to finish the edges.

Napkins are simply a hemmed piece of fabric, usually square and made in a cloth which coordinates with the tablemats or a tablecloth. Give some thought to the practical purpose of napkins and always make them from fabric which is washable. Polyester and cotton blends are a popular choice for informal napkins, but nothing beats the look of pure linen for a formal occasion.

TABLEMAT

1 Decide on the size of the tablemat and cut out two pieces of fabric. Along the short edge of one piece, mark evenly spaced points 2.5 cm (1 in) apart using a ruler and a sharp pencil. Join the points to make lines running across the fabric.

2 Cut a piece of wadding (batting) to the same size as the fabric and sandwich it between the two fabric pieces, with the wrong sides together and the marked piece on top. Pin together carefully, then work rows of tacking (basting) between alternate pencil lines.

3 Lengthen the stitch on the sewing machine slightly, then work parallel rows of machine stitching over the pencil lines using a matching or contrasting thread. Round off the corners by drawing around a cup or small plate, then trim away the surplus fabric.

4 Cut out and join the bias strips until the strip of binding is long enough to go around the edge of the tablemat. Fold the strip so that the raw edges meet in the middle and press. Open out one folded edge of the binding and pin it around the tablemat with the right sides facing and raw edges aligning. Neatly fold back the raw edges where the binding meets. Stitch along the crease of the binding.

5 Fold over the binding to the wrong side of the tablemat. Pin and stitch the binding in place by hand as shown. Turn the tablemat to the right side and strengthen the edge by working one row of machine stitching around the edge close to the inside fold of the binding.

SIZES AND FABRIC REQUIREMENTS

Tablemats
To decide on a suitable size for tablemats, first arrange a place setting with two sizes of plate plus cutlery (flatware) and measure the area these cover. The side plate and glass can be placed on the table at the edge of the mat, if preferred.

Traditionally, rectangular tablemats measure approximately 20 × 30 cm (8 × 12 in), but they can be larger – up to 30 × 45 cm (12 × 18 in). Having decided on the finished size of the tablemats, allow at least 5 cm (2 in) extra all around for working the quilting. Always trim the surplus fabric away after completing the machine quilting but before beginning to bind the edges.

Napkins
Napkins are usually square and vary in size from small napkins of 30 cm (12 in) square for tea or coffee parties to large ones measuring 60 cm (24 in) for formal occasions. However, a good all-purpose size for napkins is 40 cm (16 in) square.

RIGHT For a heavily-quilted tablemat, work two sets of parallel quilting lines across the fabric to make diamond shapes, then bind the edges with plain fabric.

NAPKIN

Cut out the fabric to the required size. Fold and press a double 5 mm (¼ in) hem all around the edge, taking care to fold the corners over neatly. Pin, tack (baste) and stitch the hem close to the inner fold.

BELOW Make a feature of a linen napkin by adding a bow of narrow ribbon and dainty fresh flowerhead.

BIAS STRIPS

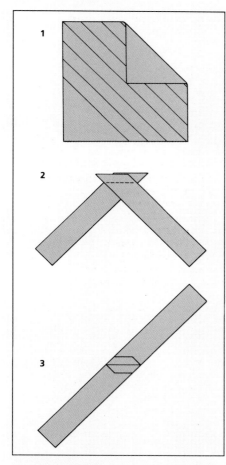

To make bias strips, mark out parallel lines the required distance apart on the cross of the fabric using a ruler and pencil (**1**). Cut out along the lines, then join the strips together with narrow seams until you have the required length (**2**). Press the seams open (**3**).

BED LINEN

Be imaginative in choosing colour schemes and pattern combinations for bed linen. A matching duvet cover and valance looks stylish, particularly when the fabric coordinates with the curtains or drapes and other bedroom furnishings.

The duvet cover is simply a large bag made from two pieces of fabric joined together around the four sides, with an opening left in the bottom edge to allow the duvet to be inserted. Close the opening with either touch-and-close fastener or press stud tape. The valance fits over the bed base, underneath the mattress, and has a frill around three sides reaching right down to floor level.

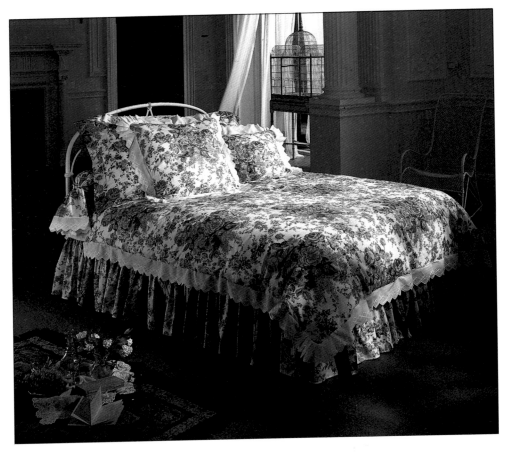

RIGHT A matching gathered valance finishes off this arrangement perfectly. Lace edging around the pillows and duvet cover adds a feminine touch.

DUVET COVER

1 Measure the length of the duvet, usually 200 cm (78 in), and add 7 cm (2¾ in) for hem and seam allowances. Measure the width and add 4 cm (1½ in) for seam allowances. Cut out two pieces of fabric. Turn and stitch a double 2.5 cm (1 in) hem along the bottom of each piece. Cut a length of touch-and-close fastener 3 cm (1¼ in) longer than the desired opening, separate the strips and pin one to the right side of the hem on each piece. Machine stitch in place around the edge of each strip.

2 Place the two fabric pieces with right sides together so the fastener strips close. Tack (baste) along the bottom hem from 3 cm (1¼ in) inside the strip of fastener and up to each corner.

3 Machine stitch through both layers at right angles to the hem 3 cm (1¼ in) inside the fastener strip to enclose the raw edges. Pivot the fabric and continue stitching along the tacked line to the edge of the fabric. Repeat at the other corner.

VALANCE

1 Measure the mattress top and add 3.5 cm (1½ in) to the length and 3 cm (1 in) to the width. Cut out one piece of fabric to this size for the panel. Round off the two bottom corners of the panel by drawing around a plate and cutting around the curves.

2 For the frill, sufficient pieces of fabric wide enough to reach from the top of the bed base to the floor, plus 6.5 cm (2½ in), are needed to make a long strip four times the mattress length plus twice the mattress width. Join the strips with French seams (see Duvet Cover, step 4) and press. Turn a double 2.5 cm (1 in) hem along the lower edge of the frill. Pin, tack (baste) and stitch as shown.

3 Divide the frill into six equal sections and mark with pins along the top edge. Work two rows of gathering stitches between the pins, leaving long thread ends.

CHOOSING FABRIC FOR BED LINEN

The best choice for bed linen is specially woven sheeting either in pure cotton or a polyester and cotton blend. Although pure cotton is cooler in summer, synthetic blends do have the advantage of needing little or no ironing. Sheeting is very wide, so joins are not necessary, and it is available in a large range of pastel and strong colours, both plain and patterned.

4 Divide the sides and bottom edge of the panel into six equal sections and mark with pins. Pull up the gathering stitches in each frill section until it fits the corresponding panel section. Pin each section in place with the right sides of the fabric facing.
Stitch the frill in place 1.5 cm (½ in) from the raw edge. Stitch again close to the first line of stitching and neaten the raw edges by machine zigzagging over them. Press the seam allowance towards the panel. Turn a double 1 cm (½ in) hem along the remaining raw edges of both the frill and panel. Pin and stitch.

RIGHT Crisply checked pillowcases and duvet cover accentuate the light and airy feel of a country-style bedroom.

4 Turn so that the wrong sides are facing. Make a French seam around the remaining three sides, as follows. Pin and stitch 5 mm (¼ in) from the raw edge. Trim the seam close to the stitching, then open the fastener and turn the cover so that the right sides are facing. Stitch around the three sides again to enclose the raw edges and complete the seam. Turn the cover to the right side.

STORAGE

Finding suitable storage space around the house for all the personal and household belongings every family accumulates can be quite a challenge. One difficulty is making a sensible compromise between tidiness and accessibility; it is no good having a place for everything if that means spending hours each day laboriously taking things out and putting them back again.

The solution is to tailor-make storage to suit its purpose. Some things need a temporary resting place where they remain readily accessible. Others need long-term storage, perhaps being retrieved and used only occasionally. And there is a third storage category, that of display – simply to show things off.

In a typical home, possessions are stored in one of three main ways: on shelves, in cupboards (closets) or in drawers. These may be combined in a variety of storage or display units, and the amount of each type of space that is required will vary from house to house. For example, the avid bookworm will have miles of shelves, while the clothes horse will need more wardrobe space.

The storage that is needed can be provided in one of two ways. One is to buy or make pieces of freestanding furniture that match the required storage function. The other is to use raw materials such as wood and manufactured boards plus the appropriate hardware to create built-in storage space – arrays of shelving, cupboards in alcoves and so on. The former is the best solution for those who value furniture more than function, since the pieces can be moved from one house to another. However, built-in storage is generally more effective in providing the most space for the least money, since the house walls can often be used as part of the structure. The following pages look at some of the storage options available.

Apart from obvious places such as kitchen units (cabinets) and bedroom wardrobes, there are many places in the main rooms of the house where items can be stored. This can be done without spoiling the look of the room. Properly planned storage space can be not only practical and capacious, but positively elegant.

The kitchen

Storage is a serious business here, and what is needed and how it is provided depends on what kind of kitchen it is and how it is used. The fully fitted kitchen is still popular, because it packs the most storage into the least space, although there is now a discernible movement back to farmhouse-style kitchens with freestanding rather than built-in furniture. This is suitable only for people who are either very tidy and well organized or, on the other hand, happy to live in chaos. The style of such kitchens restricts the amount of storage space they can offer at the expense of the look of the room, so for those who have a lot of kitchen utensils and like to keep large stocks of food, a fitted kitchen is a better idea. However, there is one big advantage with freestanding furniture: it can be taken along when moving house.

In deciding what is wanted, analyze storage needs thoroughly. Think about food, cooking utensils and small appliances for a start; all need a place close to cooking and food preparation areas. Move on to items like china, cutlery and glassware; do they need to

BELOW No corner is too small to provide either some useful extra storage space or an attractive display of kitchenware.

ABOVE If the fully fitted kitchen does not appeal, a central food preparation area can restore the period kitchen look and provide useful storage space too.

LEFT Fitted kitchen storage units (cabinets) offer much more than a home for provisions and pots and pans. Tailor-made units can now store and display everything from wine bottles to the family china.

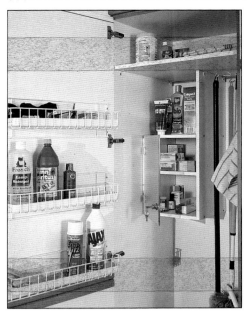

ABOVE Use can be made of every inch of cupboard (closet) space by adding internal shelves and fitting racks on door backs.

ABOVE Pull-out baskets are often more accessible than traditional shelving in kitchen base units (cabinets).

RIGHT Shelf support strips make it easy to put up single shelves or shelving groups wherever they are needed. The shelves are securely gripped along their rear edges and can be easily repositioned.

be in the kitchen at all, or would the dining room be a better place to keep them? Then consider non-culinary items – things like cleaning materials, table linen and so on – and make sure there is enough space for them.

Remember that ceiling-height cupboards (closets) are always a better bet than ones that finish just above head height, even if some small steps or a box are needed to reach them. It is best to use the top shelves for storing seldom-used items.

Always aim to make the best possible use of cupboard space. Fit extra shelves where necessary, use wire baskets for ventilated storage, hang small racks on the backs of cupboard doors and use swing-out carousels to gain access to corner cupboards.

If there is a separate laundry room, it is often easier to split cooking and non-cooking storage needs by moving all home laundry and cleaning equipment out of the kitchen

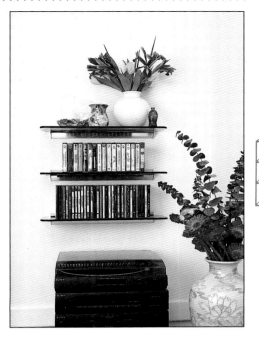

altogether. Such a room can also act as a useful back porch if it has access to the garden.

The living room

Here storage needs are likely to be firmly leisure-oriented. There has to be room for books, records, tapes, compact discs and videotapes, not to mention display space for ornaments and other treasures. The choice is again between freestanding and built-in furniture, and is a much freer one than in the kitchen

STORAGE IN THE HALLWAY

Simple hooks and an umbrella stand are the bare minimum, but consider having an enclosed cupboard (closet) that is built-in rather than freestanding. It is simple to borrow some porch or hall floor space to create a suitable enclosure. If it is fitted with a door to match others leading to the rest of the house, it will then blend in perfectly. Make sure it is ventilated so that damp clothes can dry.

Wall-mounted shelving provides an unobtrusive home for the telephone.

BELOW Alcoves are the perfect site for built-in shelving for books or display and storage cupboards for music cassettes and discs, videos, hi-fi equipment and the like.

While planning living-room storage, pay particular attention to working requirements for power points (receptacles), especially if you have a lot of hi-fi equipment, and for any concealed lighting in the unit.

The dining room

Here storage needs relate mainly to providing places for china, glassware and cutlery – especially any that is kept for special occasions. Think too about storage for table mats, cloths and other table accessories. There may also be a need for somewhere to store small appliances such as toasters, coffee makers and hotplates. Once again, the choice is between built-in storage units and freestanding furniture; this is largely a matter of taste.

The bedrooms

Now take a look at storage requirements upstairs, starting with the bedrooms. Here the main need is for space to store clothes, and this is one area where built-in (and ideally, walk-in) storage is the perfect solution. Space can often be poached between

because here looks are as important as performance.

Built-in furniture can make optimum use of alcoves and other recesses. A more radical option is a complete wall of storage units which could incorporate space for home entertainment equipment, as well as features such as a drinks cupboard. This also offers the opportunity to include a home office – some desk space, plus somewhere to file all the essential paperwork which every family generates.

USING THE ROOF SPACE

Except in older houses, the roof space is usually cluttered with all the woodwork that makes up a modern trussed-rafter roof and is of little use for storage. However, it is still worth boarding over the area immediately around the access hatch so that luggage, boxes and the like can be put there. If the roof construction permits, however, there is a chance to create almost unlimited storage capacity for everything from hobby materials to the summer's fruit crop. Fit a proper fixed ladder for safe and easy access.

RIGHT A high-level plate rack is a traditional way of storing and showing off the best china. It can be used to display other treasures too.

LEFT Built-in furniture is becoming increasingly popular in bedrooms as a way of maximizing the use of precious space.

BELOW A beautifully tiled bathroom is further enhanced with an attractive vanity unit, which can offer valuable storage space for toiletries.

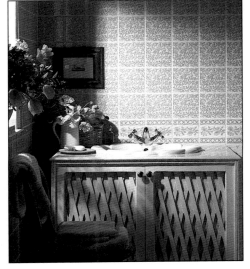

bedrooms by forming a deep partition wall, accessible from one or both rooms; this can actually save money in the long run, as there is no furniture to buy. An alternative if overall upstairs floor space permits is to create a separate dressing room, at least for the master bedroom.

Bedrooms built under the roof slope offer an unparalleled opportunity to make use of the space behind the room walls by creating fully lined eaves cupboards (closets). These are

ABOVE Clothes organizers offer the maximum storage flexibility when space is limited, especially in built-in wardrobes.

particularly useful for long-term storage of items such as luggage which may be needed only occasionally, as well as providing a home for toys and games in children's rooms.

Do not just restrict bedroom storage to clothes and bedlinen, though. There is no reason why it should not also allow for books, ornaments, or even a small portable television.

The bathroom

Finally, look at the bathroom. Here requirements are likely to be relatively low-key – somewhere to keep toiletries and cleaning materials, for example. It is not a good idea to store towels and the like in a potentially damp and steamy atmosphere. The choice is likely to be between a floor-standing vanity unit and some wall-hung cupboards (cabinets), although if space permits some thought might be given to the growing number of fully fitted bathroom furniture ranges.

Where space is very limited, use might be made of 'hidden' space such as that behind a removable bath panel to store small items such as children's bath toys.

WORKSHOP STORAGE

An area where some storage space is certainly needed is the workshop, whether this is a spare room, an area at the back of the garage or a separate building. The basic need is for shelf space, to take everything from cans of paint to garden products, and also some form of tool storage to keep everything in order.

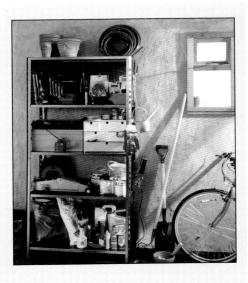

Freestanding utility shelving is the ideal way of providing sturdy and compact garage or workshop storage.

FITTING FIXED SHELVING

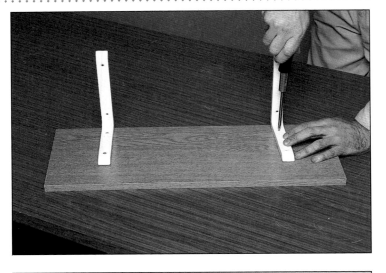

Wall-mounted shelving is one of two basic types – fixed or adjustable. With fixed shelving, each shelf is supported independently of others using two or more shelf brackets, which are fixed to the wall and to the underside of the shelf itself. With adjustable shelving, the shelves are carried on brackets, studs or tongues which are slotted or clipped into vertical support strips screwed to the wall.

Fixed brackets are ideal for putting up a single shelf – over a radiator, for example – although they can equally well be used to support several shelves. They come in many styles, shapes and colours. Metal brackets are the most usual, but wooden ones in various finishes are also available.

Shelves can be of natural wood or manufactured boards. Ready-made shelves can be bought from do-it-yourself stores; they are usually made of veneered or plastic-coated chipboard (particle board). The latter traditionally have either a white or imitation woodgrain finish, but subtle pastel shades and bold primary colours are becoming more widely available. Otherwise shelves can be cut from full-sized boards: chipboard, plywood, MDF (medium-density fibreboard) and blockboard are all suitable.

SHELF SUPPORT STRIP

This is an ingenious support for single shelves. It consists of a specially shaped channel which is screwed to the wall at the required position; then the shelf is simply knocked into place with a soft-faced mallet. The channel grips the shelf securely, and can support surprisingly heavy loads. Various sizes are available.

USING SHELF BRACKETS

1 Select the correct bracket spacing, then attach the shorter arm of each bracket to the underside of the shelf, flush with the rear edge.

2 Fix the shelf to the wall with a screw driven through one bracket, then check that it is horizontal and mark all the remaining screw positions.

3 Let the shelf swing downwards on its first fixing screw, then drill the other holes. Insert plugs for masonry wall fixings if needed.

4 Swing the shelf back up into position and drive in the remaining fixing screws. Tighten them fully so the screw heads pull the brackets against the wall.

USING SHELF SUPPORT STRIPS

1 Hold the support strip against the wall at the desired level, and mark the position of the central screw hole. Drill the hole and attach the strip.

2 Place a spirit level on top of the strip. Swivel the strip until it is precisely level, and mark the positions of the remaining screw holes.

3 Swivel the strip out of the way and drill the other holes. Then secure it with the remaining screws and slot the shelf into place.

4 Small shelf support blocks are also available for mounting small display shelves. The shelf is clamped in place by tightening a locking screw underneath.

RIGHT Individual brackets can be used to mount more than one shelf, as long as there is no need to change the shelf spacing in the future.

FITTING ADJUSTABLE SHELVING

There are many different patterns of adjustable shelving on the market, with uprights and brackets usually of metal but occasionally of wood. All operate on broadly the same principle. Start by deciding on the position and spacing of the uprights; this will depend on what sort of shelf material is used, what load it will carry and what is to be stored there. Then hang the uprights on the wall, making sure that they are perfectly vertical and set level with each other. Finally, clip in the brackets and fit the shelves.

Adjustable shelves may also be wanted inside a storage unit. There are two options. The first involves drilling a series of carefully aligned holes in each side of the unit, then inserting small plastic or metal shelf support studs. The second uses what is known as bookcase strip – a metal moulding with slots into which small pegs or tongues are fitted to support the shelves. Two strips are needed at each side of the unit.

PUTTING UP ADJUSTABLE SHELVES

1 Decide where to position the shelves, then fix the first upright to the wall by driving a screw through the topmost hole. Do not tighten it fully.

2 Hold a spirit level alongside the upright and pivot it until the upright is vertical. Mark the position of all the other fixing holes on the wall.

3 Swing the upright aside and drill the rest of the holes. Fit wall plugs for masonry wall fixings if needed, and drive in the remaining screws.

4 Use a spirit level to make a mark on the wall, level with the top of the first upright and at the required distance from it. Fix the second upright there.

PLANNING SHELVES

Think of how to make best use of the new storage area. It is a good idea to make a rough sketch of the plans, in order to take account of things like the height of books or record sleeves, or the clearance that ornaments or photographs will require. Aim to keep everyday items within easy reach – in practice, between about 750 mm (2 ft 6 in) and 1.5 m (5 ft) above the floor. Position deep shelves near the bottom so that it is easy to see and reach the back. Allow 25–50 mm (1–2 in) of clearance on top of the height of objects to be stored, so that they are easy to take down and put back.

Think about weight too. If the shelves will store heavy objects, the shelving material must be chosen with care, since thin shelves will sag if heavily laden unless they are well supported. With 12 mm (½ in) chipboard (particle board) and readymade veneered or melamine-faced shelves, space brackets at 450 mm (18 in) for heavy loads or 600 mm (2 ft) for light loads. With 19 mm (¾ in) chipboard or 12 mm (½ in) plywood, increase the spacing to 600 mm (2 ft) and 750 mm (2 ft 6 in) respectively. For 19 mm (¾ in) plywood, blockboard, MDF (medium-density fibreboard) or natural wood, the bracket spacing can be 750 mm (2 ft 6 in) for heavy loads, 900 mm (3 ft) for light ones.

5 Mark the upright positions on the rear edge of each shelf. Align the back of each bracket with the edge of the shelf and with the mark, and screw it on.

6 If the shelves are to fit flush against the wall, cut notches at the upright positions to fit around them and then attach the brackets as shown.

7 Position all the shelf brackets. Simply insert their tongues into the slots in the uprights. The weight of the shelf will lock them in place. Adjust the shelf spacings as wished.

USING BOOKCASE STRIP

1 Mark the positions of the top ends of the strips to ensure that they are level, then mark the screw positions to a true vertical and screw on the strips.

2 Insert pairs of pegs into the strip at each shelf position, checking that their lugs are properly engaged in the slots. Then lift the shelf into place.

USING SHELF SUPPORTS

1 Use a simple pre-drilled jig to make the holes for the shelf supports in the sides of the unit. A depth stop avoids drilling too deep.

2 Drill two sets of holes in each side of the unit, with the top of the jig held against the top of the unit to guarantee alignment. Insert the supports.

FREESTANDING SHELVING

Freestanding shelf units have several advantages over wall-mounted or built-in ones. They can easily be moved if the room layout is changed. They can be moved away from the wall to allow painting or papering. They can even be taken along when moving house. However, they have drawbacks too. Some manufactured shelving and display units are rather flimsy, and may twist out of square or sag if they are heavily loaded. In general, better results come from building units from stronger materials such as natural wood and plywood. The other problem is getting them to stand upright against the wall; skirtings (baseboards) prevent

standard units from being pushed back flush with the wall surface, and carpet gripper strips make them lean forwards slightly. The answer is to design the side supports on the cantilever principle with just one point of contact with the floor, as far as possible from the wall, so that the unit presses more firmly against the wall as the load on the shelves is increased.

Since a shelf unit is basically a box with internal dividers, it can be constructed in several different ways, using simple butt joints or more complicated housings. Perhaps the best compromise between strength and ease of construction is to use glued butt

joints reinforced with hardwood dowels, which give the joints the extra rigidity they need in a unit of this sort.

Start by deciding on the dimensions of the unit, then select materials to suit the likely loading the shelves will have to support. Mark up and cut matching groups of components to length in batches to ensure that they are all precisely the same size. Pre-drill all the dowel holes, using a drill stand and depth stop for holes in the board faces and a dowelling jig for those in the board ends. Insert the dowels and make up the joints. A thin plywood or hardboard backing panel can be nailed on to give the unit extra rigidity.

1 Clamp groups of identical components together. Mark them to length and cut them in one operation to ensure that they are all the same length.

2 Mark the positions of the shelf dowel holes on the unit sides, ensuring that they match. Drill them all to the required depth, using a drill stand if possible.

3 Use a dowelling jig to drill the dowel holes in the shelf ends. This ensures that the holes are correctly positioned and centred, and are drilled straight.

4 Glue the dowels and tap them into the holes in the shelf ends. Check that they all project by the same amount, and cut down any that are overlong.

5 Assemble the unit by gluing one end of each of the three shelves and joining them to one of the side panels. Then glue the other ends and add the second side panel.

6 Cut a hardboard or plywood backing panel. Check that it is perfectly square, then pin it to the back of the unit.

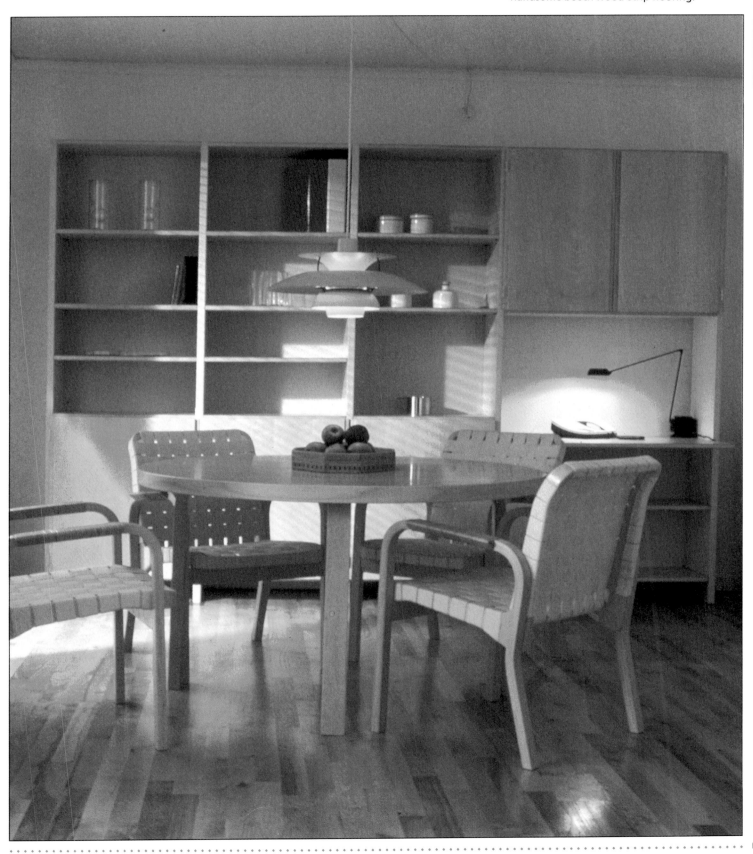

FITTING SHELVES IN ALCOVES

Alcoves beside chimney breasts (fireplace projections) or other obstructions make a perfect site for shelves, since the back and side walls can be used as supports. Although it is easy to use fixed shelf brackets or an adjustable shelving system to support shelves here, it is cheaper to fix slim wood or metal support strips directly to the alcove walls and rest the shelves on these.

If using wooden supports, cut their front ends at an angle so that they are less noticeable when the shelves are fitted. Paint them the same colour as the walls (or to tone with the wall covering) to make them even less obtrusive. If using L-shaped metal strips for the supports, choose a size that matches the shelf thickness so they are almost invisible once the shelves have been fitted.

The actual job is quite simple. Mark the shelf level on the alcove walls, cut the supports to the required lengths and screw them to the walls. Then cut your shelf to size and slip it into place, resting on the supports. It can be nailed, screwed or glued in place for extra stability. The only difficult part is in making the shelf a good fit, since the alcove walls may not be truly square. Accurate measuring of the alcove width at front and back, plus some careful scribing of the rear edge of the shelf, will ensure good results.

1 Decide on the shelf positions, then use a spirit level to mark the position of the first shelf support on one alcove wall.

2 Drill clearance and countersink holes in the supports, and use the first one to mark the fixing hole positions on the wall. Drill the holes and fix this support.

3 Rest a shelf on the first support, get it level and mark the shelf position on the opposite wall of the alcove. Then prepare the second shelf support.

4 Screw the second support in place after using it as in step 2 to mark the positions of the fixing holes on the wall. Check again that it is level.

5 Make up a set of pinch rods from scrap wood, held together as shown with a rubber band. Extend the rods to span the rear wall of the alcove.

6 Lift the rods out carefully without disturbing their positions and lay them on the rear edge of the shelf. Mark the width of the alcove on it.

RIGHT Alcove shelving can be put to practical or decorative use. Here, painted shelves form a focal point in the room for the display of wooden boxes and wicker baskets.

7 Repeat the operation in step 5 to measure the width at the point where the front edge of the shelf will be, then transfer the measurement to the shelf.

8 Cut the shelf to width and lay it on the supports. If the fit is poor against the back wall, use a block and pencil to scribe the wall outline on it.

9 Saw carefully along the scribed line with a power jigsaw (saber saw). Sand the cut edge smooth and then fit the shelf back in position.

MAKING CABINETS

Freestanding storage units consist simply of a basic box, fitted out internally as required. For example, these can include one or more shelves, vertical dividers, hanging rails, drawers and doors. All this applies to units as diverse in scale as a small hi-fi cabinet and a large double wardrobe. A pair of boxes can be placed under a counter top to create a desk or dressing table.

Units will probably be made from manufactured boards. It is difficult to get natural wood wider than about 225 mm (9 in), which rather restricts its scope; it is also more expensive. The most popular material for making box furniture is chipboard (particle board), especially the veneered and melamine-faced varieties which are sold in planks and boards of various sizes with the long edges (and sometimes the ends) already veneered or faced. Its main

disadvantage as a constructional board is its weakness – it will sag under its own weight across spans of more than about 900 mm (3 ft).

Stronger alternatives are plywood, MDF (medium-density fibreboard) and blockboard. Blockboard is the strongest – a 19 mm (¾ in) thick board can be used unsupported over spans twice as great as for chipboard. Sheets of blockboard sold as door blanks usually have the long edges faced.

Plywood offers the best of both worlds – it is almost as strong as blockboard, and has edges that can be neatly finished. It is also available in thicknesses from 4 mm (just over ⅛ in) up to 19 mm (¾ in), so there should be a perfect match for any application.

MDF is a popular choice for box furniture as well as shelves as it cuts beautifully without the need for

finishing sawn edges. It is a medium-strength material and its very smooth surface finish can be painted, varnished or stained, as wished. Available in 2440 × 1220 mm (8 × 4 ft) sheets and in thicknesses ranging from 6 to 25 mm (¼ to 1 in), MDF falls into the medium price range.

Those who are inexperienced in using power tools to make rebates and housing joints will be making up boxes using glued butt joints, nailed or screwed for extra strength. These are adequate for small items, but will need reinforcing on larger pieces. The ideal way of doing this is with hardwood dowels. It is advisable to use dowels for chipboard, in which nails and even screws will not hold well. Alternatives, for light loads only, are special chipboard screws, or ordinary screws set in glued-in fibre wall plugs.

MAKING BUTT JOINTS

1 To make a box, take measurements and start by cutting the components to size. Use a circular saw or a jigsaw (saber saw) to ensure clean, square edges.

2 While cutting the various components, label each piece in pencil and mark both halves of each joint with matching letters to avoid mix-ups during assembly.

3 To make a straightforward glued butt joint, spread woodworking adhesive along the edge of one component. Assemble the joint and clamp it to keep it square.

4 Reinforce a glued joint with nails driven in so they pass into the centre of the panel underneath. Use a damp cloth to remove any excess adhesive.

5 Screwed joints are stronger than nailed ones. Place the edge component against the face component and mark its position on the latter.

6 Mark the screw positions carefully, especially if the joint is a T-joint rather than a corner. Double-check all measurements from nearby edges.

7 Drill clearance holes through the face component, then pilot holes in the edge component. Countersink the clearance holes and drive in chipboard (particle board) screws.

USING DOWELS

1 Draw a pencil line along the centre of the joint position, then align the two components and mark corresponding dowel hole positions on both pieces.

2 Drill the dowel holes in the face component, using a depth stop to avoid drilling too deep. Use a dowelling jig to drill holes in board edges.

3 Insert glued dowels in the holes in the edge component, then glue this to the face component. Add glue along the joint line too for extra strength.

4 A back panel will give any box extra strength, and also helps to resist skewing. Cut the panel fractionally under size and then nail it in place.

FIXING DOORS AND DRAWERS

Adding doors and drawers to a basic storage box will turn it into a cupboard (cabinet) or a chest. Doors can be hung on any one of the many types of hinge available, but two of the most versatile are the *flush hinge* and the *concealed hinge*. The former has one leaf fitting into a cutout in the other, and so can be surface-mounted to the door edge and the frame, without the need to cut recesses.

The concealed hinge is a little more complex to fit – the hinge body sits in a round hole bored in the rear face of the door, while the hinge arm is attached to a surface-mounted baseplate fitted to the side of the cabinet carcass – but it can be adjusted after fitting to ensure perfect alignment on multi-door installations, as in kitchens.

When it comes to adding drawers to your cabinets, the simplest solution is to use plastic drawer kits. These consist of moulded sections that interlock to form the sides and back of the drawer, special corner blocks to allow a drawer front of any chosen material to be attached, and a base (usually of a piece of enamelled hardboard). The drawer sides are grooved to fit over plastic runners that are screwed to the cabinet sides. The sides, back and base can be cut down to size if necessary.

FITTING FLUSH HINGES

1 Mark the hinge position on the door edge, then make pilot holes and screw the smaller flap to the door. Check that the hinge knuckle faces the right way.

2 Hold the door in position against the cabinet carcass, and mark the hinge position on it. Mark the screw holes too, and drill pilot holes for the screws.

3 Reposition the door and attach the larger hinge leaf to the carcass. Check the door alignment carefully, then attach the other hinge in the same way.

FITTING A CONCEALED HINGE

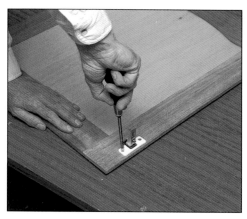

1 Mark the centre line of the hinge baseplate on the side wall of the cabinet, then lay the door flat against the carcass and extend the line onto it.

2 Use a power drill with an end mill, held in a drill stand, to cut the recess for the hinge body to the required depth in the rear face of the door.

3 Press the hinge body into the recess, check that the arm is at right angles to the door edge, and make pilot holes for the fixing screws. Drive these in.

S T O R A G E

MAKING UP A DRAWER KIT

1 Cut the sides and back to size if necessary, then stick the side and back sections together, using the clips and adhesive provided in the kit.

2 Cut the base down in size too if the drawer size was altered. Then slide the panel into place in the grooves in the side and back sections.

3 Screw the two corner joint blocks to the inner face of the drawer front, stick on the drawer base support channel, and glue the front to the sides.

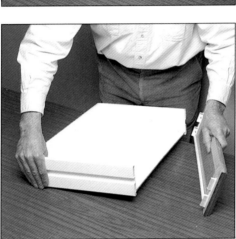

4 Hold the drawer within the cabinet to mark the position of its side grooves on the side walls. Then attach the plastic drawer runners.

4 Next, attach the baseplates to the side wall of the cabinet, centred on the guidelines drawn earlier. Check that they are fitted the right way around.

5 Hold the door against the cabinet, slot the hinge arm over the screw on the baseplate, and tighten it to lock the hinge arm in place.

TIP

Make in-out adjustments to the door by loosening the mounting screw and repositioning the door. Make side-to-side adjustments by using the smaller screw.

The walls of a room can be used to create larger storage spaces. These can range from filling in an alcove, through a unit in the corner of a room, to one running right across the room to the opposite wall. If the room has a central chimney breast (fireplace projection) with an alcove at either side, both alcoves can be used for storage and the chimney breast can be concealed with a dummy door.

In each case, the most important part is a frame to support the doors; these can be conventionally hinged or suspended from ceiling-mounted track. Remember that hinged doors allow unlimited access but need floor space in front of them so they can be opened easily. Sliding doors do not need this floor space, but they do have the minor disadvantage that access to the interior is sometimes restricted – when one door is open, it blocks access to the next section. Sliding doors can also catch on things such as suitcases inside the unit.

Such a flexible structure affords an opportunity to plan storage needs precisely. Start by selecting the depth needed to allow clothes to hang freely on hanging rails, then work out what width should be given to hanging space and what to shelving, drawers or basket space for storing other items of clothing. The space at the top level is suitable for storing seldom-used items. Shoe racks can be added at floor level.

Doors can either be made into a feature of the room, or else painted or covered to blend unobtrusively with the room's colour scheme. Large flat-surfaced doors become almost invisible if decorated with a wall covering.

FITTING SLIDING DOORS TO STORAGE UNITS

1 Decide on the unit depth required, then locate the positions of the ceiling joists and screw a track support strip to them. Use packing to level it.

2 Next, screw the top track to the support strip, making sure that it is fitted parallel with the strip. Leave a gap next to the wall for the side upright.

6 Realign the side upright with the positioning marks made earlier, and screw it to the wall. Repeat the process at the other side of the opening.

7 Cut the doors to size if necessary, allowing for clearances or overlaps as required in the door gear instructions, and then fit the door hangers.

8 Hang the doors by engaging the hanger wheels on the track as shown and then lowering the door to the vertical position. Finally, fit the floor guides.

3 Hold the length of wood that will form the side frame uprights against the wall, and mark on it the profile of the skirting (baseboard) on it.

4 Use a coping saw or power jigsaw (saber saw) to cut away the waste wood from the foot of the upright, then test it for fit against the wall.

5 Use a spirit level to check that the side upright is vertical, then mark its position on the wall and drill the necessary clearance and fixing holes.

9 Conceal the track and door hangers by pinning (tacking) a decorative moulding to the track support batten. Some tracks come complete with a metal pelmet strip.

10 Finish off the installation by pinning slim wooden mouldings to the front edges of the side uprights. These hide any slight gaps when the doors are closed.

FITTING A CLOTHES ORGANIZER

In both freestanding and built-in wardrobes (closets), best use of the interior space can be made by creating tailor-made hanging and shelving sections. Clothes organizers of this kind can be professionally made to measure, but in fact they can be constructed from the simplest of materials, at a great saving in cost. A wardrobe up to 2.4 m (8 ft) wide can be 'organized' with just four standard lengths of veneered or plastic-coated chipboard (particle board), a length of clothes pole and some 75 × 25 mm (3 × 1 in) wood to act as shelf supports.

Start by marking up and cutting out the components. All are 300 mm (12 in) wide. There are two uprights 1930 mm (6 ft 4 in) long, two shelves long enough to span the wardrobe or alcove, and six small shelves 300 mm (12 in) square. Sand all the cut edges.

Next, cut two sets of shelf supports to fit the back and side walls of the wardrobe or alcove. Nail or screw the first supports in place so that their top edges are 2140 mm (7 ft) above the floor. Add the second set 1930 mm (6 ft 4 in) above the floor. Then make up the central shelf unit, using the two uprights and the six small shelves and spacing these to suit the storage requirements. Notch the top rear corners of the unit so that they will fit around the lower shelf support, and stand it in place. Add the lower shelf first, then the upper one, and complete the unit by adding upper (and, if desired, lower) hanging rails at each side of the central unit.

1 Start by fixing the upper set of shelf supports to the sides and back of the wardrobe or alcove, with their top edges 2140 mm (7 ft) above floor level.

2 Add the lower set of shelf supports with their top edges 1930 mm (6 ft 4 in) above floor level. Check that they are all horizontal with a spirit level.

5 Cut down the shelves and uprights to the length required with the circular saw. Then cut the six small squares for the central shelf unit.

6 Make up the central shelf unit by gluing and nailing or screwing the shelves into place between the uprights. Space the shelves as required.

3 Next, mark up and cut the components to width, using a circular saw with a fence or a guide strip clamped across it to keep the cuts perfectly straight.

4 Mark the height of the uprights and the length of the shelves required on the components. Square a cutting line across them, using a try square.

7 Stand the unit against the back of the wardrobe or alcove. Mark the position of the lower shelf supports on it. Cut notches to fit the supports.

8 Reposition the central shelf unit, then lay the lower shelf on its supports. Nail or screw down through it into the supports and the shelf unit.

9 Fit hangers to support the clothes rail beneath the lower shelf. Add a second lower rail if wished. Complete the unit by adding the top shelf.

MAKING UTILITY SHELVING

Storage space in workshops, garages, basements and attics is best provided by building simple but sturdy shelves from inexpensive materials. Use wood that is sawn, not planed (dressed), for the framework, and cut the shelves from scrap plywood. Damaged boards and offcuts are often available cheaply from timber merchants (lumberyards).

The shelving units shown here are made from 50 mm (2 in) square wood, with shelves of 19 mm (¾ in) plywood. The only other materials needed are some scraps of 9 mm (⅜ in) thick plywood for the small triangular braces that help to stiffen the structure.

Start by working out how big the unit is to be. Uprights should be spaced about 760 mm (2 ft 6 in) apart so that the shelves will not sag; they can reach right up to ceiling level if desired. Match the depth of the unit to what is to be stored and to the amount of space available. Remember that it can be difficult reaching things at the back of deep shelves. After measuring up and estimating how many uprights and shelves are needed, buy all the materials and start work.

Make the uprights like a ladder, with glued and nailed butt joints reinforced with plywood triangles measuring about 100 mm (4 in) along the edges forming the right angle. Space the horizontals to suit storage requirements and cut plywood shelves to fit.

Stand the uprights against the wall at the appropriate spacing and screw them to the wall – either into the wall studs, or into wall plugs or masonry anchors if it is solid masonry. Then cut the shelves to length; each 'rung' of the ladder will support two shelves except at the ends of the run, so cut the latter to span between the centres of the rungs. Notch the shelf corners so that they fit around the uprights and are locked in place.

1 Start by deciding on the height the uprights should be, and on how many 'ladders' are needed. Cut them all to length with a power saw.

2 Make up the ladders by gluing and nailing the rungs between pairs of uprights. Reinforce the joints by gluing and screwing on plywood triangles.

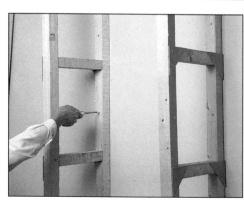

3 Stand the assembled ladders against the wall, check that they are truly vertical, and screw them to the wall – into wooden studs or masonry anchors.

4 Cut as many plywood shelves as are needed so they span between the centre lines of the rungs; notch the corners so they will fit neatly around the uprights.

MAKING A TOOL CABINET

This tool storage rack is basically a wall-mounted backing board of 19 mm (¾ in) thick plywood. Tools are hung on various supports, as shown in the illustration. These are located in, and slide along, horizontal channels formed by pinning 38 mm (1½ in) wide strips of 12 mm (½ in) plywood to the backing panel and then pinning 75 × 19 mm (3 × ¾ in) softwood strips to the plywood. Make the trays for small tools from 12 mm (½ in) plywood, and use hardwood dowel pegs or old wire coat hangers to make support hooks for larger tools. Slide the back plate of each support into its channel at the sides of the rack, and move them along to where they are needed.

MAKING A GARAGE STORAGE WALL

The garage is a favourite place to store all manner of things, including tools and materials for do-it-yourself, gardening and car maintenance. Unless these are kept under control, they will spill over until there is no room for the car. The solution is to build a shallow full-height storage unit along either the side or the end wall of the garage, tailor-made to suit whatever will be stored there.

The design concept of the storage wall is quite simple, and is based around creating bays offering different storage facilities. One can have floor-to-ceiling shelves, another a drawer system using plastic washing-up bowls (washbowls) sliding on wooden support strips. The next bay can offer full-height open storage for stepladders and scaffold boards, and another wider one provides space to store sheet materials neatly on edge beneath a wall-mounted rack for hanging up things such as a portable workbench or a set of car ramps. Simply select whatever types of bay are needed, and arrange them in any order.

The structure is based on ladder frames fixed to the wall to support shelves, drawers and whatever else is required. The frame is made mainly from 50 mm (2 in) square sawn softwood, with 75 × 25 mm (3 × 1 in) wood for the shelves and the slatted hanging rack. The hinged section drops down to allow sheets of plywood and the like to be placed on edge behind it, and is held shut with a simple hasp and staple at each side. The wall-mounted rack allows heavy items to be hung out of the way yet readily to hand on metal S-hooks.

1 Start by securing the uprights to the garage wall to form the various bays. Check that each is vertical before fixing it in place.

2 Set sole plates on something damp-proof (here sheet vinyl flooring), and screw them down into wall plugs in holes drilled in the garage floor.

3 Simply nail components together as required to form the frames making up each bay. Add horizontals to support shelves or plastic bowl drawers.

4 To make up the drop-down flap for the sheet materials storage bay, hinge the two front uprights to their baseplates and add a cross rail.

5 To make up the wall rack, nail on the slats, using an offcut as a spacer. Make the shelves in the same way, nailing the slats to 50 × 25 mm (2 × 1 in) bearers.

75 × 50 mm (3 × 2 in) fascia board

38 × 25 mm (1½ × 1 in) drawer runners

50 mm (2 in) square posts

75 × 50 mm (3 × 2 in) cross tie

webbing strap

100 × 25 mm (4 × 1 in) slats fixed 25 mm (1 in) apart

38 × 25 mm (1½ × 1 in) shelf supports

100 × 25 mm (4 × 1 in) shelf slats fixed 12 mm (½ in) apart

75 × 50 mm (3 × 2 in) fascia board

50 mm (2 in) square uprights

50 × 25 mm (2 × 1 in) cross rails

50 mm (2 in) square bottom rails

100 × 25 mm (4 × 1 in) shelf slats fixed 12 mm (½ in) apart

A   B   C   D   E   F   G

The garage storage wall offers a variety of options. Bay A is a full-height space ideal for storing stepladders and lengths of wood and mouldings, copper or plastic pipe and the like.

Bay B provides a raised platform for sacks of cement or garden fertilizer, which must be kept clear of the floor in case of damp; a sturdy webbing strap keeps them in place.

Bay C, above the platform, has a series of parallel runners supporting plastic baskets, which slide in and out like drawers and provide storage for a host of small and easily lost items.

Bay D has a slatted back on which large items such as car ramps or a portable workbench can be hung on wire hooks.

Bay E provides a wide compartment designed for storing sheet materials – boards, plastic laminates, etc. – on edge and clear of the damp floor. A simple fold-down front frame prevents the sheets from falling forward and can be quickly released when necessary.

Bays F and G complete the structure, offering full-depth shelf storage space for items like paint, garden chemicals and car lubricants.

MAINTENANCE AND REPAIRS

Creating a well-appointed home is a thoroughly satisfying leisure activity pursued by millions of householders. Unfortunately, being creative is not the whole story; houses, like anything else, develop faults from time to time and need some attention to keep them in good working order. This final chapter looks at some of the everyday maintenance and repair problems which may occur in the home, and also explains how to use the right products – adhesives, mastics, fillers, repair tapes and fixing devices – to get good results.

It also deals with a subject that is of increasing importance to householders everywhere: energy conservation and the efficient use of energy resources. Many homes, especially older ones, are very inefficient; they cost a lot to heat, and leak like sieves so that much of the heat supplied is completely wasted. However, creating a well insulated and draughtproofed house is not the complete answer. Activities such as cooking, bathing and washing clothes create large amounts of water vapour, and if this accumulates in a poorly ventilated building, condensation will result. This can be more than just a nuisance, causing steamed-up windows and mouldy patches on walls and ceilings. It can actually damage the house structure and can also be bad for the health of the building's occupants. Getting the right balance of heat input, insulation and controlled ventilation is the solution. The last part of the chapter explains how to achieve it in the home.

OPPOSITE Keeping track of running repairs and updating insulation and ventilation needs are necessary tasks for the homeowner. Shown here, from left to right and top to bottom: applying flashing tape; fixing insulation tape around doorways; removing window beads; repairing wallpaper blisters; sealing cracks with mastic; laying roof insulation; insulating sash windows; insulating pipework; and repairing stairs.

MAKING FIRM FIXINGS

Before making fixings into solid masonry, make a couple of test drillings to find out whether the wall is built of brick or lightweight blocks. If brick is identified from red or yellow bore dust, use ordinary plastic wall plugs; but if grey dust suggests lightweight blocks it is better to use a proprietary block plug which is fatter and has larger 'wings' to grip the softer material. In either case the screw must be long enough to penetrate at least 38 mm (1½ in) into the masonry behind the plaster, so use screws at least 62 mm (2½ in) long. Increase this to 75 mm (3 in) for fixings that will carry heavy loads. Screw gauge 8 will be adequate for normal loads; increase this to gauge 10 for 75 mm (3 in) screws. Make sure, too, that the screw and wall plug sizes are compatible, and take care to drill the holes at right angles to the wall surface, deep enough to accept the screw length.

Making fixings to stud (dry) walls poses different fixing problems. Cavity fixing devices such as spring or gravity toggles and cavity anchors can be used only for fixings that will carry the lightest loads. For any other use, the fixing must be made either to a horizontal nogging (cross bridging) fixed between adjacent studs – difficult to fit except during construction of the wall framework – or directly to the vertical studs themselves. These will have to be located with an electronic stud finder or, less satisfactorily, by tapping and test drilling – they are usually at 400 mm (16 in) or 600 mm (24 in) centres. Make sure that pilot holes are drilled into the centre of the stud, not near its edge, since this could result in a weak fixing. Use screws 50 mm (2 in) long for medium loads, 75 mm (3 in) long for heavy ones.

MAKING FIXINGS IN MASONRY

1 Mark where the fixing is to go and use a masonry drill sized to match the wall plug. Wind some tape around the drill bit to act as a depth guide.

2 If the drill has an adjustable depth stop attachment, use it instead of the tape flag to set the drilling depth. Drill until the stop touches the wall surface.

MAKING FIXINGS IN PLASTERBOARD (GYPSUM BOARD)

1 If the fixing must be between joists or studs rather than into them, drill a clearance hole for the fixing device through the plasterboard.

2 Push a cavity anchor into the hole so it can expand against the back of the board, and drive in the screw. With toggles, thread the screw through the object first.

3 Choose a wall plug sized to match the screw being used, and push it into the hole until its rim is flush with the wall. Tap it with a hammer if necessary.

4 Thread the screw through a clearance hole drilled in the object being fixed, insert it in the mouth of the wall plug and drive it home.

5 Alternatively, use long-sleeved frame plugs. Drill holes through the wood and into the wall, insert the plug and tighten the screw to make the fixing.

MAKING FIXINGS INTO STUDS

1 Use an electronic stud finder to locate the stud or ceiling joist positions. It works by detecting the nails which secure the plasterboard (gypsum board).

2 When the stud or joist positions are marked, drill clearance holes in the object to be fixed at matching centres. Check these for accuracy.

3 Drill pilot holes through the board surface and into the stud or joist. Make sure that the drill bit is at right angles to the surface.

4 Insert screws in all the clearance holes, then offer up the object, align it with the pre-drilled holes and drive the screws home.

There is a huge range of adhesives available nowadays. Their labelling is now generally much clearer than it was a few years ago, so finding the right product is considerably easier than it used to be. Here is a guide to the types that are likely to be needed for most repair jobs.

General-purpose adhesives

These are clear solvent-based adhesives which will stick paper and cardboard, wood, leather and a few types of plastic such as solid polystyrene and ABS. They are used straight from the tube. Check the instructions carefully; some recommend applying the adhesive to both surfaces, others to just one. Whichever method is used, hold or clamp the repair for a while; the adhesive takes some time after assembly to gain full strength. The joint is generally not heat-resistant and may not be water-resistant either. Adhesive can be removed from fingers, or anywhere else it gets by mistake, with cellulose thinner, acetone or nail varnish remover – but the last will attack gloss paint, french polish, some varnishes, and any plastic that the adhesive will stick.

Adhesives for wood

The most widely used type of adhesive for general woodwork is *PVA woodworking adhesive*, often referred to as 'white glue'. It will bond softwood, hardwood and all manufactured boards, and is colourless when dry; spills can be wiped away with a damp cloth before the adhesive sets. The joint must be clamped until the adhesive hardens – for a couple of hours at least – to get the best results. Exposure to damp will weaken the adhesive and cause failure. If such exposure is likely, be sure to use one of the cross-linking versions which give a high degree of water resistance.

Adhesives for laminates

Plastic laminates, flexible sheet materials such as foam and leather, and vinyl or cork floor tiles are stuck in place with a *contact adhesive*. This is spread on both surfaces and is allowed to become touch-dry before the two are pressed together. The resulting bond is instant, and cannot normally be repositioned; but some kinds offer a degree of slip – they are often called *thixotropic adhesives*. Contact adhesive is also moderately heatproof and water-resistant.

Most contact adhesives are solvent-based, and the fumes are both inflammable and noxious to inhale, so work with good ventilation and no naked lights. Clean up spills with the manufacturer's own solvent, cellulose thinner, acetone or nail varnish remover. Water-based contact adhesives are also available, and these are much safer and more pleasant to use; spills can be removed while still wet with a damp cloth.

Adhesives for plastics

Some plastics are very difficult to stick with adhesives. Two which cannot be stuck by any means are polythene (polyethylene) and polypropylene, the bendy plastics used for such things as washing-up bowls (wash bowls) and buckets; they must be fused by heat. Flexible PVC – used for seat covers, sunbeds and beach balls, for example – can be stuck with special *vinyl repair adhesive*. *Polystyrene cement* or general-purpose adhesive will mend rigid polystyrene – used for some kitchen and bathroom accessories – and the similar but tougher ABS. Do not use it for expanded polystyrene ceiling tiles or coving (crown molding), though, as

SILICONE MASTIC Use silicone mastic to seal around bathroom fittings. Push the nozzle along the gap so it leaves a neat concave finish to the mastic bead.

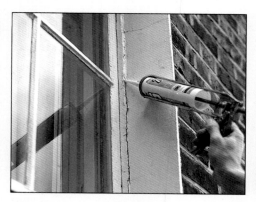

ACRYLIC MASTIC Use acrylic mastic indoors and frame sealant outdoors to seal gaps between wood and masonry where a rigid filler would tend to crack and fall out.

REPAIR TAPE Use repair tapes to make temporary repairs to cracked glass, or to waterproof glazing bars on glass roofs. Simply press the tape into place.

the adhesive will eat these away. Always use a special adhesive paste made for the purpose.

For other plastics, experiment with epoxy resin adhesives, two-part acrylics or cyanoacrylates (see right).

Mastics and repair tapes

Mastic is a permanently flexible adhesive filler that is used to seal joints indoors and outdoors. The material comes in cartridges, and is usually extruded by using a hand-held gun. The resulting bead of mastic is simply piped into place, and may be smoothed out with a wet finger or a filling knife (putty knife) if necessary. Various types are available: *acrylic* types are used as a general-purpose decorating filler indoors; *silicone* types are best for such jobs as waterproofing joints around bathroom and kitchen fittings; and *frame sealants* are designed for filling and sealing gaps around window and door frames.

Repair tapes of various types are used to make temporary repairs to things such as cracked glass, leaky glazing bars and porous flashings. As with mastics, choose the type appropriate to the task in hand.

Adhesives for glass, china and metal

Three types of adhesive can be used for repairing these materials. Each has advantages and disadvantages.

Epoxy resin adhesives are two-part products, prepared by mixing equal quantities of resin and hardener, and generally applied to both surfaces. Quick-setting types set hard in a few minutes, others take about half an hour, with full bond strength developing more slowly. Once set, the bond is heat- and waterproof, and the adhesive will fill gaps; however, it does leave a noticeable glue line, and this may darken with time. Clean up spills with white spirit (paint thinner) or methylated spirit (wood alcohol), and trim off dried adhesive with a sharp utility knife.

Cyanoacrylate adhesives, also known as superglues, are liquids which are applied sparingly to just one surface. The resulting glue line is very thin, so they are ideal for repairing china and glass, but apart from the newer gel types the adhesive has negligible gap-filling properties so the parts must be a good fit. With most brands, the joint is not waterproof, but some are specially

formulated for repairing items that will have to be washed or must hold liquids. Avoid skin contact when using this type of adhesive; if fingers, or anything else, get stuck together, instantly immerse them in hot soapy water and gently peel the stuck areas apart. Some manufacturers supply a special release agent with the adhesive. Always keep glues away from children, but especially this type.

Two-part acrylic adhesives are not mixed directly; instead adhesive is applied to one surface and hardener to the other, and the two brought together to form the bond. This sticks immediately, and reaches full strength in a few hours. The adhesive has good heat resistance and is fairly waterproof, but does not fill gaps very well. Wipe up spills with a dry cloth or use methylated spirits. Alternatively, trim off dried adhesive with a sharp knife.

Speciality adhesives

The shelves of a do-it-yourself store will also contain all kinds of special-purpose adhesives, clearly labelled as to their use. These include *wallpaper paste*, *ceramic tile adhesive* and *coving (crown molding) adhesive*.

1 **FLASHING TAPE** Use flashing tape to seal porous felt or metal flashings. Start by brushing on a coat of special primer; use an old paintbrush and wear protective gloves.

2 Unroll the flashing tape, peel off the release paper and press the strip into position over the band of primer, bedding it well into the roof/wall angle.

3 To ensure that the tape bonds well to the wall and roof surfaces, run a wallpaper seam roller firmly along both edges of the strip.

CURING DOOR PROBLEMS

A well fitted door should have a long and trouble-free life. If it does misbehave, the problem is generally the door binding against its frame and, in extreme cases, failing to shut properly. There is likely to be one of three causes: a build-up of paint on the door and frame surfaces after years of repainting, expansion due to atmospheric conditions – the door sticks in damp weather as moisture causes it to swell slightly, but it shrinks and closes freely in dry weather – and hinge faults caused either by wear and tear or bad fitting.

Where a paint build-up is to blame, the remedy is quite simple; strip off the old paint from the door edge back to bare wood, and repaint from scratch.

If atmospheric conditions are to blame, the solution is to plane down the door edges slightly to increase the clearance between door and frame. The door will have to be taken off its hinges to do this unless it is only the leading edge that is binding.

Hinge faults that can cause binding include hinge screws standing proud or working loose, and hinge recesses being cut too deep or too shallow. In each case the cure is relatively simple; the biggest problem is often trying to undo the old hinge screws, especially if they have become encrusted with paint over the years. Clean out the slots in the screw heads thoroughly before trying to remove the screws; paint remover is useful for this. Then position the screwdriver in the slot and give the handle a sharp blow with a hammer to help free the grip of the threads in the wood.

1 If the hinge screws show signs of pulling out, remove them, drill out the screw holes and hammer in glued dowels. Then drill new pilot holes.

2 If the door is striking the frame because it has expanded, close it and mark a pencil line on the door face against the edge of the frame.

5 If the door binds on the hinge side of the frame, the hinge recesses may be too deep. Remove the hinge and pin some packing into the recess.

6 Drill fresh pilot holes for the screws through the packing piece, and drive the fixing screws back into place. Make sure their heads fit in the countersinks.

MAINTENANCE AND REPAIRS

3 Take the door off its hinges, remove the handles and latch mechanism, and plane the leading edge of the door down until the pencil line has disappeared.

4 If the door is binding at the top or bottom, take this opportunity to plane off a little wood there too. Plane inwards from the corners to avoid causing splits.

7 Alternatively, relocate the hinges in a new position. Chisel out the new recesses and refit the hinge.

8 If the hinge recesses are too shallow the hinge leaves will bind and stop the door from closing. Remove the hinges and chisel out the recesses slightly.

CURING WINDOW PROBLEMS

By far the commonest window problem is a cracked or broken pane, caused by a flying object or by the window being allowed to slam. Make a temporary repair to cracked glass with a clear waterproof repair tape – not household adhesive tape – but aim to replace the pane at the earliest opportunity. If the glass is broken, lift out all the loose pieces for safety's sake and make a temporary repair by fixing heavy-duty polythene (polyethylene) sheet or a piece of board over the opening.

When measuring up for the replacement glass, measure all four sides in case the rebate in the frame is not perfectly square, and use the smaller of each pair of figures. Subtract 3 mm (⅛ in) from each one to allow for clearance all around, and note which way the pattern ran if the glass was obscured rather than clear. Take a piece of patterned glass when buying a replacement so as to be sure of getting the correct type.

The other problems that windows suffer from are similar to those affecting doors – paint build-up, expansion or warping. They may also pull out of square if the frame corner joints start to open up, causing the casement to bind in its frame and possibly also cracking the glass. The trouble can be cured by strengthening the frame corners with small L-shaped metal repair plates; cut shallow recesses for them and disguise their presence with filler and a coat or two of paint.

TIP

Always dispose of broken glass safely, by wrapping it in newspaper and then packing it in a box so it cannot injure anyone.

REPLACING BROKEN GLASS

1 When a window breaks, remove all the loose glass immediately for safety's sake. Wear stout gloves to protect hands and dispose of the glass safely.

2 Use an old chisel or a glazier's knife to remove all the old putty from the rebate in the frame. Take care not to cut into the wood while doing this.

3 Use a pair of pincers or pliers to pull out the old glazing sprigs all around the frame. Metal frames have glazing clips; save these and reuse them.

4 Knead some putty with the hands to warm and soften it, then press it into the rebate by extruding it between thumb and forefinger.

5 Set the replacement pane in position against the bedding putty with equal clearance all around, and press it into place around the edges to compress the putty.

6 Secure the pane in the rebate by tapping in glazing sprigs at roughly 300 mm (12 in) intervals. Replace clips in their locating holes in metal frames.

7 Repeat step 4 to extrude a bead of facing putty all around the pane, then neaten it to a 45° bevel by drawing the blade of a putty knife along it.

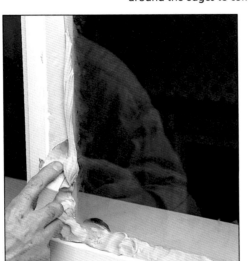

8 Trim off excess putty from the outside and inside of the pane and leave it to harden for about 14 days before painting over it to disguise and seal the joints.

CURING BINDING CASEMENTS

1 If a build-up of paint is causing the edge of the casement to bind against the frame, strip it back to bare wood. Use chemical strippers; heat may crack the glass.

2 If the frame has swollen because of moisture penetration, plane a little wood off the leading edge. Prime and paint it immediately to keep the wood dry.

3 If the corner joints of a casement show signs of opening up and the frame is pulling out of square, screw on small L-shaped metal repair plates.

PATCHING WALL AND CEILING DAMAGE

Plasterboard (gypsum board) is an immensely versatile material for lining walls and ceilings, since it provides a smooth surface for any finish and has useful sound-deadening and fireproofing properties. The one thing it does not do very well is to resist impacts, and the resulting hole cannot simply be patched with filler because the board's strength has been lost at the point of damage. The solution is either to strengthen the board or to replace a section altogether.

Very small holes can be disguised with self-adhesive scrim tape and cellulose filler (spackle), but holes more than about 50 mm (2 in) across need a more substantial repair. Use an offcut of plasterboard and cut a piece slightly narrower than the hole width and twice as long as its height to use as a patch. Pierce a hole in it, thread a piece of string through, tie one end to a nail and pull this against the face of the patch. Then butter some plaster or filler onto the other face of the patch and push it into the hole, keeping hold of the string with the other hand. Position the patch against the inner face of the plasterboard, pulling on the string to help the filler stick it in place. When it has stuck fast, fill the hole and cut off the string.

For larger holes – a foot through the ceiling, for example – in plasterboard and (in older properties) lath-and-plaster surfaces, the only solution is to cut out the damaged piece and nail on a new section in its place. Supports will need to be fixed around the edges of the opening where the damaged section has been cut out. Then fill the cut edges, apply joint tape to hide them and skim over the patch with a little plaster to complete the repair.

MAINTENANCE AND REPAIRS

PATCHING SMALL HOLES IN PLASTERBOARD (GYPSUM BOARD)

1 Cut a plasterboard patch slightly longer and narrower than the hole, and thread a length of string with a nail tied on through a hole in its centre.

2 Butter some plaster or filler onto the edges of the patch and feed it end-on into the hole, keeping hold of the string with the other hand.

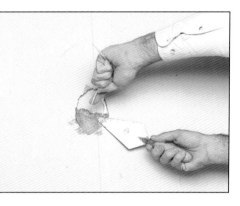

3 Pull the string to hold the patch against the rear face of the board, then fill the recess with plaster or filler and cut off the string.

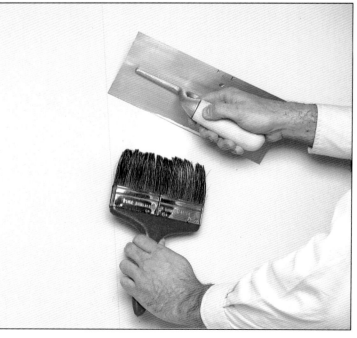

4 Complete the repair by applying a skim coat of plaster over the patch. Flick water onto it with a brush and polish it smooth with a float.

PATCHING LARGER HOLES IN PLASTERBOARD (GYPSUM BOARD)

1 If the plasterboard surface is more extensively damaged, cut through it with a sharp knife back to the adjacent wall studs or ceiling joists.

2 Cut across to the stud or joist centres, then make two vertical cuts down the centre of the stud or joist to free the damaged panel.

3 Cut two strips of wood to fit between the studs/joists, and screw or nail them into place so they will support the edges of the main board and the patch.

4 Cut a plasterboard patch to match the section removed, and nail it into place. Fill and tape the joints and skim plaster over the repair to conceal it.

REPAIRING LATH-AND-PLASTER SURFACES

1 If the wood laths are split or broken, pull them away from the surface. Remove any loose sections of plaster from around the site of the damage.

2 Continue cutting back the old plaster and the laths behind it to expose the studs or ceiling joists at each side of the hole. Square off the edges.

3 Cut a plasterboard patch to fit the hole, and nail it in place. Add two support strips as described for patching plasterboard if the panel is large.

4 Complete the repair by plastering over the patch after filling and taping the cut edges all around. Polish the repair with a steel float.

CURING FLOOR PROBLEMS

Floorboards suffer more from being lifted for access to pipes and cables beneath them than they do from everyday wear and tear. If the floor has nothing worse than the occasional creak, the trouble can generally be cured by lifting floor coverings and then nailing – or better still, screwing – the offending board down again. With a chipboard (particle board) floor, make sure that the boards are nailed to every joist they cross, not just at the edges; if they are not, the boards can bow upwards and will then bang against the joists when walked on.

Before lifting a section of floor to gain access to services below it, look first of all to see whether someone has already cut an access panel. If they have not, it will be necessary to create one. Locate the joist position closest to where access is needed – the flooring nail positions will reveal its whereabouts. Then drill a starter hole and use a jigsaw (saber saw) to make a 45° cut next to the joist. Prise up the cut end and wedge a strip of wood underneath it, then saw through the board over the centre of the next joist to free the section. To replace it, nail

one end to the joist and either skew nail (toe nail) the other angled end to its neighbour or nail a support block to the side of the joist and nail or screw the board end to that.

With concrete floors, the only repair that is likely to be needed is the filling of cracks or small potholes that may be revealed when an old floor covering is lifted. Cut back any loose edges, brush away loose material and fill the cracks with a fine mortar mix. If the floor surface is sound but uneven or out of level, lay a self-smoothing compound over it.

CREATING AN ACCESS PANEL

1 Start by locating an adjacent joist. Drill a starter hole for the saw blade. Cut through the board at 45° next to the joist with a jigsaw (saber saw).

2 Use a bolster (stonecutter's chisel) or a similar broad-bladed levering tool to prise up the cut end of the board and release its fixing nails.

3 Slide a length of scrap wood under the raised end of the board to hold it clear of the floor, and saw through it above the centre of the next joist.

4 To replace the panel, simply lay it back in position. Nail the square-cut end to its joist and skew nail (toe nail) the angled end to the neighbouring board.

5 An alternative way of supporting the cut ends of an access panel is to nail small wood blocks to each side of the adjacent joists.

6 The panel can also be screwed down onto the wooden blocks. This will allow easy access without damaging the panel.

REPAIRING A CONCRETE FLOOR

1 If cracks are found in a concrete floor after lifting old floor coverings, use a cold (box) chisel and club (spalling) hammer to undercut the edges of the crack.

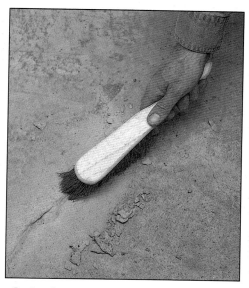

2 Brush away all loose material from the crack, then use the crevice nozzle of a vacuum cleaner to remove dust which the brush will not pick up.

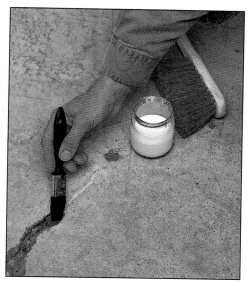

3 Dilute some PVA building (white general purpose) adhesive as recommended on the can, and brush it along the surface of the crack to help the repair mortar to bond to it.

4 Mix up some quick-setting repair mortar and trowel it into the crack, levelling it flush with the surrounding concrete. Leave it to harden.

5 If the floor has noticeable potholes in its surface, pack the hole with small pieces of stone or other non-compressible filler.

6 Patch the pothole with quick-setting mortar, using the edge of the steel float to remove excess mortar so the patch is flush with its surroundings.

CURING STAIRCASE PROBLEMS

A timber staircase consists of a series of evenly spaced horizontal *treads* which form the flight. Most staircases also have vertical *risers* which fill the space between the rear edge of one tread and the front edge of the tread above; these may be nailed in place, or may have tongued edges which slot into grooves in the treads.

The treads are supported at each side by two parallel timbers called *strings*. A *closed-string* staircase has the treads and risers set into grooves cut in the inner faces of the strings, while an *open-string* staircase has the outer string cut in a zigzag fashion so the treads can rest on the cutouts. The inner string – the one against the wall of the stairwell – is always a closed string.

At the open side of a conventional flight, a guard is fitted to run between the top and bottom *newel posts* – the main vertical timbers supporting the flight. This usually consists of a series of closely-spaced *balusters* which are fixed between the top edge of the outer string and the underside of a handrail, but it may be a solid panelled barrier. There may also be a wall-mounted handrail at the other side of the flight, and freestanding flights must obviously have a *balustrade* at each side.

Stairs creak because one of the components has become loose; a footfall then causes the loose part to move against an adjacent component of the flight. A cure is simple if the underside of the flight is accessible, but less straightforward if it is not.

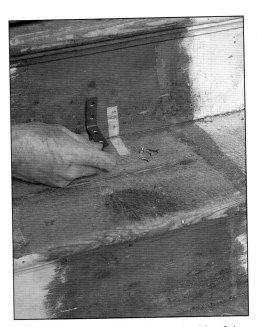

1 If there is no access to the underside of the flight, secure loose or squeaking treads by fixing metal repair brackets to tread and riser.

2 If the underside can be reached, check that the wedges securing the treads and risers to the strings are in place. Hammer them in firmly if they are loose.

3 Glue back any of the support blocks beneath the fronts of the treads if they have fallen off. Fit extra blocks beneath troublesome treads.

4 Drill clearance holes up through the rear edges of each tread, then drive screws up into the bottom edge of the riser above to lock the tread to it.

5 If the tread is found to be split, it must be replaced. Start by prising off the side moulding, then tap the balusters out with a mallet.

6 Insert a knife into the joint along the back of the tread to check if it has been nailed or screwed. If it has, use a hacksaw blade to cut the fixings.

7 Insert a crowbar or similar lever between the string and the tread, and prise it upwards and outwards to free it from the risers above and below it.

8 Use the damaged tread as a template to mark out and cut a replacement. Plane the nosing to shape, and cut notches in one end for the balusters.

9 Glue and clamp support blocks to the rear face of the riser below, and nail another block to the closed string to provide extra support for the tread.

10 Fit the new tread in place and secure it to the support blocks and to the cutout in the open string with screws rather than nails.

11 With the tread securely fixed in position, replace the balusters in their notches and nail the side moulding back on to complete the repair.

REPAIRING WALL COVERINGS

It is a simple matter to repair minor damage to painted walls and ceilings and then to cover it up with a fresh coat of paint. With wall coverings, patching damage or curing paperhanging defects requires a different approach.

The commonest form of damage to a wall covering is an impact that leaves a jagged tear. If the torn part is still attached, brush some paste onto its rear face and press it back into place, rolling it flat with a seam roller.

If the torn part is missing it will be necessary to patch the damage. If there are some offcuts from the original papering job, cut a patch from them. If not, cut and dry-strip a patch from an out-of-sight area behind a piece of furniture to use for the repair. Tear around the edges of the patch, holding it face down, to create a thin 'feathered' edge, then paste it, place it over the damaged area and flatten it with a seam roller. If the paper is a thick two-layer duplex type, try to peel away the backing paper to reduce the thickness of the patch.

Two other common problems, blisters and lifting seams, are the result of inadequate pasting during paperhanging. It is a relatively simple task to slit blisters open and lift dry seams to apply a little fresh paste and stick the covering firmly back to the wall. With fragile printed or flocked wall coverings, take care not to get paste on the surface.

PATCHING DAMAGED WALLPAPER

1 Cut a repair patch from an offcut of the original wall covering, or strip one from behind a piece of furniture. Check that it will cover the damage and match the pattern.

CURING DRY BLISTERS

1 If a dry blister appears after wallpapering, use a sharp utility knife to make two cuts through it at right angles.

2 Peel back the triangular tongues formed and apply a little paste to the wall surface and to the back of the tongues. Leave to soak for a few minutes.

3 Press the triangles back into place and run a seam roller along the cuts to bond the paper firmly to the wall and leave an almost invisible repair.

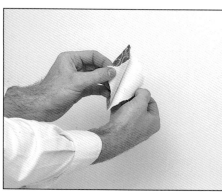

3 BELOW Some two-layer duplex papers are too thick to use as a patch. Try to separate the backing paper at a corner of the patch and peel it off.

2 ABOVE Carefully tear along the edges of the patch to reduce its thickness and create a thin feathered edge. Check that no backing paper is visible.

4 BELOW Paste the back of the patch and place it over the damaged area, aligning the pattern carefully. Then 'iron' it into place with a seam roller.

STICKING DRY SEAMS

1 If a seam has failed to stick flat, lift it with a filling knife (putty knife) and use a slip of abrasive paper to sand off the dried paste behind it.

2 Use the filling knife to hold the edge of the wall covering away from the wall, and brush a little paste onto the back and the wall surface. Leave to soak.

3 Press the seam down flat with a seam roller, then use a sponge or damp cloth to remove any paste that has oozed onto the face of the wall covering.

INSULATION AND VENTILATION

Insulation means saving energy, and that is becoming more and more essential on every level, from the personal to the global. People are increasingly conscious of the importance of environmental issues. One of the greatest contributions that any one household can make is to cut down on unnecessary waste of fossil fuels, and so to reduce the amount of carbon dioxide released into the atmosphere by burning them. This means making more efficient use of energy, and insulation has a big part to play in this. It saves money too.

Insulation is a means of reducing heat transfer from a warm area to a cold one. In temperate countries the outside air temperature is below what most

DRAUGHT EXCLUDERS Special brush draught excluders can be fitted over letter plate openings, as shown, and also to the bottoms of doors to minimize heat loss.

DOUBLE GLAZING Glass is an extremely poor insulator and secondary glazing can cut down on heat loss provided the inner panes are well sealed to their tracks.

people regard as a comfortable level for much of the year, so that heating is needed for long periods and heat is constantly lost to the outside.

All materials conduct heat to a greater or lesser extent. Wood is a good insulator, brick an average one and glass is downright poor, as anyone who has sat next to a window on a cold winter's day will testify.

Except in countries which have very cold winters, proper insulation of homes has until recently been a very low priority, both for housebuilders – who will not pay for something that provides only a hidden benefit unless they have to – and for the legislators who frame the regulations and codes with which builders must comply. At last, however, the tide is turning, and current building rules call for much higher standards of insulation than ever before. They have also recognized that over-insulation can cause condensation, both inside the rooms and within the building's structure.

Unfortunately, this will not help those people living in older properties, many of which were originally built with no thought to their insulation performance at all. Over the years, various attempts will have been made to insulate houses like these, but what was deemed adequate twenty years ago will be well below par for today.

Condensation

Condensation is a big problem in many homes. It can lead to serious health problems and can also cause damage to the structure of the home.

The air always contains a certain amount of moisture – a lot on a humid summer's day, less on a clear winter one. When the air at a particular temperature cannot hold any more

moisture, it is said to have reached saturation point, and this condition is described as a *relative humidity* of 100 per cent.

Air at saturation point is the key to the problem. If that saturated air is cooled, for example by coming into contact with a surface such as a window pane on a chilly day, it can no longer hold so much vapour. The excess moisture vapour in the air condenses into droplets of water, and these are deposited on the cold surface – first as a fine film that mists up the glass but then, as more moisture is deposited, the droplets combine to form rivulets that run down the surface to create pools of water on the window sill. This can ruin decorations and cause window sills and

ROOF INSULATION If the roof of the house is pitched (sloping), blanket insulation can be laid over the loft (attic) floor. This is one of the most cost-effective forms of insulation.

FLOOR INSULATION With suspended floors, the floorboards can be lifted and insulation blanket suspended on netting stapled to the joists. A vapour barrier, such as heavy plastic sheeting, is then laid on top.

COST-EFFECTIVENESS OF INSULATION

Before thinking about individual types of insulation, it is important to understand the concept of cost-effectiveness. Insulation costs money to install, and can bring benefits in two main ways.

It can reduce heating bills, since the home will waste less heat and the same internal temperatures can be maintained without burning so much fuel. The annual saving on the heating bill will therefore 'pay back' the cost of the extra insulation. Also, when replacing a heating system, having better standards of insulation allows a less powerful, and less expensive, boiler to be used – an indirect saving, but valuable none the less.

Alternatively, the house can be made warmer than before without increasing heating bills. In this case there will be no direct savings, just greater comfort.

The checklist below includes various ways of improving the insulation of a home. Each one has a rating that indicates how cost-effective it is. The best will pay for themselves in a year or two, while the least cost-effective (one star) are worth doing only if planning to carry out other major renovation work at the same time.

A hot water cylinder jacket ★★★★★
Pay-back period: less than 1 year.
Loft (attic) insulation ★★★★
Pay-back period: 1–2 years.
Reflective radiator foil ★★★★
Pay-back period: 1–2 years.
Draught excluders ★★★
Pay-back period: 2–3 years.
Flat roof insulation ★★(★)
Pay-back period: 2–4 years.
Floor insulation ★★
Pay-back period: 3–5 years.
Cavity wall insulation ★★
Pay-back period: around 5 years.
Double glazing ★★(★)
Pay-back period: 5 years or more.
Solid wall insulation ★
Pay-back period: over 10 years.

---

frames to rot and rust; it can also cause two further problems, both of which are potentially more serious.

The first is mould. Apart from moisture vapour, the air also contains millions of tiny spores which float around looking for somewhere to live and multiply. The one thing they need is water, and if they find a damp surface in the home they will germinate and grow there quite happily over a wide range of temperatures. The result is the patches of black, brown or dark green mould seen especially around windows, in fitted cupboards (closets) and in the upper corners of rooms which have poor insulation and ventilation and inadequate heating.

The second problem is interstitial condensation. If the materials used to build walls, roofs and other parts of a building allow water vapour to penetrate, and if the air's moisture content is high and the structure's temperature is low, condensation can occur actually inside the structure. Most building materials are porous to some extent, although in a well designed and properly maintained building the absorbed moisture can evaporate harmlessly to the outside. But if it cannot do this the affected part of the structure remains damp; this can then encourage rot to grow on wood,

CONDENSATION Constant condensation ruins paintwork and will eventually cause wooden window frames and sills to rot, unless action is taken to increase ventilation.

MOULD Poor insulation, inadequate ventilation and poor heating levels can, in extreme cases, lead to patches of mould occurring around windows and inside fitted cupboards (closets).

EXTRACTOR FANS To control ventilation in steamy rooms such as kitchens and bathrooms, extractor fans can be fitted. The types linked to humidity detectors are ideal as they activate automatically.

and may also result in frost damage to masonry in cold weather, caused by the water expanding as it freezes. What is more, a damp wall has a lower resistance to the passage of heat than a dry one, and therefore becomes colder and encourages yet more condensation.

WHERE MOISTURE COMES FROM

People themselves are a major source of the moisture in the air inside a building. Breath is moist and sweat evaporates; one person gives off 250 ml (roughly ½ pint) of water during eight hours of sleep, and three times as much during an active day.

Domestic activities create even more moisture. Cooking, washing up, bathing, washing and drying clothes and so on can create as much as a further 10 to 12 litres (about 3 gallons) of water a day, and every litre of fuel burnt in a flueless oil or paraffin heater gives off roughly another litre of water vapour. The air in the house is expected to soak up all this extra moisture invisibly. It may not be able to manage unaided. However, a combination of improved insulation and controlled ventilation will go a long way towards eliminating the problem of condensation.

INSULATING ROOFS AND PIPEWORK

In a building with a pitched (sloping) roof, where the loft (attic) space is used only for storage, it is usual to insulate the loft floor, using either blankets of glass fibre or mineral wool, sold by the roll, or else loose-fill material (vermiculite, a lightweight expanded mineral, is the most widely used). Some kinds of loose-fill insulation, usually mineral wool or fireproofed cellulose fibres, can be blown into the loft by specialist contractors.

Blanket materials are generally easier to handle than loose-fill types unless the loft is awkwardly shaped, contains a lot of obstructions or has irregular joist spacings. The rolls are generally 600 mm (24 in) wide to match standard joist spacing, and common thicknesses are 100 mm (4 in) and 150 mm (6 in). Choose the latter unless there is already some thin loft insulation, and ensure that it is laid with eaves baffles to allow adequate ventilation of the loft. It is essential to wear protective clothing when handling glass fibre insulation. Wear a face mask, gloves and cover any exposed skin with suitable clothing.

Apart from being awkward to handle, loose-fill materials have another drawback. To be as effective as blanket types, they need laying to a greater depth – usually at least an extra 25 mm (1 in). With few ceiling joists being deeper than about 150 mm (6 in), there is nothing to contain the insulation and allow for maintenance access unless strips of wood are fixed along the top edge of every joist.

When the loft floor is completely insulated, remember to insulate any water tanks and pipework within the loft, since they are now at risk of freezing. For this reason, do not lay insulation under water tanks.

LAYING ROOF INSULATION

1 Clear all stored items from the loft (attic) area, then put down a sturdy kneeling board and use a heavy-duty vacuum cleaner to remove dust and debris.

2 Always put on gloves and a face mask and wear long sleeves to handle the insulation. Unroll it between the joists, leaving the eaves clear for ventilation.

3 Butt-join the ends of successive lengths of blanket. To cut the material to length, either use long-bladed scissors or simply tear it.

6 **RIGHT** The same insulation material will lag water storage tanks too, as long as the tank has a lid. Simply wrap the blanket around the tank and tie it on.

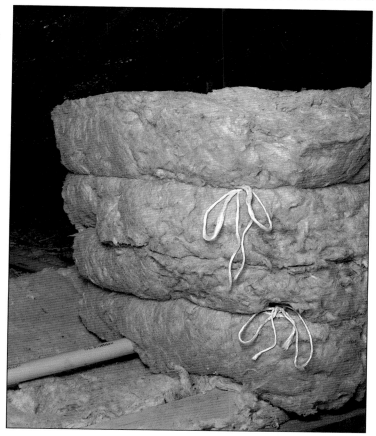

4 **ABOVE** While working across the loft, make sure that any electrical cables are lifted clear of the insulation so they cannot overheat.

5 **ABOVE** Insulate the upper surface of the loft hatch by wrapping a piece of blanket in plastic sheeting and then stapling this to the hatch door.

INSULATING PIPEWORK

1 The quickest and easiest way of insulating pipework is to slip on lengths of foam pipe insulation, which is slit lengthways.

2 To make neat joins in the insulation at corners, cut the ends at 45°, using a mitre box and a carving knife or hacksaw blade. Tape the corner joint.

3 Make a V-shaped cutout in the insulation at tee joints, then cut an arrow shape on the end of the insulation which will cover the branch pipe.

4 As with butt and corner joints, use PVC tape to secure the sections of insulation together and prevent them from slipping out of position.

5 Pipe bandage can be used instead of foam insulation. Wrap it around the pipe in a spiral, with successive turns just overlapping.

6 Tie the insulation bandage in place at the end of each length, or where the pipe passes through a wall. Simply tear the material to length as necessary.

INSULATING MASONRY WALLS AND FLOORS

House walls are the most massive part of the whole building and absorb a lot of heat, which is why a cold house takes so long to warm up. This heat can be retained by insulating the walls in one of two ways.

The traditional cavity wall consists of two 'leaves' of masonry with a gap, usually of 50 mm (2 in), between them. Their insulation performance can be improved by filling the cavity with insulating material. This is done by specialist installers who pump treated fibres, pellets or insulating foam into the cavity through holes drilled in the wall's outer leaf.

For solid walls, the most economical solution is to dry-line them on the inside with insulating plasterboard (gypsum board), fixed directly to the wall with panel adhesive or nailed to a supporting framework of treated wood strips. Alternatively ordinary plasterboard sheets can be used, with insulation blanket or boards placed between the support strips and covered with a polythene (polyethylene) vapour barrier.

For wood-framed walls, the best alternative is to remove the interior finish, install insulation batts and then cover these with a vapour barrier, such as polythene sheeting.

Insulating floors

Few people think of ground floors when considering insulation, yet a surprisingly large amount of heat can be lost through both solid and suspended wood floors.

With suspended timber floors insulation can be fixed between the joists after lifting the floorboards. One method is to cut strips of rigid expanded polystyrene and rest them on nails driven into the sides of the joists. Another is to suspend lengths of insulation blanket between them, supported on garden netting stapled to the joists. The insulation is then covered with a vapour barrier.

With direct-to-ground concrete floors (slab on grade), the commonest method of insulation involves lining the floor with polythene sheeting and placing sheets of rigid polystyrene directly on the floor surface and then putting down tongued-and-grooved chipboard (particle board) flooring over them.

INSULATING SOLID WALLS

Fix a framework of 50 × 25 mm (2 × 1 in) softwood strips to the walls with masonry nails to support the edges and centres of the insulating boards.

1 Mark cutting lines on the board surface in pencil, then cut along the line with the insulation facing downwards using a fine-toothed saw.

2 To make cutouts for light switch boxes and similar obstacles, mark their positions and cut them out with a padsaw.

3 Fix the boards by positioning them against the support framework so that adjacent boards meet over a strip, and nail them in place.

MAINTENANCE AND REPAIRS

INSULATING WOODEN FLOORS

1 To insulate beneath a wooden floor, lift all the floorboards. Then drape lengths of garden netting loosely over the joists and staple them in place.

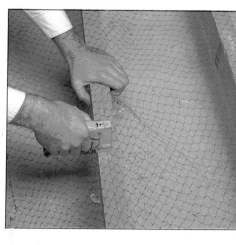

2 Lay loft insulation blanket or wall insulation batts in the 'hammocks' between the joists. If the netting sags, pull it up a little and staple it again.

3 To prevent moisture from the house condensing within the insulation, cover it with a vapour barrier of heavy-duty polythene (polyethylene) sheeting.

4 Re-lay the floorboards by nailing them to the joists. Take this opportunity to close up any joints between the boards for a neat finish.

4 At external corners, remove a strip of the polystyrene insulation as wide as the board thickness so the edges of the plasterboard (gypsum board) can meet in a butt joint.

5 Arrange the boards at external corners so that a paper-covered board edge overlaps one that has its plaster core exposed.

6 Use a simple lever and fulcrum to raise the boards to touch the room ceiling as they are fixed. A skirting (baseboard) will cover the gap at floor level.

DOUBLE GLAZING

The glass in windows is the least efficient part of the house at keeping heat in, and the only way of cutting this heat loss while still being able to see out is to add another layer of glass. Double glazing can be done in two ways: existing single panes of glass can be replaced with special double-glazed panes called *sealed units*, or a second pane can be installed inside the existing one – so-called *secondary glazing*.

Secondary glazing is the only practical course of action unless the existing windows are being completely replaced. There are dozens of types available for do-it-yourself installation, providing hinged and sliding inner panes that blend in well with most types of window; similar systems are also available from professional installers. The panes are either fixed to the window frame itself, or else fit within the window reveal on special track. An effective but flimsy alternative is clear acetate or PVC film fixed to the inside of the frame with double-sided tape.

Apart from reducing heat losses through the windows, double glazing eliminates 'cold spots' in the room next to the windows. It also helps to reduce noise penetration from outside as long as the inner panes are kept closed. It will reduce condensation too, but only if the inner panes are well sealed to their track to stop warm moist air getting into the air gap between them and the window itself. Lastly, lockable types will give a measure of additional security; burglars may tackle one pane of glass, but many will flinch at two.

As far as external doors are concerned, solid doors offer better insulation than glazed ones, so go for this type if planning a replacement. If a glazed panel is a must, choose one with a sealed double glazing unit using safety glass. Heat loss through any external door can be reduced by building a porch outside it, to create an airlock between the house and the outside world.

FITTING SLIDING UNITS

1 Measure the height and width of the window reveal at each side. If the figures differ, work from the smaller measurements for height and width.

2 Cut the track sections to length with a fine-toothed saw and sand the cut ends smooth. Make cutouts as the instructions dictate to form the corners.

3 Offer up the side track sections and screw them in place. Use thin packing to get them truly vertical if the walls are out of square.

4 Next, secure the top track section in place. Screw it directly to a wooden lintel or pre-drill holes in concrete ones and insert wall plugs first.

MAINTENANCE AND REPAIRS

FITTING THIN-FILM DOUBLE GLAZING

1 Start by sticking lengths of double-sided adhesive tape to the window frame, about 12 mm (½ in) in from the surrounding masonry.

2 Press the film onto the tape, pulling it as taut as possible. Then play hot air from a hair-drier over it to tighten it up and pull out any wrinkles.

3 When the film is even and wrinkle-free, trim off the excess film all the way around the window with a sharp utility knife.

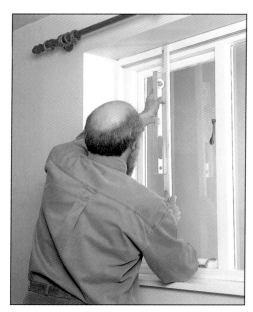

5 When positioning the bottom track on the window sill, use a straightedge and a spirit level to check that it is perfectly aligned with the top track.

6 Measure up for the glass as directed in the kit manufacturer's instructions, and order the glass. Fit cut lengths of glazing gasket to the edges of each pane.

7 Fit the first pane into the track by inserting its top edge in the top channel, and then lowering its bottom edge. Repeat the procedure for the other pane.

DRAUGHTPROOFING

Ill fitting windows and doors are a major source of heat loss, as well as causing cold draughts. Fitting efficient draught stripping around them will reduce the losses and cut down the draughts, and is a simple job to carry out. Modern self-adhesive foams are much more efficient and longer-lasting than older types, and are ideal for windows, while doors and sash windows are best draughtproofed with pin-on (tack-on) plastic or sprung metal strips or types containing a compressible rubber seal. Special draught excluders are available for door thresholds (saddles), and can be fitted to the door bottom or across the threshold. There are even excluders designed to fit over letter plate openings.

Remember that draughtproofing a home will close off many 'unofficial' sources of ventilation, turning it into a well sealed box. Fuel-burning appliances such as boilers and room heaters must have an adequate source of fresh air to burn safely, so it is wise to ask a fuel supplier to check that there is adequate ventilation in rooms containing such appliances. Often a ventilator in a window pane will solve the problem. Efficient draughtproofing may also increase condensation, especially in kitchens and bathrooms. This can be prevented by providing controlled ventilation in these rooms with an extractor fan.

DRAUGHTPROOFING DOORS

1 The simplest type of door-bottom draught excluder is a brush seal mounted in a wood or plastic strip. Simply cut it to length and screw it on to the foot of the door.

2 Alternatively, fit a threshold (saddle) strip. Cut the metal bar to length and screw it to the sill, then fit the compressible rubber sealing strip in the channel.

3 Draughtproof a letter plate opening by screwing on a special brush seal. Check that it does not foul the letter plate flap if this opens inwards.

4 Draughtproof the sides and top of the door frame by pinning (tacking) on lengths of plastic or sprung metal sealing strip. Pin the edge farthest from the door stop bead.

5 Alternatively, stick lengths of self-adhesive foam excluder to the stop bead against which the door closes. At the hinge side, stick it to the frame.

6 A third option is to use lengths of self-adhesive brush strip excluder. These three types can also be used for draughtproofing hinged casement windows.

MAINTENANCE AND REPAIRS

DRAUGHTPROOFING SASH WINDOWS

1 To fit sprung metal strip excluder to a sliding sash window, first prise off the staff bead (window stop) that holds the inner sash in position, and swing it out.

2 Measure the length of strip needed to fit the height of the window, and cut it to length with scissors. Beware the sharp edges of the metal.

3 Pin (tack) the strip to the side of the frame so it will press against the edge of the sliding sash. Pin it through the edge facing towards the room.

4 Use the special wheeled springing tool provided with the excluder to make a small groove in the strip, causing it to spring outwards.

5 Pin a strip along the inner face of the top sash meeting rail (mullion), and 'spring' it so it presses against the outer face of the bottom sash rail.

6 Draughtproof the bottom edge of the lower sash and the top edge of the upper one by sticking on lengths of self-adhesive foam excluder.

PROVIDING CONTROLLABLE VENTILATION

In every house stale, moist air must be removed and replaced with fresh air from outside. This happens not only in an obvious way when a window is opened or an extractor fan switched on, but all the time. For example, air passes up chimney flues, or finds a way out through the inevitable small gaps in the house structure.

Unless power ventilated, most modern houses have very little chance of such ventilation because improved standards of insulation and draughtproofing have made them much more airtight than formerly. Of course

this reduces heating bills and keeps the house's occupants warm and comfortable, as long as they do not create too much moisture for the air to hold. If they do, condensation will be the inevitable result, and extra ventilation will be needed.

This reduction in natural ventilation not only causes trouble within the house, it can also affect its structure. Two particular problem areas are roof spaces and under-floor voids. To prevent it, more ventilation must be provided via ridge and eaves-level vents in roofs, and airbricks in walls.

For ventilating rooms, what is needed is some controllable means of getting rid of excess moist air without wasting too much valuable heat. In habitually steamy rooms such as kitchens and bathrooms, an extractor fan is the best solution. It will extract the moist air quickly, and will also help to get rid of unwanted smells. In other rooms, fitting small 'trickle' ventilators at the top of window frames and putting in extra airbricks will often supply enough ventilation to allow the moist air to disperse before condensation becomes a problem.

FITTING AN EXTRACTOR FAN

1 Decide on the fan position, then mark the outline of the ducting on the wall outside. Drill holes right through the wall to mark it on the inside too.

2 Drill a series of closely spaced holes through the wall from inside, working within the guide holes drilled from outside. Repeat on the wall outside.

3 Chop out the brickwork with a wide bolster (stonecutter's chisel) and club (spalling) hammer, again working from inside and outside the house.

4 Use ducting for a cooker hood. Line the hole with a short length of pipe, then use connectors as required to connect the hood to the outlet.

5 Wall-mounted fans usually need a round hole. Cut it out, line it with a short length of sleeving and make good around it inside and outside the house.

6 Fit the fan into the sleeving, ready for its electrical supply to be connected. Fit a cover grille to the outside end of the ducting.

FITTING EXTRA AIRBRICKS

SAFE VENTILATION

There are two very important points to remember concerning ventilation. Firstly, many fuel-burning appliances need an adequate supply of fresh air to work efficiently and safely, so rooms where they are sited must contain provision for this if they are well sealed against natural draughts. Secondly, disused flues must be ventilated at top and bottom; if they are not, condensation can occur within the flue, which may show up as damp patches on the internal chimney walls.

1 Airbricks are the same size as one, two or three bricks. To fit one, start by drilling a series of closely spaced holes through the wall.

2 Then use a club (spalling) hammer and a wide bolster (stonecutter's chisel) to cut out the brickwork. With solid walls, drill holes right through and work from inside too.

3 Fit a cavity liner if the wall is of cavity construction, then trowel a bed of fairly wet mortar onto the bottom of the opening.

4 Butter mortar onto the top of the airbrick and slide it into the opening. Push mortar into the gaps at the sides and pack it down well.

5 Use drier mortar to point neatly all around the airbrick. Inside, make good the wall with plaster and cover the opening with a ventilator grille.

6 As an alternative to a terracotta airbrick, fit a two-part plastic type. The sleeves interlock to line the hole as the two parts are pushed together.

7 Slide the outer section into place, and point around it. Then slide the inner section into place from inside the house, and fit its cover grille.

MANUFACTURERS AND SUPPLIERS

Most of the manufacturers listed here supply their products to good independent retailers, major stores and DIY multiples. Try your local outlets first; they will usually be able to help you and can be found in the area business directory. If you have difficulties in obtaining specific items, contact the relevant company head office for more information.

TOOLS AND BASIC MATERIALS

Black & Decker Ltd *Power tools* Westpoint, The Grove, Slough, Berkshire SL1 1QQ, UK. 0753 511234

General Woodwork Supplies (SN) Ltd *Timber, tools and hardware* 76–80 Stoke Newington High St, London N16 5BR, UK. 071-254 6052

Gripperrods plc *Carpeting tools and accessories* Wyrley Brook Park, Walkmill Lane, Bridgtown, Cannock, Staffordshire WS11 3XA, UK. 0922 417777

Hobbs & Co Ltd *Builders Merchants* 88

Blackfriars Road, London SE1 8HA, UK. 071-928 1891

Mosley Stone *Painting and decorating tools* Wellington Road, Leeds LS12 1DU, UK. 0532 630221

Plasplugs Ltd *Tiling tools* Wetmore Road, Burton-on-Trent, Staffordshire DE14 1SD, UK. 0283 30303

Stanley Tools *Woodworking, Painting and decorating tools* Woodside, Sheffield S3 9PD, UK. 0742 768888

Whincop & Son Ltd *Timber and builders merchants* 32/40 Stoke Newington Church St, London N16 0LU, UK. 071-254 5044

Allway Tools Inc *Hand tools* 1255 Seabury Avenue, Bronx, New York, New York 10462, USA. (212) 792 3636

Black & Decker *Power tools* Communications Department, 702 East Joppa Road, Towson, Maryland 21286, USA

Robert Bosch Power Tool Corporation *Power Tools* 100 Bosch Blvd, New Bern, North Carolina 28562, USA

Home Building & Lumber Co Inc *Lumber* 1621 Ave H, Rosenberg, Texas 77471, USA. (713) 342 4282

Skil Corporation *Tools* 4300 West Peterson Avenue, Chicago, Illinois 60646, USA

Stanley Tools *Woodworking, painting and decorating tools*

Road, Springvale, Victoria 3171, Australia. (03) 547 9033

H J Reece Pty Ltd *Hand tools* 2 Barney Street, North Parramatta, NSW 2151, Australia. 008 01 8606 (toll free)

Stanley Works Pty Ltd *Woodworking, painting and decorating tools* PO Box 10, 400 Whitehorse Road, Nunawading, Victoria 3131, Australia

Wreckair Pty Ltd *Power tools* 2 Chisholm Road, Regents Park,

NSW 2143, Australia. (02) 645 4000

Nees Hardware Ltd *Tools* 11–15 Pretoria Street, Lower Hutt, New Zealand

Stanley Tools (NZ) Ltd *Woodworking, painting and decorating tools* PO Box 12-582, Penrose, Auckland, New Zealand

Tuf Tools CC *Woodworking, painting and decorating tools* PO Box 212, Maraisburg 1700, Transvaal, South Africa

PAINTS & WOOD FINISHES

Laura Ashley Ltd 150 Bath Road, Maidenhead, Berkshire SL6 4YS, UK. 0628 770345

Cuprinol Ltd Adderwell, Frome, Somerset BA11 1NL, UK. 0373 465151

Crown Paints Crown House, Hollins Road, Darwen, Lancs BB3 0BG, UK. 0254 704951

Dulux (ICI plc Paints Division) Wexham Road, Slough, Berkshire SL2 5DS, UK. 0753 550000

Arthur Sanderson & Sons Ltd 100 Acres, Oxford Road, Uxbridge, Middx UB8 1HY, UK. 0895 238244

Builders Square Inc *Decorating store* 9725 Datapoint Drive, San Antonio, Texas 78229, USA. (512) 616 8000

Wilson W A & Sons Inc *Decorating store* 6 Industrial Park Drive, Wheeling, WV 26003, USA. (304) 232 2200

Dulux Australia 145 Cabarita Road, Concord, NSW 23137, Australia. (02) 736 5111

Pascol Paints Australia Pty Ltd PO Box 63, Rosebery, NSW 2018, Australia. (02) 669 2266

Sikkens (Tenaru Pty Ltd) PO Box 768, Darlinghurst, Sydney, NSW 2010, Australia. (02) 357 4500

Taubmans 51 McIntyre Road, Sunshine, Victoria 3020, Australia. (03) 311 0211

ICI Hutt Park Road, PO Box 30749, Lower Hutt, New Zealand

Taubmans (New Zealand) Ltd 10 Portsmouth Road, PO Box 14064, Kilbirnie, Wellington, New Zealand. 0800 735 551 (toll free)

Dulux (Pty) Ltd 8 Juyn Street, Alrode, PO Box 123704 Alrode, South Africa

WALL COVERINGS

Laura Ashley (*see Paints*)

Crown Berger Ltd (*see Paints*)

Forbo–CP (Fablon) Ltd Station Road, Cramlington, Northumberland NE23 8AQ, UK. 0670 718300

Forbo–Kingfisher Ltd Lune Mills, Lancaster, Lancashire LA1 5QN, UK. 0524 65222

Harlequin Wallcoverings Ltd Cossington Road, Sileby, Nr Loughborough, Leicestershire LE12 7RU, UK. 0509 816575

Monkwell Fabrics and Wallpapers 10–12 Wharfdale Road, Bournemouth, Dorset BH4 9BT, UK. 0202 752944

Arthur Sanderson & Sons Ltd (*see Paints*)

Muriel Short Designs Hewitts Estate, Elmbridge Road, Cranley, Surrey GU6 8LW, UK. 0483 271211

Today Interiors Hollis Road, Grantham, Lincolnshire NG31 7QH, UK. 0476 74401

Crown Wallcovering Corp 20 Horizon Boulevard, South Hackensack, New Jersey 07606, USA. (201) 440 7000

Mazer's Discount Home Centers Inc *Decorating store* 210 41st Street S, Birmingham, Alabama 35222, USA. (205) 591 6565

Pratt & Lambert Inc *Decorating store* 75 Tonawanda Street, Buffalo, New York 14207, USA. (716) 873 6000

North American Decorative Products Inc 1055 Clark Boulevard, Brompton, Ontario, Canada L6T 3W4

Davro Interiors 616 Hay Street, Holimont, WA 6014, Australia. (09) 387 4888

International Paints Birmingham Avenue, Villawood, NSW 2163, Australia. (02) 728 7577

TILES

The Amtico Company Ltd *Vinyl tiles* 1177 St George Street, London W1R 9DE, UK. 071-629 6258

Castelnau Tiles *Wall and floor tiles* 175 Church Road, Barnes, London SW13 9HR, UK. 081-741 2452

Corres Mexican Tiles *Ceramic wall tiles* 219–221 Chiswick High Road, London W4, UK. 081-994 0215

Fired Earth Tiles plc and **The Merchant Tiler** *Ceramic, terracotta, stone and slate tiles* Twyford Mill, Oxford Road, Adderbury, Banbury, Oxfordshire OX17 3HP, UK. 0295 812088/812179

Stanley Tools (NZ) 1000 Stanley Drive, New Britain, Connecticut 06053, USA

Seco Tools Canada Inc *Hand tools* Mississanga, Ontario, Canada. (416) 568 4080

Parburyss Building Products *Wood merchants* 30 Bando

H & R Johnson Tiles Ltd *Ceramic floor and wall tiles* Highgate Works, Tunstall, Stoke-on-Trent ST6 4JX, UK. 0782 575575

Daniel Platt Ltd *Natural clay products* Brownhill Tileries, Canal Lane, Tunstall, Stoke-on-Trent ST6

4NY, UK. 0782 577187

Westco Ltd *Vinyl, cork and wood-block floor tiles* Penarth Road, Cardiff, South Glamorgan CF1 7YN, UK. 0222 233926

Wicanders (GB) Ltd *Cork floor and wall tiles* Stoner House, Kilnmead, Crawley, West Sussex RH10 2BG, UK. 0293 527700

American Olean Tile Company 1000 Cannon Avenue, Lansdale, Pennsylvania 19446, USA. (215) 855-1111

Armstrong World Industries PO Box 3001, Lancaster, Pennsylvania 17603, USA. (800) 233-3823

Crossville Ceramics Box 1168, Crossville, Tennessee 38557, USA. (615) 484-2110

Latco Tiles 2948 Gleneden Street, Los Angeles, California 90039, USA. (213) 664-1171

Summitville Tiles Inc Box 73, Summitville, Ohio 43962, USA. (216) 223-1511

Greenbank Tertech Pty Ltd *Ceramic tiles* 5 Hereford Street, Berkeley Vale, NSW 2259, Australia. (043) 88 4522

Bruce Floor (Vic) Pty Ltd *Linoleum tiles* 60 Punt Road, Windsor, Victoria 3181, Australia. (03) 51 5222

FLOOR COVERINGS

Crucial Trading Ltd *Natural floor coverings* 4 St Barnabas Street, London SW1, UK. 071-730 0075

Forbo Nairn Ltd *Cushioned vinyl and linoleum* PO Box 1, Kirkcaldy, Fife, Scotland DY1 2SB. 0592 261111

Heuga UK Ltd *Carpet tiles* The Gate House, Gate House Way, Aylesbury, Buckinghamshire HP19 3DL, UK. 0296 393244

Junckers Ltd *Hardwood strip flooring* Wheaton Court Commercial Centre, Wheaton Road, Witham, Essex CM8 3UJ, UK. 0376 517512

Kosset Carpets Ltd Tofshaw Lane, Bradford, West Yorkshire BD4 6QW, UK. 0274 681881

Tomkinsons Carpets Ltd PO Box 11, Duke Place, Kidderminster, Worcestershire DY10 2JR, UK. 0562 820006

Westco Ltd *Wood-block floor tiles* (see Tiles)

Woodward Grosvenor & Co Ltd *Carpets* Stourvale Mills, Green Street, Kidderminster, Worcestershire DY10 2AT, UK. 0562 820020

Kentile Floors Inc 58 Second Avenue, Brooklyn, New York, New York 11215, USA

Stark Carpet Corporation 977 Third Avenue, New York, New York 10022, USA

Dorsett Carpet Mills Inc 502 11th Avenue, Dalton, Georgia 30721, USA. (706) 278 1961

ETC Carpet Mill Ltd 3100 S Susan Street, Santa Ana, California 92704, USA. (714) 546 5601

Bruce Floor (Vic) Pty Ltd *Carpets* (see Tiles)

Carpet and Decor Centre 26 Central Road, Fordsburg 2092, Johannesburg, South Africa. (011) 833 2311

FEATURES & FITTINGS

J D Beardmore & Co Ltd *Architectural hardware* 3–4 Percy Street, London W1P 0EJ, UK. 071-637 7041

Richard Burbidge Ltd *Timber mouldings, shelving and fire surrounds* Whittington

Road, Oswestry, Shropshire SY11 1HZ, UK. 0691 655131

Fireplace Designers Ltd *Fire surrounds and accessories* 157c Great Portland Street, London W1N 5FB, UK. 071-580 9893/4

Harrison Drape *Curtain poles and accessories* Bradford Street, Birmingham B12 0PE, UK. 021 766 6111

Hodkin & Jones (Sheffield) Ltd *Decorative plaster mouldings* Callywhite Lane, Dronfield, Sheffield S18 6XP, UK. 0246 290888

Fixture Hardware Co Inc 4711 N Lamon Avenue, Chicago, Illinois 60630, USA. (312) 777 6100

Handy Hardware Wholesale Inc 8300 Tewantin Drive, Houston, Texas 77061, USA. 97130 644 1495

SOFT FURNISHINGS

Laura Ashley Ltd (see Paints)

Forbo–Kingfisher Ltd (see Wall Coverings)

Harlequin wallcoverings Ltd (see Wall Coverings)

Monkwell Fabrics and Wallpapers (see Wall Coverings)

Arthur Sanderson & Sons Ltd (see Paints)

Muriel Short Designs (see Wall Coverings)

Today Interiors (see Wall Coverings)

Decor Home Fashion Inc 140 58th Street, Brooklyn, New York 11220, USA. (718) 921 1030

Southwest Quilted Products Inc 18100 Kovacs Lane, Huntington Beach, California 92648, USA. (714) 841 5656

North American Decorative Products Inc (see Wall Coverings)

Tissus Rosedale Inc D'Anjou, Quebec,

Canada. (514) 351 8402

Nichimen Australia Ltd 3rd Floor, 60–70 Elizabeth Street, Sydney, NSW 2000, Australia. (02) 223 7122

STORAGE

Addis Ltd Ware Road, Hertford, Hertfordshire SG13 7HL, UK. 0992 584221

Cliffhanger Shelving Systems 8 Fletchers Square, Temple Farm Industrial Estate, Southend-on-Sea, Essex SS2 5RN, UK. 0702 613135

MFI Southon House, 333 The Hyde, Edgware Road, Collingdale, London NW9 6TD, UK. 081-200 0200.

Silver Lynx Products Ltd Lynx House, 10/11 Amber Business Village, Amber Close, Tamworth, Staffordshire B77 4RP, UK. 0827 311888

Spur Shelving Ltd Otterspool Way, Watford, Hertfordshire WD2 8HT, UK. 0923 226071

Shelves & Cabinets Unlimited 7880 Dunbrook Road, San Diego, California 92126, USA. (619) 578 4200

Bernhard Woodworking Ltd Inc 3670 Woodhead Drive, Northbrook, Illinois 60062, USA. (708) 291 1040

Caringbah Sheet Metal (Aust) Pty Ltd 42 Cawarra Road, Caringbah, NSW 2229, Australia. (02) 524 0791

Algoran Shelvit (Pty) Ltd Botha Street, Alrode, Alberton, South Africa. (011) 640 864 3900

SUNDRIES

Concord Lighting Ltd Alton House, High Holborn, London WC1, UK. 071-497 1400

Ideal-Standard Ltd *Bathroom equipment, furniture and accessories* PO Box 60, National Avenue, Hull HU5 4JE, UK. 0482 46461

Mazda Lighting Miles Road, Mitcham, Surrey CR4 3YX, UK. 081-640 1221.

Oracstar Limited *Plumbing and ventilation products* Weddell Way, Brackmills, Northampton NN4 0HS, UK. 0604 702181

Philips Lighting Ltd PO Box 298, City House, 420/430 London Road, Croydon, Surrey CR9 3QR, UK. 081-665 6655

INDEX

A

Adhesives, types of, 224–5
Arches, papering, 83
Architraves, 143, 146
  replacing, 155
Assessment of interior, 10–11
Attic
  conversion of, 13
  space, use of, 12
Austrian blinds, 183

B

Baseboards, 143, 146
  replacing, 154
Bathroom
  assessment of, 11
  lighting, 22–3
  storage space in, 199
Bed linen
  duvet cover, 192–3
  fabric, choosing, 193
  valance, 192–3
Bedroom
  assessment of, 11
  lighting, 11, 24–5
  storage space in, 198–9
Blinds
  Austrian, 183
  fabric requirements, calculating, 183
  rollerblind, putting up, 147
  Roman, 182–3
Border, applying, 87

C

Cabinets
  butt joints, 208
  concealed hinge, fitting, 210
  doors and drawers, fixing, 210–11
  dowels, using, 209
  drawer kit, making up, 211
  flush hinges, fitting, 210
  making, 208–9
  tool, making, 217

Carpet laying
  carpet tiles, 129
  foam-back carpet, 128
  tools and equipment, 120
  stair carpet, 132–3
  woven carpet, 130–1
Carpet tiles, 116–17
  cutting, 129
  laying, 129
Carpets
  foam-backed, 121, 128
  stretching, 131
  types of, 116
  underlays, 121
  widths, 116
Ceilings
  painting, 46
  papering, 82–3
  preparing for covering, 71
  rose, 145, 153
  textured finishes, removing, 70
Ceramic tiles
  adhesive, 94
  cutting, 100–1
  edges, 91
  feature panels, 91
  floor, laying, 110
  floors, for, 91–2
  grout, 94
  grouting, 102
  history of, 89
  Holland, made in, 89
  mosaics, 92–3, 106–7
  removing, 71
  tiling *see* Tiling
  tools and materials, 94–5
  types of, 90
  walls, for, 90–1
  worktops, for, 91–2
Chair rails, 143, 146
  angled joins in, 151
  putting up, 150–1
Closet
  built-in, fitting, 212–13
Clothes organizer, fitting, 214–15
Colour
  advancing and receding, 14
  complementary, 15
  contrast, 15
  harmony, 15
  primary, 14
  secondary, 14
  tertiary, 14
  tricks with, 16
  wheel, 14–15
Colour washing, 55
Condensation, 238–9

Cork tiles, 93
  laying, 112–13
  sealing, 113
  tools, 95
  using, 106–7
Cornices, 143–5
  cutting, 149
  putting up, 148–9
Crown mouldings, 143–5
  cutting, 149
  putting up, 148–9
Curtain poles, 147
  fitting, 164
Curtain tracks, 147
  fitting, 164–5
Curtains
  fabric requirements, 177
  headings, 174–5
  lightweight, 178–9
  lined, 176–7
  styles, 177
  tie-backs, 181
  wires, on, 178
Cushion covers
  bolsters, 187
  box, 186
  French seams, 186
  frills, 185
  piping, 187
  round, 185
  square, 184

D

Dado rails, 143, 146
  angled joins in, 151
  putting up, 150–1
Dining room
  assessment of, 10
  lighting, 20–1
  storage space in, 198
Doors
  binding, 226–7
  draughtproofing, 246
  fittings, 147, 162
  glazed, 160

The publishers would like to thank Jan Eaton for devising and writing the Soft Furnishings section; Fiona Skrine for devising and demonstrating the special paint effects on pages 52–57; and Pat Murphy for demonstrating the carpet laying sequences on pages 128–131. Many thanks also to New Islington & Hackney Housing Association for the use of one of their properties which was awaiting repair.

In addition, the publishers would like to thank the companies listed below for their generous help in either loaning or providing materials and equipment for use in the production of this title. For more details, see the Manufacturers and Suppliers list.

J D Beardmore & Co Ltd
Black & Decker
Crown Paints
Fireplace Designers Ltd
Forbo Nairn Ltd
General Woodwork Supplies Ltd
Gripperrods plc
Hobbs & Co Ltd
Hodkin & Jones (Sheffield) Ltd
Ideal-Standard Ltd
H & R Johnson Tiles Ltd
Junckers Ltd
Kosset Carpets Ltd
Mosley-Stone
Oracstar Ltd
Plasplugs Ltd
Daniel Platt Ltd
Stanley Tools
Whincop & Son Ltd

The publishers would like to thank the following companies for their kind permission to reproduce the following pictures in this book; they apologize for any unintentional omissions and will be happy to rectify this in future editions.

t = top; b = bottom; c = centre; l = left; r = right.

Addis Ltd: page 197 cl.
The Amtico Company Ltd: page 93 br.
Laura Ashley: pages 146 tl, 196 br, 176 t, 178 r, 181 br, 184 bl, 193 br.
Richard Burbidge Ltd: pages 14, 146/7, 194.
Castelnau Tiles: pages 92 br, 145 tr.
Concord Lighting Ltd: pages 18 b, 19 cl cr b, 23 tl b, 24 r, 25 bc br, 27 br.
Corres Mexican Tiles: page 90 cr.
Cliffhanger Shelving Systems: pages 196 tl, 197 tr.
Crown Paints: pages 30, 34 tr cr, 62/63, 63 cr br.
Cuprinol Ltd: pages 35 bl br, 119 b.
Dulux: pages 2/3, 6 bl, 8, 10 b, 11 tl, 15 tr, 16 tl, 32/33, 32, 33, 34 tl, 35 t, 144, 146 b, 179 br, 188 bl, 198 b, 207 t.
Cristal (H & R Johnson Tiles) Ltd: pages 6 br, 12 b, 90 bl, 199 tr.
Crucial Trading Ltd: pages 7 bc, 117 b.
Fired Earth Tiles plc: pages 88, 90 tr, 91, 92 t bl.

Fireplace Designers Ltd: page 145 tl.
Forbo–CP (Fablon) Ltd: pages 7 bl, 10 t, 22, 60 b, 62 l, 63 bl, 147 b.
Forbo–Kingfisher Ltd: pages 12 t, 60 t, 61 t, 167 r, 189 tr.
Forbo–Nairn Ltd: pages 93 t, 117 tr, 118 t, 135.
Harlequin Wallcoverings Ltd: 7 br, 15 tl, 58, 61 b, 146 b, 185 t, 186 br.
Harrison Drape: pages 15 b, 174 t, 175 t.
Hayloft Woodwork: pages 11 b, 198 t.
Heuga: pages 117 tl, 129 bl br.
Junckers Ltd: pages 13 b, 21 cr, 118 b, 119 t, 141, 205.
Kevin MacPartland: page 147 tr.
Mazda Lighting: pages 18 t, 19 t, 20, 21 tl tr cl, 23 tr, 24 l, 25 t bl, 26, 27 t.
The Merchant Tiler: page 108.
MFI: pages 6 bc, 11 tr, 13 t, 196 bl, 199 tl.
Monkwell Fabrics and Wallpapers: page 17 b.
Mr Tomkinson: pages 114, 116.
Philips Lighting Ltd: page 27 bl.
Sanderson: pages 16 tr b, 127 b, 180 t, 192 t.
Muriel Short Designs: page 187 br.
Silver Lynx Products: page 199 c.
Spur Shelving Ltd: pages 197 b, 199 b.
Today Interiors: pages 17 t, 168.
Wicanders: pages 93 cr, 118 c.
Elizabeth Whiting and Associates: page 183 br.